Cambridge English

MINDSET
FOR IELTS

An Official Cambridge IELTS Course

Student's Book 1

MAP OF THE BOOK

UNIT 1 – p8
RELATIONSHIPS

UNIT 2 – p24
PLACES AND BUILDINGS

UNIT 3 – p44
EDUCATION AND EMPLOYMENT

UNIT 4 – p64
FOOD AND DRINK

READING

UNIT 1 — p8

Exam skills:
- Short answer questions

Learning strategies:
- Identifying words in a question
- Scanning for details

Language focus:
- Uses of the Present simple
- Adverbs of frequency
- Vocabulary to describe family

UNIT 2 — p24

Exam skills
- Sentence completion

Learning strategies:
- Skimming and scanning a text
- Understanding paraphrase

Language focus:
- Present simple and Past simple
- Vocabulary to describe houses and buildings

UNIT 3 — p44

Exam skills:
- Multiple choice questions

Learning strategies:
- How to find the answer
- Finding words with similar meanings
- Identifying the main idea

Language focus:
- Vocabulary for work and study
- Present perfect

UNIT 4 — p64

Exam skills:
- Matching information
- Sentence completion

Learning strategies:
- Locating information
- Dealing with paraphrase

Language focus:
- Vocabulary for food and drink
- Countable and uncountable nouns

WRITING

UNIT 1 — p12

Exam skills:
- Describing a process (Part 1)

Learning strategies:
- Understanding a diagram
- Writing overviews and introductions

Language focus:
- Using sequencing expressions
- Using the Present simple passive

UNIT 2 — p30

Exam skills:
- Describing maps and places (Part 1)

Learning strategies:
- Describing changes in a map

Language focus:
- Prepositions of place
- Vocabulary for map tasks
- Past simple (regular and irregular)
- Past simple (active and passive)

UNIT 3 — p49

Exam skills:
- Graphs, bar charts and pie charts (Part 1)

Learning strategies:
- Describing changes in numbers
- Studying a model answer

Language focus:
- Prepositions with numbers

UNIT 4 — p70

Exam skills:
- Two diagrams in one question (Part 1)

Learning strategies:
- Introduction and overview
- Describing numbers in a pie chart
- Describing diagrams without exact numbers
- Avoiding outside information

Language focus:
- Making comparisons
- Countable and uncountable nouns

LISTENING

UNIT 1 — p16

Exam skills:
- Multiple choice (Part 1)

Learning strategies:
- Identifying speakers
- Listening for numbers

Language focus:
- Pronunciation of numbers

UNIT 2 — p35

Exam skills:
- Short answer questions (Part 1)

Learning strategies:
- Spelling names
- Checking for accuracy
- Understanding categories

Language focus:
- Vocabulary for places in a town

UNIT 3 — p54

Exam skills:
- Sentence completion (Part 3)

Learning strategies:
- Identifying key words
- Following a conversation
- Synonyms and paraphrases

Language focus:
- Describing jobs and courses

UNIT 4 — p75

Exam skills:
- Classification tasks (Part 1)
- Matching tasks (Part 1)

Learning strategies:
- Synonym and paraphrase

Language focus:
- Vocabulary for cooking methods

SPEAKING

UNIT 1 — p19

Exam skills:
- Speaking about your family (Part 1)

Learning strategies:
- Answering Part 1 questions
- Extending Part 1 answers

Language focus:
- Adjective and noun collocations for family
- Adverbs of frequency

UNIT 2 — p39

Exam skills:
- Speaking about your hometown (Part 1)

Learning strategies:
- Lexical resource and accuracy

Language focus
- Prepositions to describe a town
- Adjectives to describe a town
- Present simple / Present perfect / Past simple
- Pronunciation of past tenses

UNIT 3 — p58

Exam skills:
- Speaking about work and study (Parts 1 and 2)

Learning strategies:
- Organising your talks
- Using the headings in questions

Language focus:
- Adjectives to describe feelings
- Adjectives to describe experiences

UNIT 4 — p80

Exam skills:
- Talking about food and meals (Part 1 and Part 2)

Learning strategies:
- Expressing opinions
- Using the preparation time in Part 2
- Organising a Part 2 talk

Language focus:
- Vocabulary for food and cooking
- Countable and uncountable nouns

ANSWER KEY – p167

LISTENING SCRIPTS – p177

UNIT 5 – p86
CONSUMERISM

Exam skills: p86
- Matching headings

Learning strategies:
- Skim reading
- Topic sentences
- Main and supporting ideas
- Paraphrase

Language focus:
- Vocabulary connected with shopping
- Future forms (will and going to)

Exam skills: p92
- Agree or disagree essay (Part 2)

Learning strategies:
- Overview of Part 2 essay types
- Writing an introduction
- Developing an argument
- Structuring your essay

Language focus:
- Language for expressing opinions
- Language for introducing ideas

Exam skills: p98
- Multiple choice (Part 2)

Learning strategies:
- Identifying distractors
- Recognising paraphrase
- Recognising synonyms

Language focus:
- Vocabulary to identify places

Exam skills: p102
- Describing a shop (Part 2)

Learning strategies:
- Developing ideas in Part 2

Language focus:
- Using effective intonation

UNIT 6 – p106
LEISURE TIME

Exam skills: p106
- True / False / Not Given
- Summary completion

Learning strategies:
- Developing strategies

Language focus:
- Vocabulary for sports and hobbies
- Comparatives

Exam skills: p112
- Opinion based essay (Part 2)

Learning strategies:
- Coherence and cohesion

Language focus:
- Free time collocations
- Linking words and phrases
- Comparing the past and present

Exam skills: p117
- Map labelling (Part 2)

Learning strategies:
- Understanding map questions
- Finding places on a map
- Recognising distractors

Language focus:
- Prepositions of place
- Prepositions of movement

Exam skills: p121
- Sports and hobbies (Part 2)

Learning strategies:
- Extending your talk
- Dealing with Part 2 follow-up questions

Language focus:
- Describing experiences
- Language to give reasons
- Pronunciation of strong and weak words

UNIT 7 – p126
FAME AND THE MEDIA

Exam skills: p126
- Matching features
- Yes / No / Not Given

Learning strategies:
- Skim reading
- Scan reading
- Identifying the writer's views

Language focus:
- First conditional

Exam skills: p132
- Discussion essay (Part 2)

Learning strategies:
- Organising paragraphs
- Giving specific examples
- Supporting your points

Language focus:
- Vocabulary connected with the media
- Pronouns

Exam skills: p137
- Flow-chart completion (Part 4)

Learning strategies:
- Predicting the answer
- Dealing with scientific and technical language

Exam skills: p142
- A famous person (Part 2)
- Fame and the media (Part 3)

Learning strategies:
- Linking ideas in Parts 2 and 3
- Analysis of differences between Parts 2 and 3

Language focus:
- Linking words
- Vocabulary for giving reasons

UNIT 8 – p146
NATURAL WORLD

Exam Skills: p146
- Note completion
- Matching sentence endings

Learning strategies:
- Finding the relevant information
- Paraphrase

Language focus:
- Vocabulary for the natural world
- Vocabulary for the environment
- Modals of possibility and probability

Exam skills: p152
- Problems and solutions essay (Part 2)

Learning strategies:
- Writing a conclusion
- Linking the main ideas and conclusion

Language focus:
- Environmental collocations
- Present perfect and Past simple

Exam skills: p156
- Note completion (Part 4)

Learning strategies:
- Using headings to help you
- Signposting words

Language focus:
- Vocabulary for the natural world

Exam skills: p161
- The natural world (Parts 2 and 3)

Learning strategies:
- Developing answers for Part 3

Language focus:
- Vocabulary for the natural world
- Language for giving examples
- Language for giving reasons

MEET THE AUTHORS

With a thorough understanding of the essential skills required to succeed in the IELTS test, let our team of experts guide you on your IELTS journey.

Greg Archer

Greg Archer is an experienced, DELTA-qualified teacher and teacher trainer who began teaching *IELTS* at International House in London, where he trained and qualified as an *IELTS* Examiner in both Writing and Speaking. After moving to Cambridge in 2013, he has been working at an international college, at various times managing the English Language department, developing appropriate courses to run alongside A Level and GCSE study, and primarily teaching *IELTS* and English for Academic Purposes classes to students whose ambition is to enter a UK or English-speaking university.

Lucy Passmore

Lucy began teaching English in 2002 in the UK and Spain, where she prepared young learners for Cambridge English exams. She has been a tutor of English for Academic Purposes since 2008, and has taught on *IELTS* preparation courses in addition to preparing international students to start degree courses at Brunel University and King's College London. Lucy is currently based at King's College London, where she teaches on foundation programmes for international students, provides in-sessional support in academic writing for current students and contributes to materials and course design.

The *Mindset for IELTS* authors have extensive experience teaching in the UK and globally. They have helped prepare students for the *IELTS* test from all over the world, including:

China, UK, Pakistan, Middle East, Republic of Korea, Italy, Indonesia, Sri Lanka, Kazakhstan, Greece, Russia, Spain

Peter Crosthwaite

Peter has worked in the TESOL and applied linguistics fields for 13 years. His previous experience includes writing and consultancy work with various publishers, two sessions as Director of Studies for language schools in the UK, over six years' experience in the Korean EFL context, and teaching and supervision experience at the University of Cambridge. He worked as an Assistant Professor at the Centre for Applied English Studies (CAES), University of Hong Kong, where he is the coordinator of the MA Applied Linguistics (MAAL) and the MA TESOL. He is currently working at the School of Languages and Cultures at the University of Queensland. He has worked on *IELTS* test preparation, publishing and materials development for over 10 years, with 4 years of experience as a qualified *IELTS* Examiner.

Natasha De Souza

Natasha has been involved in the ELT industry for 15 years – as a teacher, Director of Studies, Examiner and an Examinations Officer. She started teaching *IELTS* in 2006, when she worked on a University Pathway and Foundation Programme for a language school in Cambridge. More recently, as a Director of Studies and an Examinations Officer, she was responsible for giving guidance to students and teachers on how the *IELTS* test works and how best to prepare for it.

Jishan Uddin

Jishan has been an EFL teacher since 2001. He has taught on a range of courses in the UK and Spain, including general English, exam preparation and English for Academic Purposes (EAP) courses and is currently an EAP lecturer and academic module leader at King's College, London. He has extensive experience teaching *IELTS* preparation classes to students from around the world, particularly China, the Middle East and Kazakhstan. He also has experience in designing resources for language skills development as well as exam preparation and administration.

Susan Hutchison

Susan Hutchison has been an ESOL teacher and examiner for more than 30 years. She has taught overseas in Italy, Hungary and Russia. She now lives and works in Edinburgh, Scotland as an ESOL teacher in an independent school for girls. She has co-authored a number of course books, preparation and practice materials for both Cambridge English Language Assessment and *IELTS*. She has also developed online and interactive *IELTS* practice materials for the British Council.

Marc Loewenthal

Marc has been teaching for 35 years, mostly in the UK but also abroad in Greece, Russia, Middle East, Indonesia and Pakistan. He has taught in the public sector since 1990, mostly in further education and adult education, and more recently on pre-sessional EAP university courses. He has been a Speaking and Writing Examiner for over 25 years and has expert knowledge of *IELTS* requirements for university admission.

Claire Wijayatilake

Claire has been teaching English since 1988. She spent much of her career in Sri Lanka, including 16 years at British Council, Colombo. She became an *IELTS* Examiner in 1990 and examined regularly in Colombo and Malé, Maldives for almost 20 years. She worked as the *IELTS* Examiner Trainer for Sri Lanka, recruiting, training and monitoring examiners. She then moved into training and school leadership, serving as Teacher Trainer and Principal at various international schools. She returned to the UK in 2013 and worked for Middlesex University, where she started her materials writing career. She is currently a Visiting Lecturer at Westminster University, which allows her time to write. She has a PhD in Applied Linguistics and English Language Teaching from the University of Warwick.

HOW DOES MINDSET FOR IELTS WORK?

AVAILABLE AT FOUR LEVELS

FOUNDATION LEVEL	**LEVEL 1** Target Band 5.5	**LEVEL 2** Target Band 6.5	**LEVEL 3** Target Band 7.5

CORE MATERIAL

- Student's Book (print and digital).
- Online skills modules for Reading, Writing, Listening, Speaking plus Grammar and Vocabulary.

ADDITIONAL MATERIAL

- Customised online modules for specific L1 groups that focus on areas where help is most needed, informed by the Cambridge English Learner Corpus.
- Academic Study Skills online module that prepares students for the challenges of studying a university-level course taught in English.

TAILORED TO SUIT YOUR NEEDS

Mindset for IELTS gives teachers the ultimate flexibility to tailor courses to suit their context and the needs of their students.

GIVES TEACHERS CHOICE

- Course design means teachers can focus on either the skills or the topics that their students need the most help with.

CUSTOMISATION

- Online modules can be used in the classroom as extension work or as extra practice at home, allowing the teacher to customise the length and focus of the course.
- Additional online modules designed for specific L1 learners can be incorporated into the course.

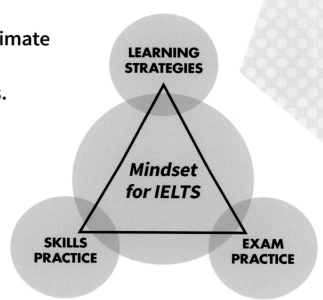

COURSE CONFIGURATIONS

The *Mindset for IELTS* course comprises 5 key components:

CORE TOPICS & SKILLS	**Student's Book (print and digital)** 8 topic-based units, organised by skill, provide 60-90 hours of teaching per level (levels 1, 2 and 3)
ONLINE SKILLS MODULES	**8 hours of practice per skill, per level:** • Speaking • Writing • Reading • Listening • Grammar and Vocabulary
ACADEMIC STUDY SKILLS	**6 hours of practice to get ready for the challenges of studying a university-level course taught in English**
LANGUAGE SPECIFIC AND PLUS MODULES	**6 hours of practice per module:** • Pronunciation and Speaking for Chinese speakers • Spelling and Writing for Chinese speakers • Spelling and Vocabulary for Arabic speakers • Writing for Arabic speakers • Speaking Plus • Writing Plus
ONLINE PRACTICE TESTS Test**bank**	**Access to Cambridge English authentic IELTS Academic practice tests online**

01▶ SKILLS MODULES

8 hours of practice per skill, including Reading, Writing, Listening, Speaking plus Grammar and Vocabulary.

RECEPTIVE SKILLS Focus on sub-skill	**PRINT** Reading Listening	**ONLINE** Different topic

PRODUCTIVE SKILLS Focus on active production	**PRINT** Writing Speaking	**ONLINE** Same topic

02▶ LANGUAGE SPECIFIC MODULES

Extra practice for areas that need the most work, informed by the Cambridge Learner Corpus.*

ARABIC
• Spelling and Vocabulary
• Writing

CHINESE
• Pronunciation and Speaking
• Spelling and Writing

Plus modules focus on common areas of weakness and are suitable for all first languages.

PLUS
• Speaking
• Writing

*Currently the same module is used for Level 1 and Level 2.

UNIT / 01: RELATIONSHIPS

READING

IN THIS UNIT YOU WILL LEARN HOW TO

• answer questions using up to three words

• identify key words in a question

• scan a text to find specific information.

LEAD-IN

01 ▷ **In pairs, explain the words in the box.**

Example: sister *My sister is my parents' daughter / other daughter.*

~~sister~~	brother	cousin	father-in-law	grandfather	uncle
aunt	nephew	niece	great-aunt	grandmother	

Tell your partner who you live with. Which other family members are you close to?

02 ▷ **You are going to read about some advantages of living in an extended family (i.e. not just parents and children living together). Which of the following advantages do you think are the most important?**

1 Older people are fun to live with.

2 Older people are patient and experienced.

3 You can save money by living together.

4 Grandparents are not as busy as parents.

5 Children get plenty of love and attention.

Read the text quickly and check which are mentioned. Ignore the highlighted words.

TIP 02

Don't worry if you don't know a word in the text. You can often guess the meaning by reading the other words in the sentence. And you may not need to know the meaning to answer the questions.

BLOOD IS THICKER THAN WATER

A Blood is thicker than water. This means that family is more important than anyone else. Many young people, though, spend more time with their friends than with their family. They value their friends' opinions more and enjoy their company. When it's time to visit grandma or go to a cousin's wedding, teenagers often prefer to be left at home. But are they missing out?

B In Asia, the Middle East, South America and Sub-Saharan Africa over 40% of children live in families with other adults such as aunts, uncles and grandparents in addition to their parents. In South Africa, it is almost 70%. On the other hand, in Europe, Australia and North America, less than 25% of children live in extended families. Is the lack of close contact with relatives putting some children at a disadvantage?

0 3 ▸ Match the highlighted words from the text with their meanings. Start with words you already know. Use the context (the sentence it is in and other words around it) to work out the meaning.

1 value	**a**	worried; not able to relax
2 (have an) influence (on)	**b**	dealt with, had experience of
3 stressed	**c**	get (something positive)
4 handled	**d**	be grateful for
5 selfish	**e**	a well-known phrase giving advice
6 gain	**f**	caring only about yourself and not other people
7 proverb	**g**	(have an) effect (on)
8 appreciate	**h**	believe something is important

SHORT-ANSWER QUESTIONS

In this type of task you have to answer questions using **up to three words**, or **up to two words and/or a number**. The instructions tell you how many words you can use. Short-answer questions test if you can find the right part of the text quickly and understand the information.

FINDING INFORMATION

0 4 ▸ To practise finding information quickly, have a race with your partner to find the following phrases in the text. They are not in order.

- grandparents' stories
- cousin's wedding
- young adults
- extended families
- come and go
- Italian proverb

How did you do this? Can you explain to another student how to find information quickly?

C The people they live with have a great influence on the way children grow up. Those who live with their extended family have many advantages. They usually get lots of love and attention. Grandparents often have more time to read to children and play with them. As they are often retired, they are not always busy and stressed as many parents are. They have learnt to be patient and they have already handled most of the problems children and young people face.

D It is good for children to grow up to understand the needs of older people: they may become more caring and less selfish if they spend time helping their grandparents. Children learn about the past from grandparents' stories. Sometimes they feel closer to their grandparents than to their parents.

E Young adults often feel that living alone will be exciting, but they forget that it can also be lonely. By remaining with the family during this stage of their lives, they can avoid this. They can also save money for their education and future.

F Young people whose grandparents live far away can gain some of these advantages by keeping in close contact by phone, email, letters and visits. It is nice to know there is someone you can go to if you have a problem. As the Italian proverb says, *'Se non sta andando bene chiamare la nonna.'* – 'If things aren't going well, call your grandmother.'

G Friends are important to young people, but friends come and go. Your family is always on your side. Grandparents won't be there forever. Appreciate them while you can.

IDENTIFYING THE KEY WORDS IN A QUESTION

0 5 ▷ Identify the key words in these questions.

1 What percentage of children live in extended families in Asia, the Middle East, South America and Sub-Saharan Africa?

2 Why are grandparents often less busy and stressed than parents?

3 What do young adults often think living alone will be like?

SCANNING A TEXT

0 6 ▷ Answer the questions in exercise 5. Follow the advice in the box.

0 7 ▷ Read this exam task and the answers to the questions. What is wrong with the answers? Match the answers 1–4 with the advice a–d below.

*Answer these questions. Choose **NO MORE THAN TWO WORDS AND/OR A NUMBER** from the passage for each answer.*

Question 1 What percentage of children in South Africa live with their extended family?

Answer 1: 20%

Question 2 What helps children in extended families learn about the past?
Answer 2: grandparents storys

Question 3 What negative word can describe how it sometimes feels to live alone?
Answer 3: Living alone can be lonely.

Question 4 According to the Italian proverb, who should you phone when you have a problem?
Answer 4: your gran

a Don't write more than the number of words you are given. You mustn't write full sentences.

b Make sure that you use the correct information when you answer a question.

c Don't change words in the text. Remember, the instructions tell you to **choose words from the text**.

d Be careful with spelling. You can lose marks if your spelling is wrong.

0 8 ▷ Now correct the answers in exercise 7.

GRAMMAR FOCUS: TENSES

0 9 ▷ Answer these questions.

1 What tense are most of the verbs in the text?

2 Choose the correct reason for the choice of tense.

   a The verbs describe events which are happening now.

   b The verbs describe things that are generally true.

   c The verbs give the writer's opinion.

 Before you look for the answer to a question, it helps if you find the **key words** – the most important words – in the question. This will help you find the information you need.

Example: What do <u>young people</u> often <u>think</u> about <u>older family members</u>?

 When you are answering a question:

- Decide on the key words in the question and think of words with a similar meaning.

- Move your eyes quickly across and down the text, looking for the key words, or words that mean the same. Don't read every word. This is called 'scanning'.

- If the text has headings, use them to help you decide which part of the text to look at first.

- When you find a key word, read the text around it to make sure you have found the right information.

TIP 0 7

Some grammar words (e.g. *a*, *the*, *some*) can be omitted in order to get the right number of words.

10 Identify the frequency adverbs in these sentences from the text.

1 Your family is always on your side.
2 Teenagers often prefer to be left at home.
3 As they are often retired, they are not always busy …
4 They usually get lots of love and attention.
5 Sometimes they feel closer to their grandparents than to their parents.

11 Study the <u>position</u> of the frequency adverbs in the sentences in exercise 10. With a partner, work out some rules on the position of frequency adverbs.

*Grandparents **often** have more time to read to children.*

Often is an adverb of frequency. It gives us an idea of how often something happens. The present simple tells us about regular events, and adverbs of frequency are common with this tense.

EXAM SKILLS

 GO FURTHER ONLINE

12 Read the passage and answer the questions below.

SOCIAL MEDIA AND THE MEANING OF FRIENDSHIP

There have been a lot of scientific studies into what makes a friendship. It seems today that ideas of what friendship is are also changing. A study in 1993 at the University of Oxford showed that people could only maintain 150 relationships. However, with the explosion of social media since then, many people now have over 300 people who they think of as friends. Some people think that these friends are not real friends, but others believe that social media has helped us to expand and keep our friendships because we have more time and opportunities.

Another change from the past is that people don't stay in the place where they were born. They go to different cities and countries for education and jobs. People are in general more geographically mobile nowadays. This means that we have more chances to meet and make friends with people from different cultures and different backgrounds. People still often make friends at college who remain friends for life, but making new friends at work is more difficult. People now have less security at work and this also means that they find it harder to build new relationships.

As people get older, they sometimes also have less free time. They become busier with their jobs and families and have less time to spend with friends. Friendships can be very different when we are at different ages. Young children often choose their friends because of convenience, for example, they go to the same school, they live near each other or their parents are friends. As we get older, friendships are more connected with having similar interests and opinions.

One thing is definitely true though, it doesn't matter how old we are or how many friends we have on social media, friendship is good for our health. People who spend time with friends have fewer mental health problems and are generally happier and in a better physical state of health than people who spend their free time alone.

*Answer the questions below. Choose **NO MORE THAN THREE WORDS** from the passage for each answer.*

1 What has enabled people to have more friends than in the past, according to some people?
2 What phrase does the writer use to describe people who don't stay in the same place?
3 What work-related problem do people have that makes them less likely to form friendships?
4 What frequently influences the friendships of young children?
5 What are people with friends less likely to suffer from?

WRITING

IN THIS UNIT YOU WILL LEARN HOW TO

- describe a process (Writing Part 1)
- use sequencing expressions to describe the order of stages in a process
- use the present simple passive to describe a process
- write an introduction and overview.

LEAD-IN

01 ▷ What foods do you eat at a family celebration? Do you know how to prepare them? Do you need any special equipment?

02 ▷ In Sri Lanka, a family meal often includes stringhoppers. To make stringhoppers you need some special equipment. Choose the best description of each piece of equipment.

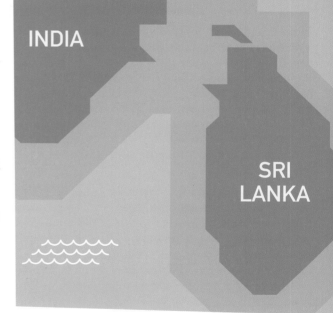

INDIA

SRI LANKA

1 Stringhopper press

   A It has two parts which are different in shape but the same size. It is made of a light material such as plastic.

   B It's made of heavy metal and has two parts which are similar in shape. The centre is round and there are handles on each side. One part fits into the other.

   C It has two parts and one goes on top of the other. It is square in shape and made of wood.

2 Stringhopper mats

   A These are round shallow baskets made of thin pieces of wood. The wood is in a criss-cross pattern to form large holes.

   B These are cloth triangles with very small holes in them.

   C These are thick pieces of wood with rectangular holes in them.

3 Rice grinder

   A It is made of metal and the top and bottom are the same size and shape.

   B It is a metal machine with a wide base and a narrow tray on top.

   C It is a machine made of metal with a wide tray at the top and a narrower base.

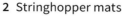

03 ▸ Complete the chart with words from exercise 2.

Materials	Parts	Shapes
plastic	handles	round

TIP 04

Don't worry if you don't know about the topic. The notes and pictures give you the ideas and vocabulary you need.

PART 1: DESCRIBING A PROCESS

04 ▸ The pictures show the process of making stringhoppers. Match the short instructions to the pictures.

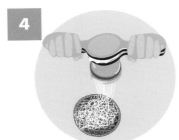

a push through the stringhopper press onto the stringhopper mats

b add water to the flour

c put the rice into the grinder and grind into flour

d cook in a steamer

e serve with spicy curries

f mix well to form a dough

◎ We use the present simple passive to describe a process.

We make them with rice. → They are made with rice.
You mix it with water. → It is mixed with water.

GRAMMAR FOCUS: THE PRESENT SIMPLE PASSIVE

05 ▸ Complete the sentences about tea. Use the verbs in brackets in the present simple passive.

1 Tea leaves _____ (**pick**) by hand.

2 Only the best leaves _____ (**use**).

3 A lot of water _____ (**need**) to grow tea plants successfully.

4 A lot of tea _____ (**grow**) in China and India.

GRAMMAR FOCUS: SEQUENCING WORDS

0 6 ▶ Complete the sentences about making stringhoppers with words from the box.

| After | Finally | First | Next | The next stage | Then |

1 _____ , the rice is put through a grinder.
2 _____ that, water is added to the flour.
3 _____ it is mixed and made into a dough.
4 _____ is to push the dough through the stringhopper press.
5 _____ the stringhoppers are placed in a steamer.
6 _____ , they are served with spicy curries.

TIP 0 6

When describing the stages in a process, it is important to use sequencing expressions, for example *first*, *then*, *next*, to clearly show the order of the stages.

WRITING AN INTRODUCTION AND OVERVIEW

0 7 ▶ Which of these is an introduction and which is an overview?

a There are six stages in the process of making stringhoppers, beginning with grinding the rice and making a dough and ending with using a steamer to cook the stringhoppers.

b The diagram demonstrates the process of preparing stringhoppers, a kind of noodle.

0 8 ▶ Which of these are NOT overviews?

a The process of making blue cheese can be seen in this series of pictures.

b To make a perfect omelette you need fresh ingredients, the right equipment and the correct technique. You must also cook it for the correct amount of time and pay attention to the temperature.

c The production of tea involves a range of stages, from picking the leaves from the plant to drying and distributing it.

d The diagram shows the various stages in the process of making strawberry jam. The first stage is to pick the strawberries when they are ripe.

◎ In Writing Part 1 your answer should include an introduction and an overview. The **introduction** is usually the task question rewritten in your own words. The **overview** is a summary of the process.

STUDYING A MODEL ANSWER

0 9 ▶ Study the Model answer opposite and find:

1 the introduction
2 the overview
3 sequencing expressions
4 verbs in the present simple passive
5 descriptions of the equipment
6 vocabulary from the short instructions in exercise 4

MODEL ANSWER

The diagram demonstrates the process of preparing stringhoppers, a kind of noodle dish. There are six main stages in the process, beginning with grinding the rice and making a dough and ending with using a steamer to cook the stringhoppers.

First, the dry rice is put into a rice grinder to make it into flour. Next, the flour is mixed with water and formed into dough. After that, the dough is put into a stringhopper press, which is a metal piece of equipment with two handles and holes in it. The dough is pushed through the holes and it comes out as thin noodles. The noodle 'nests' are placed onto individual stringhopper mats, which are round baskets made of thin pieces of wood. They are then cooked in a steamer until they are ready. The final stage is to serve the stringhoppers with a variety of spicy curries.

10 ▶ Look at the pictures, which show the process of making cherry jam.
Complete the sentences with a verb from the box in the correct form.

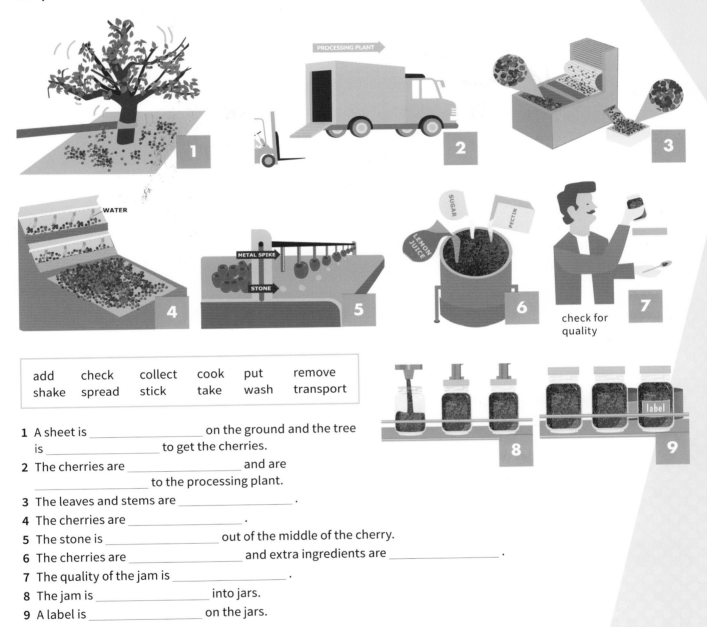

check for quality

| add | check | collect | cook | put | remove |
| shake | spread | stick | take | wash | transport |

1 A sheet is _____ on the ground and the tree
   is _____ to get the cherries.
2 The cherries are _____ and are
   _____ to the processing plant.
3 The leaves and stems are _____ .
4 The cherries are _____ .
5 The stone is _____ out of the middle of the cherry.
6 The cherries are _____ and extra ingredients are _____ .
7 The quality of the jam is _____ .
8 The jam is _____ into jars.
9 A label is _____ on the jars.

EXAM SKILLS

11 ▶ The pictures show the process of making cherry jam.

Describe the process.

Remember to:
• include an introduction and an overview
• use the present simple passive
• use sequencing expressions
• write 150 words.

TIP **11**

Use the words on the pictures and diagrams in your answer. They are there to help you.

GO FURTHER ONLINE

UNIT /01: RELATIONSHIPS

LISTENING

IN THIS UNIT YOU WILL LEARN HOW TO

- identify the speakers in a conversation
- listen for numbers
- answer multiple-choice questions.

01▶ In Section 1 of the Listening test you will hear two people talking in everyday situations.

Tick TWO situations that could be in Section 1 of the Listening test.

A Discussing a course assignment
B Describing changes in family life over time
C Choosing a gift
D Arranging a birthday celebration

02▶ Listen and match the conversations with two of the situations above.

Conversation 1 _____   Conversation 2 _____

IDENTIFYING THE SPEAKERS

03▶ Listen to the conversations again and pay attention to the speakers.
For questions 1–4, write M for male and F for female next to the people.

	Male or female?	Information wanted
Conversation 1	manager **1** ___ customer **2** ___	**5** The customer would like to … **A** book a table. **B** order a meal.
Conversation 2	shop assistant **3** ___ customer **4** ___	**6** The customer wants to buy … **A** a necklace. **B** earrings.

In Section 1 of the Listening test you will hear two speakers. In Section 3, there will be two or three speakers. In each case the speakers' voices will sound different from each other to help you easily identify who is speaking. The answers could be given by any of the speakers. In Section 1, there is normally one person who has to find out information from the other.

04▶ Listen again and for questions 5 and 6, choose the correct answer, A or B.

LISTENING FOR NUMBERS

05 ▷
🎵 03

Listen and circle the number you hear in each pair.

a 1st / 3rd   e 19 / 90
b $10.50 / $10.15   f 52 / 62
c 6th / 5th   g £110 / £810
d 17 / 70   h 22nd / 27th

Listen again and practise saying the numbers.

06 ▷
🎵 04

Listen to the next part of conversation 1 and choose the correct answer.

1 How many people does the woman want to make the booking for?

A 8   B 12   C 16

2 What is the date of the booking?

A 12th   B 16th   C 17th

TIP 06

You will usually hear all the numbers given in the options but only one will be correct. It is important to listen carefully for key phrases, so that you can choose the correct one.

07 ▷

Look at the following phrases taken from the recording. What number is missing?

1 No, no, it's the day after – the _____ .
16th / 17th

2 The private room can seat up to _____ people.   12 / 20

08 ▷
🎵 05

Now listen to the rest of conversation 1 and choose the correct answer.

How much is the total cost of the booking?

A £218   B £318   C £380

09 ▷
🎵 06

Listen to the second part of conversation 2 and answer the questions.

1 The price of the earrings now is …

A £10   B £20   C £30

2 How much does the customer pay for the gift wrapping?

A £4   B £5   C £7

10 ▷
🎵 07

Listen again and complete this part of the conversation.

Customer Oh, really? So, how much are they?

Assistant Well, they *were* **1** _____ pounds, but actually we've got a sale on at the moment, so they're a little cheaper – only **2** _____ pounds. So you can save **3** _____ pounds!

In Section 1 of the Listening test you need to listen for specific details. These details often include numbers.

[MULTIPLE-CHOICE QUESTIONS]

 In multiple-choice tasks, you choose the correct answer from three options, A, B or C.

There are two types of multiple-choice question:

a a question followed by three possible options
b an unfinished statement followed by three possible endings

1 1 ▶ Match the words and phrases 1–5 to words and phrases a–e, which have a similar meaning.

1 a goodbye party
2 a soccer game
3 a celebration
4 brother and sister
5 work in the same office

a members of the same family
b colleagues
c a leaving party
d a birthday party
e a football match

1 2 ▶ Read questions 1–6 in the Exam skills task below and match them with the topic areas in the box.

| Colour | Food | Presents | The meaning of something |
| The relationship between the people | | | The type of event |

> **TIP 1 1**
> The words in the questions and options (A, B, C) may not be the same as the words you hear on the recording. You need to listen for words with a similar meaning. It can sometimes help to rephrase the question in your own words before you listen.

EXAM SKILLS]

> **TIP 1 3**
> Use the questions to help you to follow the recording. Multiple-choice questions are in the same order as the information in the recording. You will hear the answer to question 2 before you hear the information which gives you the answer to question 3.

1 3 ▶ Listen to the conversation and choose the correct letter, A, B or C.

08

1 Who are the two speakers?
   A good friends
   B work colleagues
   C family members

2 What celebration are they talking about?
   A a birthday party
   B a graduation
   C a wedding

3 What colour hat do baby girls wear at the event in Korea?
   A black and silver
   B black
   C red and silver

4 The purse represents
   A good health.
   B good fortune.
   C wealth.

5 What food do guests have at the event?
   A oranges
   B vegetables
   C rice cakes

6 What does the baby receive from the guests?
   A a candle
   B some money
   C some tea

 **GO FURTHER ONLINE**

UNIT /01: RELATIONSHIPS

SPEAKING

IN THIS UNIT YOU WILL LEARN HOW TO

- use simple adjective–noun collocations relating to family
- answer simple questions about your family
- give full answers to Part 1 questions.

01▶ Talk to a partner about these members of your family for 20 seconds each. Try to keep talking for the full 20 seconds.

| father | mother | brother | sister | grandmother | grandfather |

USING ADJECTIVES AND NOUNS TO DESCRIBE YOUR FAMILY

02 ▶ **Listen to Hoi Chin talking about her family and read the first part of what she says. Which collocations does she use to describe her family?**

09

Examiner Let's talk about family. So, tell me about your family.

Hoi Chin My family? Well, my family isn't a large family. It's quite a small family, in fact – and quite a typical family for my country. Just my parents, my older brother and me. So, I'm the baby of the family! I think we're a close, happy family. We do a lot of things together, particularly preparing food – and eating it of course!

03 ▶ **Which adjective in the box can you NOT use in this sentence?**

We are a _____
family.

best	close	happy
large	small	typical

With a partner, describe your family using the collocations in the box.

GRAMMAR FOCUS: ADVERBS OF FREQUENCY
SOMETIMES, OFTEN, NEVER, RARELY AND ALWAYS

04 ▶ **Listen to a candidate talking about the things he does with his family. Answer the questions.**

10

1 How often does he go out with his family?
2 What days of the week does he go out with his family?
3 Where do they often go?
4 What do they usually do when they get to the park?
5 Who sometimes comes with them?

05 ▶ **With a partner, use the questions above to discuss how often you do these things with your family.**

eat out	go bowling	go to the cinema

Many words in English often 'go together' with other words. This is called 'collocation'. For example, we say *a fast car*, but we **don't** say *a quick car*.

TIP 02

It is a good idea to use collocations in the Speaking test. This shows the examiner that you have a good vocabulary.

TIP 03

It is a good idea to make a list of useful words and add to the list as you meet new words when you read and listen, and also to write down words which go together. You may want to group words under headings to help you remember them.

[ANSWERING PART 1 QUESTIONS]

06▶ **Look at questions a–d below on the topic of family. Which question:**

1 asks you about your likes and dislikes?
2 asks you about your personal preferences?
3 asks you how regularly you do something?
4 asks you to talk about who you are like in your family?

a Are you more similar to your mother or your father?
b How often do you go out with your family?
c What do you enjoy doing with your family?
d Do you prefer spending time with your family or your friends?

Now, ask and answer these questions with a partner.

 In Part 1 of the Speaking test the examiner will ask you a few questions about yourself, for example about your family, your likes and dislikes, where you live.

 TIP 06

It is important to listen carefully to the questions that the examiner uses. Make sure you answer the question that is asked.

07▶ **Listen again to Hoi Chin talking about her family and giving more information. Complete the notes below.**

11

· Her parents and **1** _____older_____ brother
· They are a **2** _____ , happy family.
· They like preparing food and **3** _____ it.
· Her father is a better **4** _____ than her mother.
· Her brother is getting **5** _____ next year.
· Hoi Chin would like to have a **6** _____ or **7** _____ one day.

Tell your partner what you remember about Hoi Chin's family. Is your family similar or very different to hers?

08 ▶ Listen to three students answering the question *Who are you most similar to in your family?*

12

1 Which student's answer was too short?

2 Which student didn't answer the question?

3 Which student's answer was the best?

◉ You can add information to your answer by adding a reason, extra details or combining information:

*I don't see my grandparents very often **because** they live in the north of the country.*
*I don't see my family very often **but** I miss them very much.*
*I have a twin brother, **so** I am very close to him.*
*I look very much like my father, **although** we have very different personalities.*

09 ▶ Use one of the words in the box to help you complete the sentences with ideas of your own. Try to use a different word from the box in each sentence.

also	and	because	but	so	even though

1 I visit my parents every weekend …

2 We have a large family …

3 My sister is getting married next year …

4 My father works very long hours, …

5 My brother likes the same things as me, …

PRONUNCIATION

10▷ **What is the third person singular form of the words in the box?**

Example: *have – has She **has** a small family.*

ask	choose	enjoy	keep	play	talk	want	watch

13 **Listen to the words and group them under /z/, /s/ or /ɪz/ according to how the end is pronounced.**

/s/ _____

/z/ _____

/ɪz/ _____

11▷ **Listen and repeat the sentences. Be careful of the pronunciation of verbs with 's' endings.**

14

Is there anyone in your family who annoys you sometimes?

– My father watches football on TV and shouts a lot.

– My brother plays on the computer all the time.

– My mother keeps telling me to tidy my room.

12▷ **With a partner, ask and answer the following questions.**

1 What activities do different members of your family enjoy doing?
   My father enjoys mending old cars. My mother enjoys running and reading books.

2 What do your mother and father want you to do in the future?

3 What type of films do different members of your family watch?

4 What do different members of your family talk to you about?

EXAM SKILLS

13▷ **With a partner, ask and answer the questions below about *your* family. Try to talk for about 20 seconds for each question.**

1 Do you come from a large family?

2 Is there anything you usually do together with your family?

3 How often do you see your grandparents?

4 Who do you like the most in your family?

5 Would you like to spend more time with your family?

When your partner is speaking, make notes about any interesting vocabulary (particularly collocations) that you hear. Then, ask and answer the questions again.

 **GO FURTHER ONLINE**

READING

IN THIS UNIT YOU WILL LEARN HOW TO

- respond to sentence completion questions
- skim read a text
- recognise paraphrase
- practise using the present simple and past simple.

LEAD-IN

01 ▷ Tell your partner about the house or apartment you live in.

> Is it big or

> How many bedrooms

> Is it old or

> Does it have a

02 ▷ What kind of house would you like to live in?

a luxury apartment in the city

a house in the country

a caravan

0 3 ▶ **Find these in the pictures on this page.**

| igloo   treehouse   houseboat   shipping container homes |

Which ones would you like to live in?

SKIMMING AND SCANNING A TEXT

The skills of skimming and scanning are very important in the Reading test.

Skimming is reading the passage quickly to get an idea of what it is about.

Scanning is also reading the passage quickly, but this time looking for particular information in the text, for example, the answer to a question.

- Before you look at the questions, read through the passage quickly. Don't spend more than a minute on this.
- *Skim* over (don't spend time on) words like *the, they, our, through*.
- Notice the 'content' words, such as nouns and verbs, to get an idea of what the passage is about.
- Read the questions.
- *Scan* the passage for the answers. Let your eyes move quickly over the text until you see one of the key words from the question, or words that have a similar meaning.
- Read that part of the passage carefully until you find the answer.

04 ▸ **What is the passage about? Read it in ONE minute and choose one of the options.**

a Life in different cities around the world
b Unusual places to live or stay around the world
c The type of houses and flats most people live in

05 ▸ **Read the passage again to find the words from the box in exercise 3 as quickly as you can.**

06 ▸ **Which of the two activities you have just done practised scanning? Which practised skimming?**

AMAZING HOMES

Most people live in a house or a flat. When they go on holiday they stay in a hotel or a guest house. But some places where you can live or stay are a bit different.

A One unusual place to live is a houseboat. Amsterdam in Holland is famous for its houseboats – there are about 2,500 of them. They have everything that a normal house has: a living room, bedroom, kitchen, bathroom and even sometimes a terrace on the roof. They are cheaper than houses and people who live on houseboats enjoy being close to nature. Some houseboats can be moved to other parts of the river, while others are permanently in one place.

B In Tokyo, Japan, there is a see-through house. It is like a normal Japanese house but all the walls are made of glass. There is plenty of daylight but no privacy. Architect Sou Fujimoto designed it for a couple to make their home. He based his ideas on early man living in trees. It wouldn't suit everyone but the couple who live there love the feeling of being surrounded by the natural world.

C All around the world, people live in homes made from shipping containers. Some use only one container, while others are made from several containers joined together. One house in Chile was built from 12 containers. They are cheap to buy and eco-friendly. They can also be placed in the garden or drive as guest rooms, studies or utility rooms.

D In Germany, you can stay in a one-metre-square house, the smallest house in the world, called the House NA. Van Bo Le-Mentzel, a refugee from Laos, built it to draw attention to the world housing shortage. It is a wooden structure on wheels and weighs 40 kg. It has a locking door and a window. You can turn it onto its side when you want to lie down. Franz from Munich spent the night in one recently 'just to see what it was like'. He found it a bit uncomfortable!

E For an unusual holiday you can stay in an igloo, a house made of ice. These can be found in several countries including Sweden, Norway and Finland. They are built new every winter. Jenny and Callum, visitors from Australia, told us, 'We slept in an igloo last night. It's so cold here – minus 5 degrees centigrade. We used reindeer skins to keep warm!'

F Another couple, Shaun and Rachel from Manchester, enjoyed a recent holiday in a treehouse in Sussex, England. They said, 'It was right up in the trees and had everything we needed, even wifi! It had a small kitchen and we did our own cooking. It was the perfect place to get away from our busy lives.'

UNDERSTANDING PARAPHRASE

 In the Reading test, it is very important to be able to understand paraphrase (when the same idea is given using different words). The words used in the questions won't be exactly the same as the ones in the passage.

07 ▸ **Match these words and phrases from the text (1–6) with their paraphrases (a–f).**

1 houseboats
2 permanently
3 privacy
4 surrounded by the natural world
5 uncomfortable
6 Sweden, Norway and Finland

a not being watched by others
b not feeling pleasant
c homes on the water
d Nordic countries
e forever, always
f having nature all around

08 ▸ **Choose the best paraphrase for these sentences from the text.**

1 The treehouse had everything we needed.
   A We needed some more things for our stay in the treehouse.
   B The treehouse was very well equipped.
   C We need everything for the treehouse.

2 Some houseboats can be moved to other parts of the river.
   A Not all houseboats are permanently fixed in one place.
   B Only some parts of the river have houseboats.
   C You can move to a houseboat in another part of the river.

3 One house in Chile was built from 12 containers.
   A There are 12 houses in Chile made from containers.
   B 12 containers were used to make one house.
   C You need 12 containers to make a house in Chile.

SENTENCE COMPLETION

◎ In this task type you have to complete a sentence with a maximum of three words (or two words and/or a number) taken from the passage. The instructions tell you how many words you are allowed to use.

Look at this example: *Houseboat occupants like living* _____ .

This is a paraphrase of the following sentence from the passage:

People who live on houseboats enjoy being close to nature.

Because you have to use the exact words from the passage in your answer, the answer is *close to nature*.

0 9 ▶ **Follow the steps in the box opposite and complete the sentences. Choose NO MORE THAN TWO WORDS from the passage for each answer.**

1 The two people who live in the transparent house love it, but it wouldn't _____ .

2 The designer of the smallest house hopes to _____ to the lack of houses all over the world.

3 People who stay in igloos sometimes protect themselves from the cold by making use of _____ .

4 People who have _____ would find a holiday in a treehouse ideal.

GRAMMAR FOCUS: PAST SIMPLE AND PRESENT SIMPLE

1 0 ▶ **Answer these questions about the *Amazing homes* passage.**

1 Which tenses does the passage use?
  a present tenses
  b past tenses
  c both present and past tenses

2 Which tenses are used:
  a to describe the houses?
  b to describe habit or things that are always true?
  c to describe people's experiences on holidays?
  d to talk about designing or building the house?

TIP 1 0

As part of your first quick look at the passage, identify whether it is written mainly in the past, present or future, and if the tense changes. This may help you understand the passage.

1 1 ▶ **Choose the correct verb, present simple or past simple.**

1 Most people in China **live** / **lived** in flats.
2 In the UK most houses **have** / **had** gardens.
3 In 2010, my parents **move** / **moved** to Australia.
4 Nowadays Sarah usually **spends** / **spent** her holidays in cities.
5 In the past she **prefers** / **preferred** beach holidays.

1 2 ▶ **Complete the sentences with the correct form of the verb in brackets.**

1 Farid now _____ (**share**) a flat with some other students.
2 Last year he _____ (**live**) at home with his parents.
3 Once I _____ (**stay**) on a campsite next to a lake in Italy.
4 The flat where I live _____ (**have**) two balconies.
5 In 2014 we _____ (**move**) into our new house.

◎ **How to do sentence completion questions**

- Underline key words from the sentence (*houseboat occupants*, in the above example).

- Scan the text for the key words or words that mean something similar (*people who live on houseboats* has a similar meaning to *houseboat occupants*).

- Read the sentences near the key words carefully – *like living* means the same as *enjoy being*.

- Find the words that seem to fit the sentence.

- Check that the meaning of the sentence matches the meaning of the text.

- Check the grammar of the completed sentence.

- Check if the word(s) should be singular or plural.

- Check that you have used the correct number of words.

EXAM SKILLS

HOME FROM HOME

I remember feeling the first time I left home that I would never be able to feel at home anywhere but in my home. No other place would have my mum and dad, my annoying little brother and my cat, Tilly. Nowhere would smell like my home – my mum's roast chicken in the oven and the salty, seaweed smell that drifted in from the nearby beach. The sound of seagulls squawking was the sound of home. Nowhere else would I feel comfortable enough to put my feet up under me and gaze into the log fire dreaming of the future.

I was 15 when I first went away from home on a school trip to Germany. My friends were going too, but we would all stay with different families. I was nervous about this. I knew the home I was going to would not be as comfortable as mine, the family would not be as kind, and who knew what the German food would be like? I knew I would spend three weeks, homesick and sad, missing my family back home.

We arrived in Germany late at night after a long journey by coach and boat. I was tired and hungry. We went into the school hall, where the host families were waiting to meet us. I wondered which one would be mine. Would they give me dinner at this time and would I be able to eat the unfamiliar food? Suddenly I heard my name called and the name of my exchange partner, Brigitte Schmitt. A pretty, blonde girl stepped forward, smiling widely. Behind her stood her parents, a pleasant-looking couple who were also smiling. They held out their hands and said, 'Wilkommen in Deutschland. Welcome to Germany.'

I spent three happy weeks with the Schmitt family. Brigitte had an elder brother, Hendrik, and a younger sister, Lisa. They had two cats, Ping and Pong, who sat on my lap as I looked into the fire in the evenings. The whole family were kind and welcoming. My room was cosy and warm and looked out onto a forest. The fresh clean smell of the trees and of apples baking in the oven became familiar and comforting, like the smells of home. I learnt in those three weeks that you can feel at home anywhere that people are kind to you.

Later that year, Brigitte came to stay with me in the UK. I gave her my room and moved in with my brother. I cleared space for her clothes and put fresh flowers in a vase by the bed. I asked my mum to make her famous roast chicken and an apple pie to make our guest feel at home. We made a welcome banner and put it up on the front door. I did everything I could to help Brigitte feel at home with us. I now understood the importance of a warm welcome.

1 3 ▶ **Read the passage and complete the sentences below. Choose NO MORE THAN THREE WORDS from the passage for each answer.**

1 The writer's mother often cooks _____ .
2 She thought the visit to Germany would make her feel _____ .
3 Brigitte came to pick up the girl with _____ .
4 The Schmitt family's pets' names are _____ .
5 From her bedroom the girl could see a _____ .
6 The girl and her family tried hard to make Brigitte _____ .

GO FURTHER ONLINE

UNIT / 02: PLACES AND BUILDINGS

WRITING

IN THIS UNIT YOU WILL LEARN HOW TO

- describe changes over time as shown on a map
- use prepositions to explain location
- use past tense verb forms (active and passive) to describe change.

LEAD-IN

01 ▷ Which of these facilities do you expect to find on a university campus?

bank	bus stop	car park	halls of residence
gym	library	laboratories	lecture theatres
cafés	post office	tennis courts	recreation area

02 ▷ Look at the maps of Sunnyhills University campus in 1995 and today. Which facilities can you see?

Sunnyhills University 1995

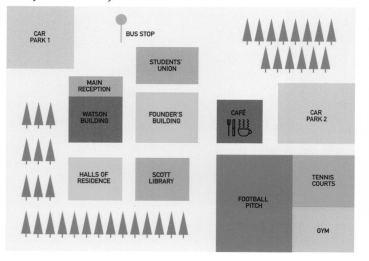

Sunnyhills University today

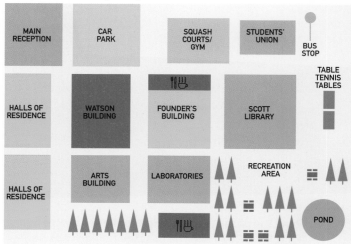

GRAMMAR FOCUS: PREPOSITIONS OF PLACE

0 3 ▶ Look again at the map of Sunnyhills University campus today. Which of these sentences are true?

1 The Founder's Building is between the Watson Building and the Scott Library.
2 The bus stop is in the upper right-hand corner of the campus.
3 The halls of residence are opposite the Students' Union.
4 There are two car parks on the campus.
5 There are two places to eat on the campus.
6 The main reception is in the middle of the campus.
7 The Students' Union moved to a different building between 1995 and today.
8 The car park was moved towards the bottom of the campus.

TIP 0 3

Prepositions are important in any task including maps. It is important to say exactly where things are located in relation to other places.

0 4 ▶ Complete the sentences about the 1995 campus map using the prepositions in the box.

between	in	next to	of	of	on	opposite	to

1 The tennis courts were _____ the football pitch.
2 The Founder's Building was in the middle _____ the campus.
3 The Scott Library was _____ the halls of residence and the football pitch.
4 The café was _____ the football pitch.
5 There were two car parks _____ the campus.
6 The gym was _____ the bottom right-hand corner of the campus.
7 The Watson Building was _____ the left of the Founder's Building.
8 The main reception was part _____ the Watson Building.

0 5 ▶ Complete the sentences to describe the map of the campus today to your partner. You can use the expressions in the box.

between	in front of	in the top right-hand corner
next to	on the left	opposite

1 The halls of residence …
2 The laboratories …
3 The bus stop …
4 The recreation area …
5 The table tennis tables …
6 The Students' Union …

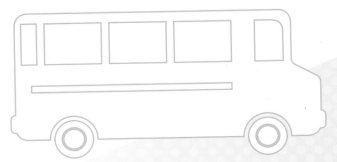

DESCRIBING CHANGES IN A MAP

06 Read this Writing Part 1 task.

You should spend 20 minutes on this task.

Look at the two maps of Sunnyhills University campus in 1995 and today.

Summarise the information by selecting and reporting the main features, and make comparisons where relevant.

You should write at least 150 words.

07 There are three important parts in a Part 1 essay. Match the parts 1–3 with their meanings a–c. Then find them in the model answer.

1 The introductory sentence
2 The concluding sentence
3 The overview

a A summary of the main points
b A description of what the data shows
c Writing the most important points again in different words

VOCABULARY

08 Find these in the model answer:

1 verbs describing change
2 expressions describing where things are

09 The underlined words in the model answer are useful for any essay. Among them, find two expressions which:

1 mean 'and'
2 mean 'but'
3 refer to time
4 refer to what you see in the chart or diagram

10 Find words in the model answer with these meanings.

1 moved to a different place
2 made (3 words)
3 knocked down
4 got bigger (2 words)

MODEL ANSWER

The two maps show changes to the campus of Sunnyhills University between 1995 and today. We can see that the university made many changes during this period, including new buildings and recreation facilities.

In the past, the Scott Library was in front of the Founder's Building. It was relocated to the right, and in addition, it increased in size. The old library building now contains laboratories. In 1995 there was a car park in the top left-hand corner of the campus, whereas now the main reception is there. The halls of residence were moved to the far left of the campus and a new Arts Building was built opposite them.

The old sports ground, gym and tennis courts were demolished; however, in their place the university created a new recreation area with a pond, trees and seating areas. What is more, the university developed new sports facilities, including table tennis tables, a new gym and squash courts. They also built two new cafés.

So, it is clear that the university changed and expanded during this period.

TIP 09

It is important to use plenty of different words in the essay to show you have a wide vocabulary. Make a list of similar words in your notebook and try to use them when writing your practice essays.

GRAMMAR FOCUS: PAST SIMPLE – REGULAR AND IRREGULAR FORMS

1 1 ▷ Find these past tense forms in the model answer. Which of them are irregular? What are the infinitives of these verbs?

expanded	changed	created	made	built
increased	developed	moved	was	

1 2 ▷ These sentences could also be used to describe the maps. Put the verb in brackets into the past tense to complete the sentences.

1 They _____ (**cut**) down trees to build the halls of residence.
2 The old café _____ (**become**) the new library.
3 In 1995 students _____ (**catch**) the bus outside the Students' Union.
4 The university _____ (**need**) laboratories.
5 They _____ (**put**) table tennis tables in front of the Scott Library.
6 There _____ (**be**) not enough halls of residence in 1995.
7 They _____ (**dig**) a pond in the recreation area.
8 They _____ (**plant**) lots of new trees.

Two of the verbs are regular. Which ones?

GRAMMAR FOCUS: PAST SIMPLE – ACTIVE AND PASSIVE

1 3 ▷ Read the information about active and passive verbs. Are sentences 1–4 about the map active or passive?

1 The library was relocated to the right of the Founder's Building.
2 They also built two new cafés.
3 The university created a new recreation area.
4 The old gym and tennis courts were demolished.

1 4 ▷ Change these sentences from active to passive.

1 The university expanded the campus.   *The campus was expanded.*
2 They planted trees in the recreation area.
3 The authorities moved the bus stop.
4 They built a new main reception.

*The university **developed** the campus during this period.* – active

- The subject (*the university*) did the action.
- The verb is a single word (*developed*).

*New halls of residence **were built**.* – passive

- The subject (*new halls of residence*) didn't do the action (*build*), but someone else did the action to it.
- The verb consists of two words: the correct form of *be* (*were*) + past participle (*built*).

15 ▶ Answer the task below. Take as much time as you need and try to write 150 words.

The verbs in the box may be useful. Check the meaning of any unknown words.

| add | build | construct | create | develop | expand | move | plant trees |

The maps below show Colwick Arts Centre in 2005 and today.

Summarise the information by selecting and reporting the main features, and make comparisons where relevant.

2005

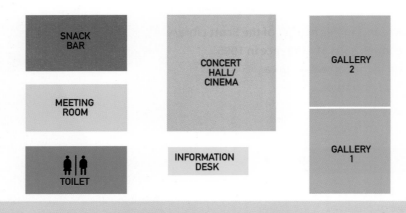

Today

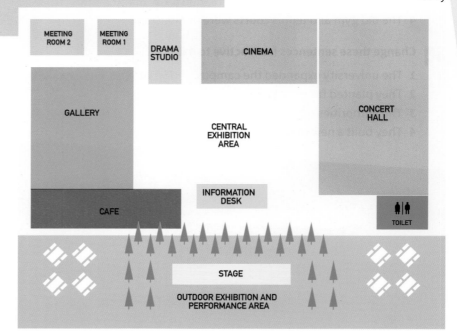

Remember to:
- write an introductory sentence
- include an overview
- use the present simple and past simple, both active and passive
- use prepositions to explain where things are/were.

GO FURTHER ONLINE

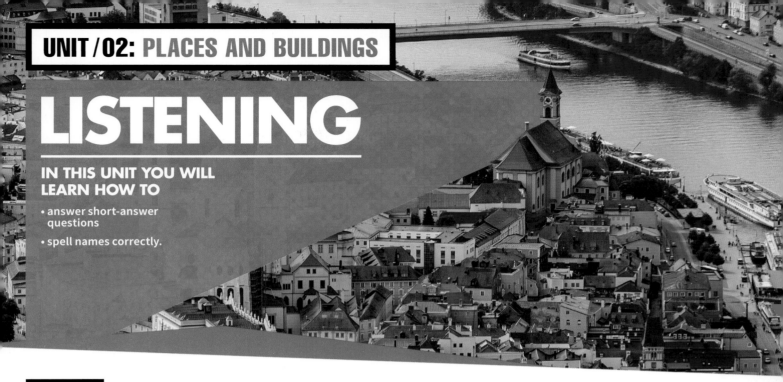

UNIT /02: PLACES AND BUILDINGS

LISTENING

IN THIS UNIT YOU WILL LEARN HOW TO

- answer short-answer questions
- spell names correctly.

01▷ Here are some pictures of places in a town. Match pictures A–G with the words in the box.

| railway station | museum | bank | harbour |
| sports centre | restaurant | bus stop | |

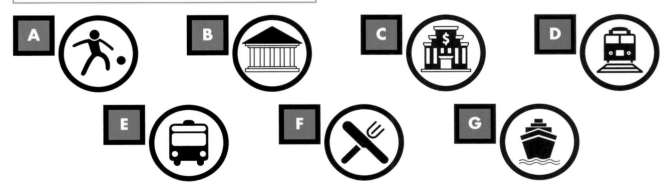

02▷ Put the words in exercise 1 into the correct group. There is an example to help you.

Travel and transport: _____harbour_____ , _____ ,

_____

Sports and leisure: _____ , _____

Arts and culture: _____

Money: _____

03▷ Listen to two short conversations. Where are the speakers?

15

Conversation 1 _____

Conversation 2 _____

SPELLING NAMES

04 ▶ **Listen to the rest of conversations 1 and 2 and answer the questions.**

16

Conversation 1

1 What is the address of the sports website?

   A www.getactive.com   **B** www.getaktive.com

Conversation 2

2 What is the man's name?   James _____

3 What is his address?   _____ Road

> In Section 1 of the Listening test you may have to write the name of a person, a place or a website. Usually the names will be spelled for you. You need to know the letters of the English alphabet so that you can write the words correctly. If you don't, your answer will be wrong. You will hear the spelling once only.

05 ▶ **Listen again and complete the extracts from the two conversations. The first letter of each word is given to help you.**

17

1 'Get active' – Is that a_____ o_____ w_____ ?

2 Is that […] w_____ an 'e' or without?

3 It's got an 'e' at the e_____ .

4 Is that […] with a d_____ 'd', did you say?

SHORT-ANSWER QUESTIONS

06 ▶ **Read the questions and underline the key words. The first one has been done for you.**

1 <u>What</u> did the speakers <u>order</u> in the restaurant?

2 How much did each person pay for their meal?

3 What time is the bus due?

4 Where is the bus stop?

5 How long did the course last?

6 Which TWO things did the speaker do on the course?

7 What is the date of the next course?

8 Who will lead the course?

> You often use short answers in note completion tasks. In this type of task you answer questions using up to three words, or two words and/or a number.

07 ▶ **Complete the table. Use the key words in the questions in exercise 6 to help you. The first one has been done for you.**

Which questions need ...	Question
• a date	7
• a price	
• a period of time	
• a time	
• a meal or a kind of food	
• a name of a person	
• the names of activities or skills	
• a place?	

0 8 ▶ Look at the table you completed in exercise 7. For which questions do you need to write a number?

0 9 ▶ Listen to the conversation and answer the questions.

18

Write NO MORE THAN ONE WORD AND/OR A NUMBER for each answer.

1 What did both speakers order? _____

2 How much did each person pay for the meal? £ _____

1 0 ▶ Read this question about a shopping trip, and choose the correct answer. Why is the other answer incorrect?

Answer the question. Write NO MORE THAN ONE WORD AND/OR A NUMBER for each answer.

What did the boy buy in the shopping mall? _____

Answer: shoes / he bought shoes

1 1 ▶ Listen to the conversation and choose the correct answers. Why are the other answers incorrect?

19

Answer the questions. Write NO MORE THAN TWO WORDS AND/OR A NUMBER for each answer.

1 What time is the bus due? _____ pm

  seven fifteen / seven fiftty / 7.15 / 7.50

2 Where is the bus stop?

  Blithe Road / Blith Road / Blythe Road / Blyth Road

TIP 1 0

It is important to check the instructions carefully to see how many words you can write in your answer.

TIP 1 1

It is important to check your spelling carefully. If you spell the word incorrectly, your answer will be marked wrong. When you need to answer a question with a number, it is easier and quicker to write it as a number rather than writing it in words. And also you are less likely to make a mistake.

1|2▸

20

Listen to Alicia telling a friend about a sailing course and answer the questions. Write NO MORE THAN TWO WORDS AND/OR A NUMBER for each answer.

1 How long did the sailing course last? _____

2 What was the first thing that Alicia learnt? _____

3 What is the date of the next course? _____

4 Who will lead the next course? _____

[EXAM SKILLS]

1|3▸ Read questions 1–8 below. For which questions do you need to write a number ONLY?

1|4▸ Find the key words in questions 1–8 below.

1|5▸ Listen and answer questions 1–8.

21

Then read your answers carefully.

- Did you check your spelling?
- Did you write numbers in digit form?
- Did you check that you have written the correct number of words?

Questions 1–5

Answer the questions below. Write **NO MORE THAN TWO WORDS AND/OR A NUMBER** *for each answer.*

1 What kind of tour did the woman do? _____

2 How did she find out about the tour? _____

3 How many people were on the tour? _____

4 What is the name of the street where the hire shop is? _____

5 How much did each student in the group pay? $ _____

Questions 6–7

Which TWO items were included in the cost of the hire?

6 _____

7 _____

Question 8

What is the website address of the hire shop?

_____

GO FURTHER ONLINE

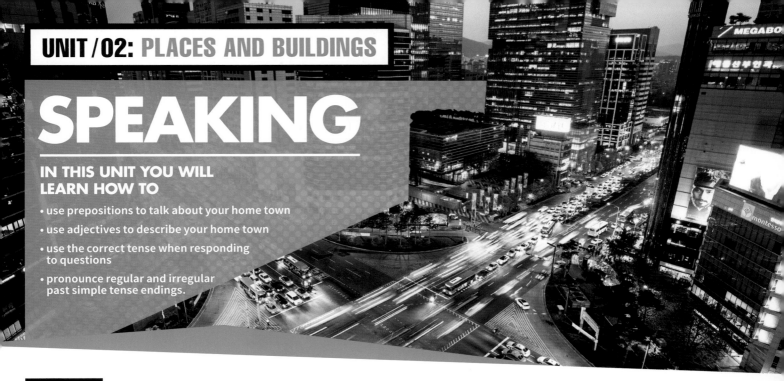

UNIT / 02: PLACES AND BUILDINGS

SPEAKING

IN THIS UNIT YOU WILL LEARN HOW TO

- use prepositions to talk about your home town
- use adjectives to describe your home town
- use the correct tense when responding to questions
- pronounce regular and irregular past simple tense endings.

---

01 ▷ What tense would you use to answer these questions? Select the correct answer A–C below.

1 Is there much for young people to do in your home town?

2 What was your home town like in the past?

3 Has your home town changed since you were a child?

A Present perfect, e.g. *Many things **have changed** in my home town over the years.*

B Present simple, e.g. *There **are** lots of things for young people to do in my home town.*

C Past simple, e.g. *There **were** more factories and the houses were smaller.*

02 ▷ Now, with a partner, ask and answer the three questions in exercise 1.

ANSWERING PART 1 QUESTIONS

0 3 ▶ Listen to a boy describing his home town and read the script.
Match the places the boy talks about with A–H on the map.

22

town hall ___H___	library _____	art gallery _____	cinema _____
shopping mall _____	harbour _____	stadium _____	swimming pool _____

Well, I live in a small town in the north of my country. It has quite a few interesting places to visit. For example, in the centre of town, on the north side of the square we have the historic town hall, which was built in 1895. In front of it, there's a beautiful fountain. Opposite the town hall there's the library. Then if you go over the bridge, we have the art gallery, a big modern building, which often has interesting exhibitions. The art gallery is actually between the cinema (to the north) and a big shopping mall, where I often meet up with my friends.

To the south of the town, there's a harbour, where you can take a boat to the islands. And then next to the harbour is the stadium, where people go to watch our local football team. And just behind it is the public swimming pool. It's an outdoor pool – lovely in summer, but very chilly the rest of the year.

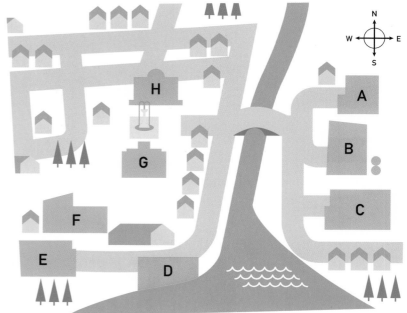

0 4 ▶ Now describe your home town. You might want to draw a map to help you.

USING ADJECTIVES TO DESCRIBE YOUR HOME TOWN

0 5 ▶ Choose the correct heading from the box for the words and phrases in the table below.

Areas	Buildings	Climate	~~Location~~	Opinion

1 Location	2 _____	3 _____	4 _____	5 _____
on the coast	busy	hot	industrial	tall
in the north-east	crowded	humid	business	historic
in the centre	dirty	mild	financial	ordinary
outdoor	exciting			modern
inland	lively			old
	quiet			

06 ▷ Look at the words and phrases in the box and write them in the correct column of the table in exercise 5.

ancient	colourful	cool	enormous	high-rise
tourist	in the south	indoor	incredible	magnificent
narrow	polluted	huge		

With a partner, add two more adjectives of your own to the table.

07 ▷ Complete the sentences with pairs of adjectives from the table in exercise 5.

1 I come from a very modern city. You can see _____ and _____ buildings everywhere.

2 In summer it's very wet and uncomfortable in my town. It's very _____ and _____ .

3 There's usually a light breeze from the sea, so it's very _____ and _____ .

4 There's a lot of rubbish on the streets. It's quite _____ and _____ .

5 There's a great atmosphere in my city, especially at night. It's very _____ and _____ .

TIP 07

It is a good idea to use pairs of words with similar meaning when you talk about your home town. This shows the examiner that you have a good range of vocabulary. For example: *A lot of people live and work in my city. It's very **busy** and **crowded**.*

08 ▷ Look at the photographs below. Try to describe each place using the headings and the words in exercise 5.

GRAMMAR FOCUS: TENSES

09 ▷ Read the questions on the examiner's card. Then match them with the verb tenses.

Let's talk about the town or city where you grew up.

1 Where did you grow up?
2 Is it a good place to live?
3 Do you think it has changed a lot? How?

| present simple | present perfect | past simple |

⊙ In Part 1 of the Speaking test the examiner will ask you questions about familiar everyday topics such as your home town. To answer the questions you might need to use a range of tenses.

TIP 09

It is important to listen very carefully to the questions the examiner asks you. This will help you to decide how to form your answer and what tense to use. One thing you can do is repeat or 'echo' the examiner's question to help you do this, but don't do this too often!

10▶ Read the Part 1 questions from different Speaking tests and choose the correct tense in the candidates' responses.

Examiner Where were you born?

Candidate 1 I (1) **am** / **was** born in Dubai, in the Middle East. It (2) **is** / **was** situated on the north-east coast of the United Arab Emirates.

Examiner Where did you grow up?

Candidate 2 I (3) **am** / **was** born in a small village in China, but I (4) **grow up** / **grew up** in Chengdu, which (5) **is** / **was** a very big city in south-west China.

Examiner Has your home town changed much since you were a child?

Candidate 3 In the last ten years Baku (6) **changed** / **has changed** a lot. Ten years ago we (7) **haven't had** / **didn't have** so many tall buildings and there (8) **isn't** / **wasn't** as much to do then. The biggest problem is that everything (9) **is** / **was** more expensive now.

Examiner Is there anything that you used to do in your home town that you don't do now?

Candidate 4 Well, I (10) **used to** / **was used to** go to the beach every summer when I (11) **have been** / **was** younger, but now I don't have time. One summer, I even (12) **used to go** / **went** fishing. I'd like to do that again. Perhaps I'll have time next summer after my exams.

Listen and check your answers.
23

11▶ Answer the examiner's questions in exercise 10 with your own ideas. Be careful with which tenses you use.

PRONUNCIATION

12▶ Listen to the sentences and tick the correct column, /t/, /d/ or /ɪd/ according to how the verb ending is pronounced.
24

◉ In the past simple, the ending of the verb can be pronounced in one of three ways: /t/, /d/ and /ɪd/.
Examples:
/t/ work – worked
/d/ play – played
/ɪd/ decide – decided

		/t/	/d/	/ɪd/
1	bought			
2	built			
3	situated			
4	called			
5	located			
6	changed			

		/t/	/d/	/ɪd/
7	developed			
8	designed			
9	discovered			
10	started			
11	used to			
12	said			

13▷ Complete the sentences with ideas of your own. Then say them to your partner, pronouncing the verb carefully.

1 Our family **bought** _____ in the middle of town.

2 The _____ was **built** in _____ .

3 Our town is **situated** _____ .

4 The _____ is **called** 'the _____'.

5 _____ is **located** across from the _____ .

6 _____ **have/has changed** over the years in my home town.

7 _____ was/were **developed** by the harbour.

8 _____ was **designed** by _____ .

9 Recently, scientists **discovered** _____ near our village.

10 Recently, many young people have **started** to _____ .

11 A long time ago many people **used to** _____ .

12 A tourist who visited recently **said** our town is _____ .

14▷ Read an examiner's questions, then listen to four students answering them. Match the speakers 1–4 with the examiner's questions a–d.

a What is your favourite place in your town?

b What do people do for fun in your town?

c Is it easy to travel around your town?

d What is the oldest part of your town?

Speaker 1 _____ Speaker 2 _____
Speaker 3 _____ Speaker 4 _____

Now ask and answer questions a–d with a partner.

[EXAM SKILLS]

15▷ Ask and answer the questions below about *your* home town with a new partner.

Listen to your partner's answers and note any new ideas or vocabulary you hear. Then, ask and answer the questions again and try to improve your answers.

1 Can you describe the town where you grew up?

2 What places of interest are there in your home town? Where are they?

3 Is it a good place for young people? Why?

4 Where do young people in your town meet their friends?

5 What is your town like at night?

6 How has your town changed in the last 10 years?

7 Have any new buildings been built?

8 A long time ago, where did people from your town used to work?

GO FURTHER ONLINE

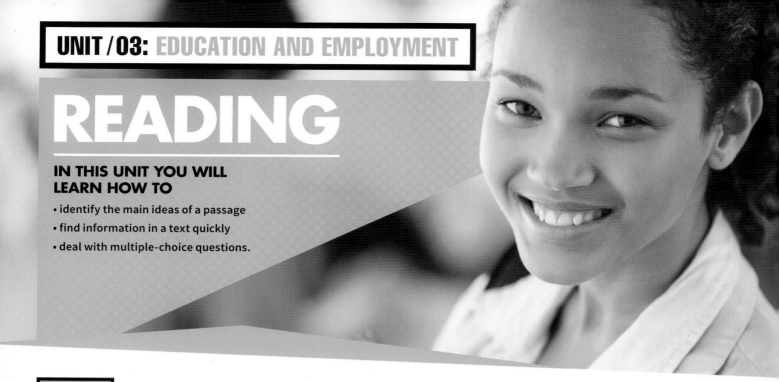

UNIT /03: EDUCATION AND EMPLOYMENT

READING

IN THIS UNIT YOU WILL LEARN HOW TO

- identify the main ideas of a passage
- find information in a text quickly
- deal with multiple-choice questions.

01 Are these words about work or studies? Put them in the correct column.

academic	blended learning	business
degree	employers	retirement
job	qualification	primary education
office	lifelong learning	seminars

TIP **01**

Divide your vocabulary notebook into topics. Leave space to add new words as you learn them.

Work	Studies

02 How many of the words can you find in the text opposite in ONE minute?

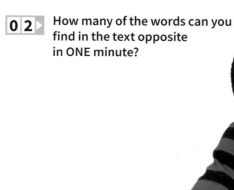

MULTIPLE-CHOICE QUESTIONS

 In multiple-choice questions, you have to choose the correct answer from four options: A, B, C, D.

In the test, you will not have time to read the whole passage in detail. You need to quickly find the part of the text that contains the answer.

First, **skim** the text (read it very quickly) so you know what it is about.

Next, look at the main part of the questions (NOT the options A, B, C, D) and decide which words will help you find the answer. These are the 'key' words.

Then, read the text again quickly. This time you are *only* looking for the key words or words which mean the same. That is the part of the text where the answer is.

FINDING THE ANSWER

03▶ **Spend another ONE minute quickly reading the text and answer this question.**

Does the text express a positive or negative view of globalisation in education?

04▶ **Quickly find which paragraph (A–F) you need to read to answer these questions.**

1 Blended learning means
   A continuing to learn throughout your life.
   B studying online or via email.
   C mixing traditional and modern methods.
   D learning in a classroom.

2 All of these are advantages of globalised education except:
   A Students in developing countries can get better jobs.
   B Students can get a degree at a cheaper price.
   C Universities benefit from international students.
   D The elite get most of the opportunities.

Do you need to read the whole paragraph to find the answers?

Choose the correct answers and explain your choices to your partner.

GLOBALISATION OF EDUCATION AND THE WORKPLACE

A Globalisation has affected most aspects of our lives. One area which has changed is education. More and more people move to different countries for their studies. At the same time, more people stay at home and study by distance learning. It is now easy to learn without attending a college or university, or attending less often. 'Blended learning' means studying partly in a traditional way in the classroom and partly online or via email. These changes also mean that there is now more interest in 'lifelong learning', the idea that we go on learning throughout our working lives and even into retirement. It is easy to attend 'webinars' or online seminars without being away from our offices. Many adults go back to college later in life because it is so easy to get a qualification without giving up work or disrupting family life.

B Different countries have benefitted from the globalisation of education in different ways. Many British, Australian and American universities run their degree programmes in countries throughout Asia, and many students, parents and employers feel this is a valuable opportunity. Students can get an internationally recognised degree at a much cheaper price than going abroad and so can improve their chances of getting a good job. At the same time, those in the countries providing world-class degrees also benefit. They have greater access to ideas and knowledge from all over the world and having international students enriches their universities.

C However, it is not good news for everyone in some developing countries. It is usually the elite – or the richest people in the large cities – who have access to international education. Many people in rural areas have not even had a primary education. Also, those areas usually do not have reliable internet connections and most people do not own a computer. It will take a bit more time for international opportunities to reach everyone in developing countries.

D One concern people have about globalisation is that it can start to mean 'westernisation'. In other words, local knowledge can be lost and money seen as more important than culture. Education should treat every culture with respect; it should not be just learning about the West, but should include different ways of teaching and approaches from around the world. The aim is to enrich and share; the flow of ideas and information should go from East to West as well as from West to East.

E Educational institutions have changed their focus due to globalisation. There are so many benefits of having overseas students that universities are competing for them, using strategies from the world of business. For example, they visit Education Fairs all over the world and spend time and money creating publicity material and advertisements. There is also more emphasis on the student experience. There is more focus on customer care, especially helping international students to settle in, improve their English and understand the academic culture of the host country.

F There are many advantages to the globalisation of education and the workplace. More people get benefits that were only available to those in the developed countries before. There is more understanding between different nations as people learn about each other's cultures. However, it is important to make sure the benefits reach everyone and don't leave many citizens of the developing world behind.

LOOKING FOR WORDS WITH SIMILAR MEANINGS

0 5 ▶ If you see these words (1–7) in a question, what words might you expect to find in the text? Choose a word or phrase from the box below. You do not need all the words.

1 abroad
2 benefits
3 disturbing
4 going to
5 make better
6 useful
7 workplaces

advantages	attending	disrupting	distance learning
enrich	globalisation	lifelong learning	offices
overseas	valuable	westernisation	

The words you don't need are examples of the type of words which are likely to be the same in both the question and the text.

- Sometimes the words in the text are the **same** as the key words in the question, for example the technical term 'blended learning'.
- Sometimes the words in the text are **different** to the key words, but they mean something similar.
- When you are looking for the key words in the text, it is important to look for words, or groups of words, that **mean the same**. We call these 'paraphrases'.

IDENTIFYING THE MAIN IDEA

0 6 ▶ Which FOUR sentences represent the main ideas of the passage?

1 There are both advantages and disadvantages to the globalisation of education.
2 Many people study after retirement.
3 It is important that globalisation should not be westernisation.
4 Universities have had to become more business-focused.
5 University fees rose dramatically in the UK in 2012.
6 Many poorer people in developing countries do not benefit from globalisation.
7 Most lecturers work part-time.

Where in the paragraph can the main ideas be found?

Questions often relate to the main ideas of the passage. It is therefore important that you are able to identify them.

TIP 0 6

Read the first paragraph and the first sentence of every other paragraph, as this is where the main ideas can usually be found.

MULTIPLE-CHOICE QUESTIONS: ANOTHER WAY TO DO THEM

 07 ▷ **Write your own answers to these questions.**

1 Who benefits from globalised education in developing countries?
2 What is the meaning of 'westernisation'?
3 How has the focus of educational institutions changed?

Look at the options and find the one closest to your answer.

1 Who benefits from globalised education in developing countries?
   A almost everyone in those countries
   B mainly well-off people in big towns
   C only those in developed countries
   D only those who own a computer

2 What is the meaning of 'westernisation'?
   A learning only about the West
   B learning local knowledge
   C not learning about culture
   D treating culture with respect

3 How has the focus of educational institutions changed?
   A They have become poor value for money.
   B Staff are not committed to their students.
   C They are focused on attracting students.
   D They only want foreign students.

Then read the passage again and answer the questions. Was it helpful to try to answer the question yourself first?

There is another way to do multiple-choice questions.

- Identify the key words (the most important words) in the question.
- Find the part of the passage that gives the answer.
- Try to answer the question yourself.
- Look at the options and find the one that matches your answer.

GRAMMAR FOCUS: THE PRESENT PERFECT

08 ▷ **Look at this example of the present perfect from the first sentence of the passage:**

Globalisation has affected most aspects of our lives.
Did this happen in the past or present?   *– It began in the past.*
Does it have results in the present?   *– Yes. We are still affected by globalisation.*

1 Look at these present perfect sentences from the passage. Do they relate to both the past and the present? How?
   a Different countries have benefitted from the globalisation of education in different ways.
   b Many people in rural areas have not even had a primary education.
   c Educational institutions have changed their focus due to globalisation.

2 Which of these tenses is used most in the passage?
   a simple past
   b simple present
   c present continuous

3 Choose the best reason for this choice of tense.
   a The situation affects people now.
   b Most of the changes happened in the past.
   c It is a constantly changing situation.

0 9 ▶ Read the text on work-based learning and answer the questions that follow.

◎
- Read (skim) the text very quickly so you understand what it is about.
- Read the main part of the questions and find the key words (the words that will help you find the answer in the passage).
- Find the key words or words that mean the same in the passage.
- Try to answer the question without looking at the options A–D.
- Find the option, A, B, C or D, that matches your answer.
- Check that the other options are incorrect.

EDUCATION
AND THE WORKPLACE
IN THE UK

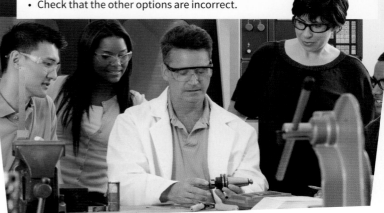

A There has been a trend towards creating a closer connection between education/training and the workplace. This is because many employers felt that school leavers were not prepared well enough and didn't have the skills they would need to do well at work. Having a close relationship between training and work is not new: apprenticeships were a common way of learning in the past. Young people learnt by working with an expert, but this was most common in trades such as builders or electricians. The trend now is for a closer connection between education and the workplace at all levels and in many different types of job.

B In 1944, the UK government created a new system of education. Education was divided into three parts. Children who passed an exam at 11 went to grammar schools. Pupils who didn't do well in the exam went to 'secondary modern' schools or technical schools. At technical schools they studied work-based subjects. In practice, however, only 0.5% of pupils went to technical schools, and this system divided students at a very young age into academic and non-academic. The system did not produce good results, and changed to a more equal system in the 1970s.

C In the 1980s the British government introduced NVQs or National Vocational Qualifications so that young people could get certificates to show their practical skills. It helps employers understand what workers can do. In 1994, the government started a programme which aimed to provide 'quality training on a work-based (educational) route'. These 'modern apprenticeships' are available at three different levels.

D At the higher levels of education, too, there has been more emphasis on work-based learning, which links academic study closely to practical experience. At degree level, companies have linked with universities to create specialised qualifications, such as the BA in Distribution run between Middlesex University and Asda Supermarket. Such partnerships also exist at Masters and even doctorate level.

E The development of technology has helped work-based learning to develop. Blended learning means part of the course can be delivered online, so people don't have to miss work to go to classes. Older or recently retired employees have been given the opportunity to develop new skills as tutors, mentors and coaches for the work-based part of these courses. This kind of work-based training was common in fields such as nursing and teaching, but has now spread to careers which were traditionally not closely linked to education.

F There are some challenges involved in work-based learning. Some lecturers might find it difficult to teach students with a lot of work experience. It may also be difficult to find teachers who can teach in different places and at different times. However, it is a positive trend as there are more ways to learn and people can study at different stages of their lives.

1 Apprenticeships
  A are a new way of learning.
  B were common in the past.
  C only existed in the past.
  D did not help people do well at work.

2 The education system introduced in 1944
  A only affected 0.5% of students.
  B taught only technical subjects.
  C was not a great success.
  D was for academically gifted students.

3 Blended learning
  A mainly benefits older or retired people.
  B involves mainly face to face classes.
  C is mainly for teaching and nursing.
  D is convenient for working people.

4 The challenges of work-based learning include
  A practical issues like when classes are held.
  B students who are not very experienced.
  C finding acceptable types of learning.
  D older people can't use computers well.

GO FURTHE ONLINE

WRITING

IN THIS UNIT YOU WILL LEARN HOW TO

- describe different types of data
- describe changes in numbers
- use prepositions with numbers.

LEAD-IN

01 ▷ Match the diagrams with their names in the box.
Which of them describe changes to numbers over time?

| table | bar chart | pie chart | line graph |

1 % of graduates in the population (UK)

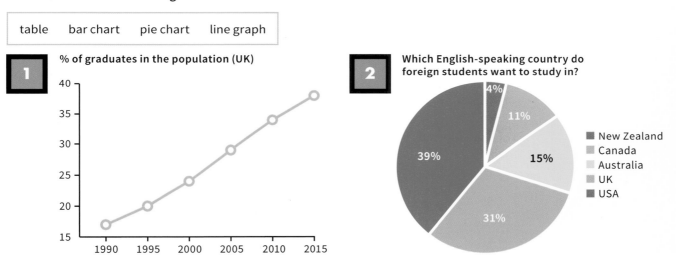

2 Which English-speaking country do foreign students want to study in?

- New Zealand
- Canada
- Australia
- UK
- USA

4%, 11%, 15%, 39%, 31%

3 Participation of 18-year-olds in education and training, 2014

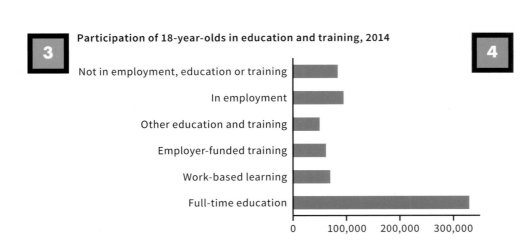

- Not in employment, education or training
- In employment
- Other education and training
- Employer-funded training
- Work-based learning
- Full-time education

0   100,000   200,000   300,000

4 New entrants to primary teacher training programmes 2007 – present

2007/08	16,540
2009/10	15,500
2011/12	17,630
2013/14	18,360
2015/16	20,480
This year	19,213

DESCRIBING CHANGES IN NUMBERS

02 ▶ Put the words into the correct column. Are they verbs (V), nouns (N) or both?

decline	decrease	drop	fall	growth	increase	rise

↑	↓

03 ▶ Write the past simple and past participle forms of the verbs.

infinitive	past simple	past participle
fall		
increase		
drop		
decrease		
decline		
rise		
grow		

04 ▶ Use the correct verb or noun form of one of the words from above to complete the sentences about the table.

New entrants to primary teacher training programmes 2007 – present

2007/08	16,540
2009/10	15,500
2011/12	17,630
2013/14	18,360
2015/16	20,480
This year	19,213

1 The number of new entrants to primary teaching _____ during the period between 2009/10 to 2011/12.

2 There was a _____ from 2007/08 to 2009/10.

3 There was a steady _____ in numbers from 2009/10 to 2015/16.

4 The numbers _____ again this year.

GRAPHS AND BAR CHARTS

05 ▷ **Which is the better description of the line graph: A or B? Why?**

A The graph shows the percentage of graduates in the UK population between 1990 and 2015. In 1990 17% of the population of the UK were graduates. This rose to 20% in 1995 and 24% in 2000. In 2005, it went up to 29%, in 2010 to 34% and up to 38% in 2015.

B The graph shows an upward trend in the % of graduates in the population between 1990 and 2015. The percentage rose gradually throughout the period. It increased by about 3 to 5% every five years, for example between 1990 and 1995 it increased from 17 to 20%.

TIP **05**

Select information that is important – don't include everything. You must include some data to support your description.

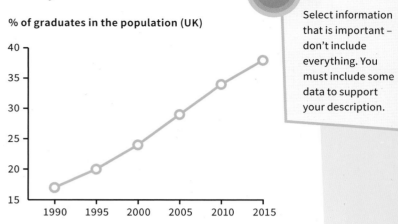

% of graduates in the population (UK)

06 ▷ **Read sentences 1–9 about the bar chart, and answer the questions.**

1 Which TWO sentences should NOT be included?

2 Which of the other sentences include the most important information about the bar chart, do you think?

1 There were about 330,000 18-year-olds in full-time education.

2 Work-based learning is really useful for young people.

3 60,000 were in employer-funded training.

4 Around 70,000 of the age group were involved in work-based learning.

5 Only about 50,000 were in the 'other education and training' category.

6 There were three times more 18-year-olds in full-time education than in employment.

7 The situation is very different in my country.

8 About 90,000 were not in employment, education or training.

9 More 18-year-olds were in employment than not in employment, education or training.

Participation of 18-year-olds in education and training, 2014

07 ▷ **Complete the sentences with a preposition from the box.**

between	in	from	of	of	to	by

1 17% _____ the population are graduates.

2 The number _____ graduates went up.

3 It rose _____ 21% _____ 29%.

4 It increased _____ about 4%.

5 _____ 1992 and 1996 there was an increase.

6 There was a rise _____ graduate numbers during the 1990s.

08▸ Read the model answer and find:

1 the introductory sentence
2 the overview
3 a description of data
4 some data to support the descriptions
5 past simple verb forms
6 a present perfect verb form

The chart below shows the percentage of unemployed recent graduates and young non-graduates aged 21 to 30 between 1990 and 2015.

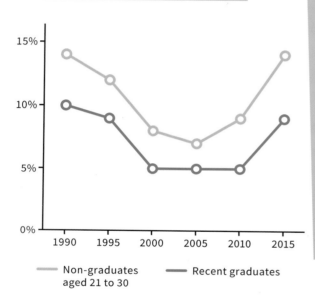

Non-graduates aged 21 to 30 — Recent graduates

Why is the past simple used more than the present perfect?

MODEL ANSWER

The line graph shows the number of unemployed recent graduates and non-graduates in the population of 21 to 30-year-olds in the years between 1990 and 2015. Overall, the numbers have not changed much: we can see a fall, followed by a rise, in both groups. The non-graduates are a larger number than the recent graduates at all points.

Between 1990 and 2000 there was a decrease in the number of unemployed recent graduates and non-graduates. The fall was small from 1990 to 1995, but greater between 1995 and 2000. There was a small change in the middle period. The number of non-graduates dropped and then grew during that period. Over the five years from 2010 to 2015, the numbers of both non-graduates and recent graduates returned almost to their 1990 figures of 14% and 10%.

Overall, it is clear that having a degree is helpful in finding employment as more non-graduates than recent graduates are out of work.

DESCRIBING A PIE CHART

09▸ Which country matches these phrases?

1 over a third
2 a little under a third
3 the lowest number of students
4 about 1 in 10
5 just under a sixth
6 the most popular country
7 the country in second place
8 the least popular country

Which English-speaking country do foreign students want to study in?

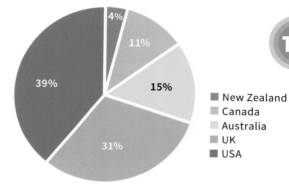

■ New Zealand
■ Canada
■ Australia
■ UK
■ USA

 A pie chart is used to show percentage or proportion.

TIP 09

In your descriptions, include phrases like these, as well as the actual numbers.

EXAM SKILLS

10 ▶ **Look at the Writing Part 1 task below. Before you start writing, answer these questions about the graph.**

1 What are the two groups in green and purple?
2 What do the vertical ↕ and horizontal ↔ axes show?
3 Which two regions had the highest literacy rates?
4 How many regions show different literacy rates for men and women?
5 Which region shows the biggest difference between men and women?
6 What are the male and female literacy rates in the least literate region?
7 What is the percentage difference between the most and least literate areas?

You should spend about 20 minutes on this task.

The bar chart shows the literacy rate (% of people who can read and write) by region and gender in 2011.

Summarise the information by selecting and reporting the main features, and make comparisons where relevant.

Write at least 150 words.

GO FURTHER ONLINE

Literacy rate by region and gender 2011

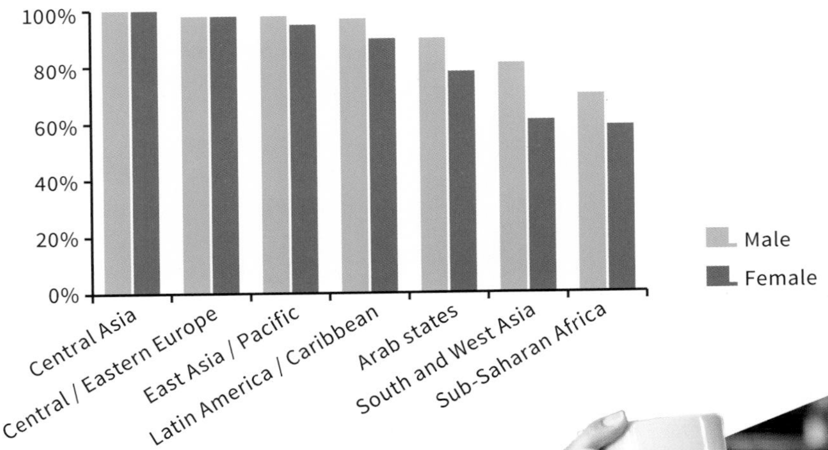

Male
Female

11 ▶ **Write your answer.**

Remember to:
- include introductory and concluding sentences and an overview
- use expressions with prepositions
- use the past simple tense.

LISTENING

IN THIS UNIT YOU WILL LEARN HOW TO

- identify key words in sentence completion tasks
- use strategies to help you answer sentence completion tasks
- follow a conversation
- recognise synonyms and paraphrase.

LEAD-IN

In the Listening test you may hear people talking about their area of work or studies. And in the Speaking test you may have to talk about your job or your course. It is important to understand and use words related to these topics to help you do this.

01 ▶ Pictures A–G show different areas of work or study. Match the pictures with the words in the box.

hotel and catering	construction	health	sports and leisure
information technology	art and design	retail	

02 ▶ Look at the words in the box. Do they describe a job or a type of course?
Put J for 'job' or C for 'course' next to each word. The first one has been done for you.

architect __J__	chef ____	building engineering ____	badminton coach ____
computing ____	doctor ____	fitness training ____	food technology ____
graphic designer ____	medicine ____	shop management ____	store assistant ____
web designer ____	textiles ____		

03 ▷ Complete the table. Use the words in exercise 2. There are two examples to help you.

	Job	Area of work or study	Course
1	graphic designer	art and design	
2		construction	building engineering
3		health	
4		hotel and catering	
5		information technology	
6		retail	
7		sports and leisure	

04 ▷ Identify the TWO correct endings for each sentence.

1 I've done a course in **computing / badminton coach / food technology**.
2 My sister has worked on a cruise ship as a **chef / medicine / doctor**.
3 Our son had a job as a(n) **architect / store assistant / building engineering**.
4 He's very keen on **web designer / fitness training / textiles**.

TIP 04

It is important to listen carefully to the ending of words. For example, words ending in -*ology* and -*tion* can be used to talk about different areas of work or study. Words that end in -*er* may refer to people and jobs.

05 ▷ Listen to two short conversations. Are the speakers talking about a job or a course? Put J for 'job' or C for 'course'.

🔊 26

Conversation 1 _____   Conversation 2 _____

SENTENCE COMPLETION]

◉ In this type of task you complete sentences by writing up to three words, or two words and/or a number, in the gaps. The instructions tell you how many words you can write.

The gaps can come
• at the beginning of the sentence
• in the middle of the sentence
• at the end of the sentence.

The sentences have a main verb and a subject.

06 ▷ Read the sentences carefully. Underline the key words before and after each gap.

1 Anna has got a job as a _____ .
2 She has recently completed a course in _____ .
3 The new name of the department which sells computers and phones is _____ .
4 The Food Photography course takes place on the _____ September.
5 There is a total of _____ places available on the course.

07 ▷ Match questions 1–5 in exercise 6 with the type of information you need to listen for, given below. The first one has been done for you.

an area of study _____
a type of job __1__
a number only _____

a name of a place _____
a date _____

TIP 06

It is useful to underline the key words in the sentence before you listen to the recording. Doing this will help you decide what kind of information you need to listen for.

08 ▷ Listen again to Anna talking to the store manager and complete the sentences. Write NO MORE THAN TWO WORDS for each answer.

🔊 27

1 Anna has got a job as a _____ .
2 She has recently completed a course in

_____ .

3 The new name of the department which sells computers and phones is _____ .

TIP 07

It is important to think about what *type* of word will go into each gap. This helps you to be ready to hear it during the conversation.

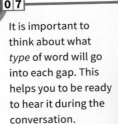

09 ▶ Choose the correct grammatical answer. Why are the other answers incorrect?

1 Anna has got a job as a **assistant / store assistant**.

2 She has recently completed a course in **informations technology / information technology**.

3 The new name of the department which sells computers and phones is **Moving Image / Moving Images / The Moving Images**.

TIP 09

Take care with singular and plural forms when you write your answers. If you use the wrong form, your answer will be wrong.

10 ▶ Listen to the student and the receptionist again and complete the sentences. Write *NO MORE THAN ONE WORD AND/OR A NUMBER* for each answer.

26

1 The course takes place on the _____ September.

2 There are a total of _____ places available on the course.

TIP 10

Pay attention to the number of words you need to write. **NO MORE THAN ONE WORD AND/OR A NUMBER** means that if you write **two** words or more, your answer will be wrong. But you can write one word and a number.

Check to make sure that you have not written 'extra' words that are already in the sentence.

11 ▶ Look at the question below and read the answers that different candidates wrote. Which answers are correct? Why are the other answers incorrect?

*Complete the sentence below. Write **NO MORE THAN ONE WORD AND/OR A NUMBER** for your answer.*

The course takes place on the _____ September.

Candidates' answers

19   19th   the 19   nineteenth of   19th of September   19 Sept

TIP 11

You can write numbers in figures or in words. It is a good idea to write them in figures as it takes less time and you will not make any spelling mistakes.

FOLLOWING A CONVERSATION

12 ▶ Read the questions carefully. Then put the topics below in the order they will be mentioned in the conversation. The first one has been done for you.

*Complete the sentences below. Write **NO MORE THAN TWO WORDS AND/OR A NUMBER** for each answer.*

1 The title of the course the speaker wants to do is _____ .

2 The course starts at _____ .

3 It lasts for a period of _____ hours in total.

4 The course aims to teach people how to use different _____ .

5 Part of the course is held at a nearby _____ .

6 The total cost of the course is _____ .

a the price of the course   _____

b the location of the course   _____

c the name of the course   1

d the starting time of the course _____

e the purpose of the course   _____

f the duration of the course   _____

The questions always follow the order of the information you hear in the conversation. This means that you will hear the answer to question 1 before you hear the answer to question 2.

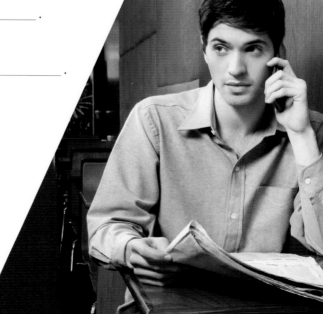

The speakers you hear often use different words to those in the questions. You may hear a synonym or paraphrase (a word or words with a similar meaning). Before you listen, try to identify key words and phrases in the sentences and think about possible synonyms for each one.

13 ▶ **Match the words and phrases 1–9 with their synonyms a–i.**

1	price	**a**	place
2	name	**b**	finishes
3	duration	**c**	reason for
4	starts	**d**	is held
5	takes place	**e**	begins
6	purpose	**f**	length
7	ends	**g**	hands-on
8	location	**h**	cost
9	practical	**i**	title

[EXAM SKILLS]

14 ▶
28

Listen to the rest of the conversation between the student and the receptionist and complete the sentences. Ignore the highlighted words for now. Write NO MORE THAN TWO WORDS AND/OR A NUMBER for each answer.

1 The title of the course the student wants to do is

_____ .

2 The course starts at _____ a.m.

3 It lasts for a period of _____ hours in total.

4 The course aims to teach people how to use different

_____ .

5 Part of the course is held at a nearby _____ .

6 The total cost of the course is _____ .

15 ▶ **Match the highlighted words in exercise 14 with the words and phrases used on the recording.**

begins	full fee	goes on	it's called
local	some	train	a range of

16 ▶ **Read your answers to the sentence completion task carefully and then answer the questions in the checklist below.**

- Have you answered ALL the questions?
- Have you written the correct number of words in each sentence?
- Have you written numbers as figures to save time?
- Have you checked your spelling?
- Have you checked whether your answer should be in the singular or plural form?

Now check your answers.

 GO FURTHER ONLINE

SPEAKING

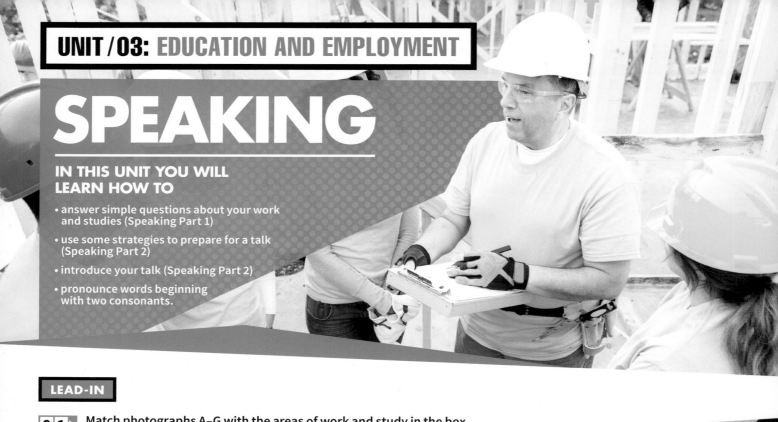

IN THIS UNIT YOU WILL LEARN HOW TO

- answer simple questions about your work and studies (Speaking Part 1)
- use some strategies to prepare for a talk (Speaking Part 2)
- introduce your talk (Speaking Part 2)
- pronounce words beginning with two consonants.

LEAD-IN

01 ▷ Match photographs A–G with the areas of work and study in the box.

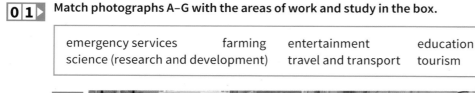

emergency services	farming	entertainment	education
science (research and development)		travel and transport	tourism

ADJECTIVES TO DESCRIBE FEELINGS AND EXPERIENCES

02▶ Look at the words in the box. Which words have a negative meaning?

tired	boring	embarrassed	challenging	fascinated
great	thrilled	not very exciting	interesting	amazed

03▶ Read the words in exercise 2 again. Which words can you use to describe your feelings? Which words can you use to describe the experience of doing the things in the photographs? Put F for 'feelings' or E for 'experience' next to each word.

Which ONE word can be used to describe both your feelings and the experience?

04▶ Complete the table. There is an example to help you.

I feel / I felt …	It is / It was
amazed	amazing
	thrilling
	boring
	challenging
fascinated	
not very excited	
	tiring
	embarrassing
interested	
great	

05▶ Choose the correct word in each sentence.

1 I've got a place on the course! I'm **thrilled** / **thrilling**!
2 It's a very **interested** / **interesting** job – I'm learning a lot.
3 I had to give a presentation in front of my colleagues. I felt really **embarrassing** / **embarrassed**.
4 She gets **boring** / **bored** easily, so she's changed jobs twice.
5 He works long hours and late nights and weekends in order to pay for his daughter's university course. It must be very **tired** / **tiring** for him.
6 She's got an **amazing** / **amazed** job. She's a journalist and she's interviewed lots of famous people.

C

F

G

06 ▶ **Look at photographs A–D and answer the questions.**

- Which of these jobs or activities have you done before?
- How did you feel about it?
- Which have you not done yet? Would like to try them? Why?

[SPEAKING TEST – PART 1]

 The examiner will ask you some simple questions about your work or your studies. It is important to try to give full answers to the questions and to say what you feel about your job or course of study. Look at the examples of Part 1 questions.

- What do you do? Do you work or are you a student?
- Are you enjoying it?
- Would you like to learn anything new in the future?
- Is there a job you would really like to do in the future?

07 ▶ **Listen to a recording of Part 1 of the Speaking test. Match the speaker, Nina, with the correct photograph A–D above. Does she work or is she a student?**

29

08 ▶ **Listen again and number the following in the order Nina talks about them.**

29

What job she would like to do in the future	☐
How many hours a week she studies/works	☐
What she does	☐
What she would like to learn in the future	☐
What she thinks about her studies/work	☐
Where she studies/works	☐

TIP 07

It is very important not to simply answer a question with 'Yes' or 'No'. Try to use your imagination and invent some ideas. Remember that the examiner is testing your ability to speak English, not your views or general knowledge. For example, if there isn't a job you would really like to do in future, don't just say 'No'. Think of any job you could talk about.

09▶ Use the headings in exercise 8 to talk about Anna.

10▶ Make notes using the headings in exercise 8 to speak about what *you* do. You may wish to use a dictionary to help you do this.

11▶ Use your notes to tell your partner about what you do. Ask each other questions.

- What do you do? Do you work or are you a student?
- Are you enjoying it?
- Would you like to learn anything new in the future?
- Is there a job you would really like to do in the future?

PRONUNCIATION: WORDS BEGINNING WITH TWO CONSONANTS

12▶ Listen and practise the sounds at the beginning of the words in bold.

30

a **st**udent – I'm a **st**udent.

a **sc**arf – a beautiful **sc**arf

I've just made a beautiful **sc**arf.

plastic – It's made out of **pl**astic.

ate – rate – **gr**eat

It's **gr**eat – I think it's **gr**eat.

It looks very **str**ange, but I think it's **gr**eat!

great close-up shots

I've learnt how to take some **gr**eat close-up shots!

SPEAKING TEST – PART 2]

◉ In Part 2 of the Speaking test, you prepare and talk about a simple topic.

The topic will be based on your own experience. This means that you should find it familiar and easy to talk about.

You have one minute to prepare your topic.

You must talk for about two minutes.

Part 2 tests your ability to organise your ideas and speak fluently.

13▶ Read the information about Part 2 and then look at the following topic areas. Which THREE do you think are Part 2 topic areas?

1 Talk about how the education system in your country has changed.
2 Talk about a time when you learnt something new.
3 Talk about your very first day at school.
4 Talk about your ideal place to study.
5 Talk about how people normally travel to work in your city.
6 Talk about the kind of jobs that people do in your home town.

14▶ Look at the information about what happens in Part 2 of the Speaking test. Can you put the stages A–F in the correct order?

A You talk about the topic in the task, including all four points on the card. ☐

B You stop talking when the examiner tells you to. ☐

C You read a card with a task on it. ☐

D You make notes on each of the separate parts of the task. ☐

E The examiner says, 'Here is your topic card. You now have one minute to prepare your talk.' ☐ 1

F The examiner asks you some questions about your talk. ☐

15▶ Look at the example of a Part 2 card. Highlight or underline the key words in each instruction. The first one has been done for you.

Describe a time when you learnt something new.

You should say:

- <u>what</u> you <u>learnt</u>
- how you learnt it
- what the result was

and explain how you felt about learning something new.

TIP 15

There are always FOUR instructions on the card, which tell you what you need to talk about. It is therefore important to identify the key words in each instruction. It is important to try to talk about all four points on the card.

16▶ Before you start your talk, the examiner will give you some paper to make notes on. You need to make sure your notes cover all the points on the card.

Match the key words with the candidate's notes.

What?   thrilled and proud of myself
How?   learnt to fly a small plane
Result?   had lessons at a flying club
How I felt?   got my pilot's licence

INTRODUCING YOUR TALK

◉ It is important that you introduce your talk. Here are some suggestions of ways you can begin.

– I'm going to talk about *a time when I learnt something new.*
– I'd like to tell you about …
– I want to talk about …

17▶ Practise introducing the following talks. Say one sentence for each.

- Describe a time when you learnt something new.
- Describe your very first day at school.
- Describe your ideal place to study.

TIP 17

It is a good idea to introduce your talk clearly and slowly. Doing this gives you time to think about what you are going to say next.

18 ▶ Look at the topic card with some student's notes on it. Complete the student's notes by adding notes a–d to the correct part of the card.

Describe a time when you learnt something new.

You should say:

- what you learnt   learnt to ski; **1** _____
- how you learnt it   **2** _____ , had great instructor!
- what the result was   **3** _____ , got a silver cup!

and explain how you felt about learning something new. proud; **4** _____

TIP 18

The points on the topic card often begin with *How* or *Wh-* question words such as *why, who, when, what* or *which*. These points are given to help you.

a was in a group
b really thrilled
c won a competition
d love snow and being active!

31 Now listen to Nina giving her talk and check your answers.

19 ▶ Make your own notes for the topic card in exercise 18. Use the key words to help you.

20 ▶ Practise your talk. Try to speak for two minutes.

GO FURTHER ONLINE

READING

IN THIS UNIT YOU WILL LEARN HOW TO

- locate and match information from a text
- complete gapped sentences
- correct common errors in the use of countable/uncountable nouns
- use *some*, *any*, *much* and *many*.

LEAD-IN

0 1 ▷ Find the foods in the pictures and then put the food words into the correct column: countable or uncountable.

burger	cereal	chips	curry	fish	mashed potato
chicken	noodle	rice	salad	toast	vegetable

Examples: *Apple* is a countable noun – we can say *three apples*.
Bread is an uncountable noun – we can't say *three breads*.

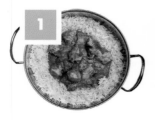

Countable	Uncountable

0 2 ▷ Answer the questions.

1 Which of the foods above do you eat regularly?
2 Which do you like/dislike?
3 What foods are typical of your country?

03 ▶ Read the text in one minute. Then cover it and tell your partner what you can remember.

FOOD
CULTURE SHOCK

A CHARLES

You would think that eating with your fingers would be easy. In the US, there are only certain things you can eat with your fingers, like burgers, for example, and that's easy enough. When I went to South India, though, I realised that it is a whole new skill to learn to eat rice and curry with your fingers. You have to mix the curries together and with the rice and form a 'ball'. Daal* is particularly helpful as a kind of glue. You use your fingertips, never the palm of your hand, and use your thumb to pop it into your mouth. I thought I knew where my mouth was, but my first few attempts were a disaster. There was food everywhere!

*Daal is a lentil curry widely eaten in the Indian subcontinent.

B ALFREDO

For me, when I travel, the 'fast food' culture always shocks me. I can't believe there are people in the world who live on 'junk food' like burgers and just grab a sandwich for lunch. Back home, food is very important to us. We cook fresh food for lunch and dinner and sit down and eat as a family at least once a day, twice at weekends. A lot of people grow their own vegetables and keep chickens. Food is part of your identity, so what are you saying about yourself when you eat some rubbish which contains chemicals and goodness knows what else? The worst thing I have seen on my travels is a baby being given a fizzy drink in a bottle. That really shocked me!

C QIANG SHI

I enjoy trying food from different countries, but what interests me more is the culture and habits surrounding food and eating. In China, when we go to a restaurant with colleagues, when we are offered something, we say 'No thanks', even though we want it, because the person will definitely repeat the offer. In other countries, though, 'no' means 'no', so if you are just trying to be polite and don't take it the first time, you will end up with nothing! To me, it feels wrong to take something the first time it is offered, so it took me a while to get used to that when I travel abroad.

D PAULINE

Being a vegetarian is so easy here in the UK that we forget that not everyone in the world understands vegetarianism. For vegans the situation is even more difficult. Probably the best place I've been to is India, as everything is divided into 'veg' or 'non veg' so you know exactly what you're getting. In many countries, they don't even realise that there is a concept of not eating meat for ethical reasons. In many parts of the world, meat equates to prosperity, so the idea of going out for a meal and not having meat is alien to them. I have travelled to places where, as a vegetarian, all I have been able to eat is salad, fruit and chips. I'm glad to get home where we have special vegetarian products.

E AILEEN

I think breakfast is the meal where food culture shock really hits you. In Australia, there are certain foods you eat for breakfast and certain foods you don't. We usually eat cereal or toast, maybe yoghurt and fruit. We would never eat chicken or vegetables. But when I travelled in Asia, I realised that in many places, there is no difference between breakfast and dinner: rice, curry, noodles, soup, steamed vegetables and fish all appeared at breakfast. Even though I love all those things, I just can't face them at breakfast!

04 ▶ **Quickly find the following information in the text.**

1 a food that can be used as a 'glue' _____
2 a meat not usually eaten for breakfast In Australia _____
3 a country where 'no' doesn't always mean 'no' _____
4 an example of a 'junk food' _____
5 a country which is easy for vegetarians _____
6 a food eaten with fingers in the US _____

◎ Some questions require you to find very specific information quickly. This exercise will help you practise this skill.

◎ **Paraphrase**

To answer some questions, you need to recognise paraphrase.

Question: Who is concerned about healthy eating?
Answer: Alfredo.

Paragraph B doesn't use the phrase 'healthy eating' but these clues help us find the answer:

… the 'fast food' culture always shocks me.
… what are you saying about yourself when you eat some rubbish which contains chemicals …?
The worst thing I have seen … is a baby being given a fizzy drink.

05 ▶ **Match questions 1–6 with the evidence a–f.**

Who:
1 realised that some people eat the same dishes for different meals?
2 dislikes the takeaway culture?
3 discusses travelling for people on a special diet?
4 talks about what is considered polite in different cultures?
5 found it difficult to learn a new way of eating?
6 talks about producing your own food?

a … we forget that not everyone in the world understands vegetarianism.
b I thought I knew where my mouth was, but my first few attempts were a disaster. There was food everywhere!
c A lot of people grow their own vegetables and keep chickens.
d I can't believe there are people in the world who live on 'junk food'
e In China, when we are offered something, we say 'No thanks' … In other countries, though, 'no' means 'no'
f But when I travelled in Asia, I realised that in many places, there is no difference between breakfast and dinner

SENTENCE COMPLETION

06▶ **Complete these sentences using a word from the text.**

1 In China, if you refuse food, the host will usually _____ the offer.
2 For Alfredo, food plays an important role in a person's _____ .
3 In India, you should not use your _____ when eating.
4 In some countries, eating meat represents _____ .
5 In many places in _____ , there is no difference between foods eaten for breakfast and dinner.

GRAMMAR FOCUS: COUNTABLE AND UNCOUNTABLE NOUNS

07▶ **Correct the errors in these sentences.**

1 Fresh fruit are healthy and we should eat them every day.
2 Chips cooked in the oven is healthier than fried chips.
3 The burgers and the pizza are the cheapest foods you can buy.
4 In the India it is easy to find the vegetarian food.
5 My favourite food is chickens.

08▶ **Complete the sentences with *some, any, much* or *many*.**

1 There are _____ mushrooms in the fridge.
2 Are _____ people vegetarian in your country?
3 I don't put _____ sugar in my tea – just half a spoonful.
4 Do we have _____ flour left?
5 Can I have _____ more cake, please?
6 How _____ rice do you eat every week?

◉ Being able to locate information quickly will help you in questions where you need to find a suitable word to complete a sentence.

FOOD TV: education or entertainment?

A Shows about cookery have become more and more popular all over the world. But what are the reasons for this, and does it make us cook more? In the UK, BBC viewers complained to the programme *Points of View* that there were too many cookery shows on TV. In one week, the BBC showed 21 hours of cookery. When shows on other channels were included, this came to an amazing 434.5 hours of food TV.

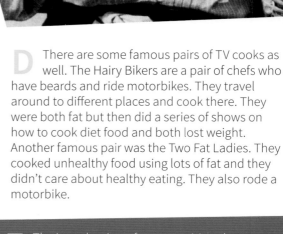

B In the past, TV cookery shows were there to teach people how to cook. One of the first famous TV cooks, Julia Child, was American. She began her career as a cook when, in 1948, she moved to Paris and learnt to cook sophisticated French cuisine because her husband loved good food. On her return home, she published a collection of French recipes made simple, for ordinary American housewives to use, which was an instant success. She was invited to do a TV show, where her humour and strong personality soon won her great fame.

C Nowadays TV chefs are famous for all sorts of different reasons. Gordon Ramsay, for example, is an interesting TV chef. He is famous for having a bad temper and using foul language. In his TV show, *Hell's Kitchen*, he shouts at his staff when they make mistakes because he wants all the food at his restaurants to be perfect. He has many restaurants in different countries. Jamie Oliver is a good-looking, working-class boy who made healthy eating fashionable. He believes children should eat healthy food and he worked with the government to make school meals healthier. His style of cooking is quick, easy and fun.

D There are some famous pairs of TV cooks as well. The Hairy Bikers are a pair of chefs who have beards and ride motorbikes. They travel around to different places and cook there. They were both fat but then did a series of shows on how to cook diet food and both lost weight. Another famous pair was the Two Fat Ladies. They cooked unhealthy food using lots of fat and they didn't care about healthy eating. They also rode a motorbike.

E The introduction of a competitive element to many cookery shows reminds us that food TV is more entertainment than education these days. Many of us love shows like *Masterchef*, where a contestant is eliminated on every show. The personalities of both the contestants and the judges are far more important than the cookery. In a popular competitive show called *The Great British Bake-Off*, there was a 'nice judge', Mary Berry, and a 'nasty judge', Paul Hollywood.

09 ▸ **Read the article about Food TV. Which paragraphs contain the following information? Write the correct letter, A–G.**

[NB You may use any letter more than once.]

1 The cooking show that affects people most
2 A TV chef who was first famous as an author
3 The number of food shows on TV
4 The role of cookery shows for enjoyment rather than learning
5 Why children should be taught to cook at school
6 Research about the amount of time people cook
7 Examples of famous cookery partners

GO FURTHER ONLINE

FLOUR

10 ▸ **Look at the following descriptions (1–7) and the list of famous chefs. Match each description with the correct chef, A–F.**

[NB You may use any letter more than once.]

1 Changed the style of cooking on some of their programmes
2 One of the first TV chefs
3 Helped to get children eating healthy food
4 The kinder of two judges
5 Cooked food that was not very good for you
6 Is very rude to the kitchen workers
7 Showed people that cooking foreign dishes need not be difficult

A Mary Berry
B Jamie Oliver
C The Hairy Bikers
D Gordon Ramsay
E Julia Child
F Two Fat Ladies

F We know that cooking at home is better for us than eating ready-made or takeaway meals. However, the fact that there is more cookery on TV doesn't necessarily mean people cook more. Different studies have produced different results, but most agree that people generally spend less time cooking than they did in the past. Certain cookery shows influence viewers more than others. One study found that the most influential show was Jamie Oliver's *15 Minute Meals*, which influenced 21% of viewers. This may be because his method is to cook quick, simple, healthy meals rather than 'restaurant-style' food.

G It seems, though, that teaching children to cook at home and at school has much more influence on healthy eating than watching TV programmes on cooking. Grandparents have an important role to play because they may have more time – and experience – than parents. Cooking with family members on a regular basis and making food preparation part of the school curriculum is likely to ensure that children become adults who can and do cook.

WRITING

IN THIS UNIT YOU WILL LEARN HOW TO

- deal with a Part 1 question with two diagrams
- describe data without exact numbers
- compare data in a pie chart
- decide what information to include.

LEAD-IN

0 1 ▷ Read the task and look at the diagrams below.

The charts below show the favourite takeaways of people in the UK and the number of Indian restaurants in the UK between 1960 and 2015.

Summarise the information in both charts by selecting and reporting the main features, and make comparisons where relevant.

Write at least 150 words.

Diagram 1

Favourite takeaways in the UK
(A *takeaway* is a meal you buy in a restaurant or shop to eat at home.)

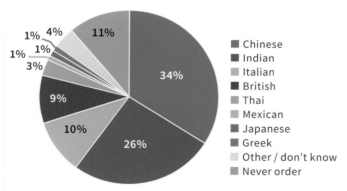

- ■ Chinese
- ■ Indian
- ■ Italian
- ■ British
- ■ Thai
- ■ Mexican
- ■ Japanese
- ■ Greek
- ■ Other / don't know
- ■ Never order

Diagram 2

Number of Indian restaurants in the UK

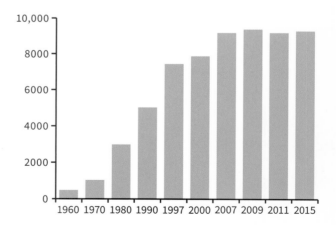

0 2 ▷ Look at the following expressions. Which are more suitable for diagram 1 and which are more suitable for diagram 2?

1 the highest proportion of people
2 only a very small number of people
3 there has been a steady increase
4 a very small drop

5 about a third of people
6 approximately a quarter of people
7 the greatest rise took place

DESCRIBING TWO DIAGRAMS

INTRODUCTION AND OVERVIEW

03▶ Complete this introductory sentence and overview. Write one word in each gap.

The **1** _____ chart shows which type of takeaway food is the most popular in the UK, while the **2** _____ chart shows how many Indian restaurants existed in the UK between **3** _____ and **4** _____ . We can see that **5** _____ and Indian takeaways are the favourites, and that the number of Indian restaurants in the UK **6** _____ steadily during this period.

◎ Sometimes you will have to write about two separate types of diagram in the same task.

TIP 03

When you are working with two diagrams, your first sentence should introduce both of them and your overview should summarise both of them.

DESCRIBING NUMBERS IN A PIE CHART

04▶ Match the percentages from the pie chart with their descriptions.

1 34%   **a** a tiny proportion
2 26%   **b** about a quarter
3 10%   **c** just over a third
4 1%   **d** one in ten

MAKING COMPARISONS

05▶ Look at diagram 1 and complete the sentences about the pie chart with the words in the box. One word is used twice.

fewer	least	less	more	most

1 The _____ popular type of takeaway is Chinese.
2 The three _____ popular types are Mexican, Greek and Japanese.
3 Italian takeaways are slightly _____ popular than British takeaways.
4 Japanese food is _____ popular than Thai food.
5 _____ people like Chinese food than Indian food.
6 _____ people like Mexican food than Thai food.

GRAMMAR FOCUS: COUNTABLE AND UNCOUNTABLE NOUNS

06▶ Choose the correct words to make true sentences.

1 *More* and *less* are used with **countable / uncountable** nouns.
2 *More* and *fewer* are used with **countable / uncountable** nouns.

07 Put the nouns into the correct column.

restaurant	coffee	farm	country	home	land
language	meat	oil	person	animal	sand

Countable	Uncountable

08 Complete the sentences with *more, less* or *fewer*. Use the information in the chart.

	China	India
land	9,596,960 square km	3,287,263 square km
percentage of population living in cities	50.5%	31.3%
official languages	Mandarin Chinese	22 official languages

1 China has _____ land than India.
2 India has _____ land than China.
3 In India, _____ people live in cities than in China.
4 India has _____ official languages than China.

GRAMMAR FOCUS: ARTICLES

09 Correct the errors with articles in these sentences about diagrams 1 and 2.

1 Number of Indian restaurants in UK has risen.
2 The Chinese food is the most popular.
3 Second most popular food is Indian.
4 There was small drop in the number of Indian restaurants in 2011.
5 There were about thousand Indian restaurants in 1970.

DESCRIBING DIAGRAMS WITHOUT EXACT NUMBERS

10 Some graphs or charts do not give the exact numbers. It is important to show that the number you use is not exact. Match these numbers with their description.

1 8950   a approximately 4000
2 2019   b about a hundred
3 500,070   c just under 9000
4 3946   d between 7000 and 7500
5 103   e around half a million
6 7223   f a little over 2000

11▶ **Look at these examples from a description of diagram 2.**

There were **about** 500 Indian restaurants in the UK in 1960.
The number rose from **approximately** 5000 in 1990 to **just under** 8000 in 2000.
The figure for 1997 was **around** 7500.
From 2007 to 2015 the number of restaurants was **between** 9000 **and** 9500.
In 1970 there were **a little over** 1000 Indian restaurants.

Use the expressions in bold to complete the sentences about diagram 3, which shows the market share of four supermarkets.

1 In 1995, Foodhall had _____ 20% of the market, while Finco had _____ 20%.
2 In 1995, Bestway's share of the market was _____ 5%.
3 In 2005, all the supermarkets had _____ 11% and 30% of the market.
4 In both 2005 and 2015, Alton's share of the market was _____ 16%.
5 Finco had the biggest market share in 2005, which was _____ 30%.

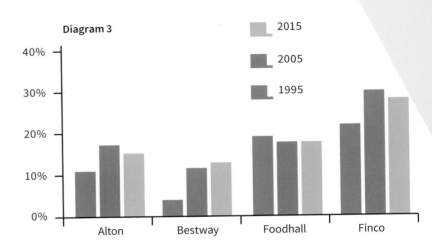

Diagram 3

2015 / 2005 / 1995

Alton · Bestway · Foodhall · Finco

STUDYING A MODEL ANSWER: AVOIDING 'OUTSIDE' INFORMATION

12▶ **Read the model answer, which is based on diagrams 1 and 2. Two sentences should not be included. Can you find them?**

13▶ **Read the model answer again and find:**

1 the overview
2 a sentence that explains the link between the two charts
3 a comparison
4 a passive form
5 a way of saying '1990 to 2000'
6 an expression meaning 'has not changed much'
7 an expression used to avoid exact numbers

TIP 13

Never include any information that is not shown in the diagram. Even if you know a lot about the data given, do not try to explain the reasons for it or give your own opinion.

MODEL ANSWER

The pie chart shows which type of takeaway food is the most popular in the UK, while the bar chart shows how many Indian restaurants existed in the UK between 1960 and 2015. We can see that Chinese and Indian takeaways are the favourites, and that the number of Indian restaurants in the UK rose steadily during this period.

The pie chart shows that Chinese and Indian takeaways are much more popular than all the others, at 34% and 26%. There are another two types that quite a lot of people like. These are Italian at 10% and British at 9%. It is not surprising that people in the UK like British food, as fish and chips is the national dish. Greek, Japanese and Mexican were only chosen by 1% of people.

The pie chart shows us that Indian food is popular and the bar chart shows how its popularity grew. Even my village has an Indian restaurant! There was a rising trend from 1960 onwards. The increase was greatest in the 1990s, from about 5000 restaurants in 1990 to almost 8000 in 2000. Since 2007, the number has remained stable at just over 9000.

EXAM SKILLS

1 4 ▶ Read the exam question below and study the charts, then answer these questions about the data.

1 What is the main trend revealed in the bar chart?

2 Which ten-year period showed the first significant increase?

3 What happened in the ten-year period after that?

4 What is the link between the two charts?

5 In 2015, what percentage of people were severely obese?

6 Which was the largest group in 2015?

You should spend about 20 minutes on this task.

The bar chart shows the percentage of adults who were overweight or obese (too fat or much too fat) in one country from 1965 to 2015. The pie chart shows the proportion of adults who were overweight, obese or severely obese in 2015.

Summarise the information by selecting and reporting the main features, and make comparisons where relevant.

Write at least 150 words.

Percentage of adults who are overweight or obese

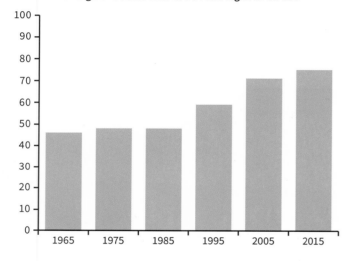

Weight range of the adult population 2015

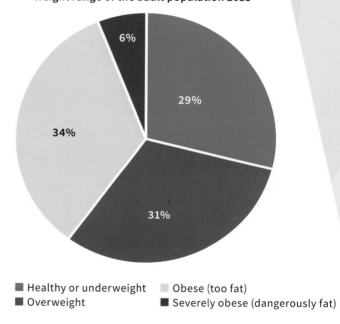

- ■ Healthy or underweight
- ■ Overweight
- ■ Obese (too fat)
- ■ Severely obese (dangerously fat)

1 5 ▶ Now write your report. Remember:

- Include an overview.
- Don't try to include all the data.
- Don't include anything from outside the data.

GO FURTHER ONLINE

UNIT / 04: FOOD AND DRINK

LISTENING

IN THIS UNIT YOU WILL LEARN HOW TO

- find synonyms and paraphrase in matching tasks
- identify 'distractors' in matching tasks
- answer classification tasks.

LEAD-IN

01▶ Label the different ways of preparing food with verbs from the box.

| bake | boil | fry | grill |

A

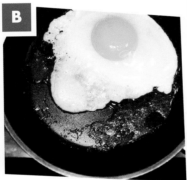
B

C

D

02▶ Match the words with the type of food they are. Put them in the correct column.

| apples | bananas | beef | biscuits | burger | cake | steak | potatoes |
| carrots | chocolate | lamb | cucumbers | pastries | pears | peas | strawberries |

Meat dishes

Vegetables

Fruits

Sweets

[MATCHING TASKS]

03 **Listen to two friends talking about a party they are planning. Match Mike's suggestions with Jane's answers.**

 In matching tasks in the Listening test, you may hear information about several of the options, but only one of the answers is correct.

Suggestions

1 What do you think about preparing a Mexican meal?

2 We could have pizza. Everybody likes pizza.

3 I know! We could have salad and roast chicken.

Answers

a I think we should have something healthier.

b That sounds like a good idea. Let's do that.

c I think it might be too spicy for some people.

What are they going to prepare?

04 ▶ **Listen to two friends talking about preparing a meal. How are they going to prepare the potatoes?**

A boil   **B** bake   **C** fry

Why are the other answers incorrect?

In matching tasks in the IELTS test:

- you do not need to use all of the letters. You should put one letter next to each numbered question.
- the questions follow the same order as the information on the recording.

05 ▶ **Listen to two friends discussing food shopping. Match the names of the shops (1–3) with the different types of food, A–D.**

1 Arcadia
2 Best Buy
3 Hampton's

Types of food
A vegetables
B meat
C fruit
D sweets

Which option didn't match any of the shops?

TIP 05

Listen carefully to what is said about all the options to make sure you choose the correct one.

0 6 ▶ You will hear a radio programme in which two people are discussing the different restaurants in a town.

Look at the names of restaurants (1–3) and the list of types of restaurant. Match each restaurant with the correct type, A–G.

Types of restaurant

1 Adam's   **A** vegetarian
2 The Duke   **B** steakhouse
3 The Tower   **C** seafood
                  D Italian
                  E international
                  F French
                  G fast food

0 7 ▶ After you have checked your answers, look at the Listening script on page 182 and check why the other options were not correct.

0 8 ▶ Look at the Listening script again and find words that mean the following:

1 crowded
2 delicious
3 cheap
4 smart
5 inexpensive

09▶ Choose the option, A, B or C which does NOT mean the same as the first sentence.

1 The price of food in the restaurant is cheap.
   A The price of a meal in the restaurant is reasonable.
   B The restaurant is excellent if you want a budget meal.
   C The food in the restaurant is overpriced.

2 Marco cooked us a really tasty meal.
   A The meal Marco prepared was delicious.
   B Marco cooked us a really unappetising meal.
   C The meal Marco made for us was mouth-watering.

3 We were served food that was cooked in the old-fashioned way.
   A The meal we had was very contemporary in style.
   B The meal we had was very traditional.
   C The meal was made from a historic recipe.

4 When I went to Thailand, I really enjoyed trying the street food.
   A I really liked tasting the food that was sold outdoors in Thailand.
   B In Thailand I loved the food we bought from stalls in the streets.
   C I enjoyed eating at restaurants when I was in Thailand.

5 The chef at the Lodge Hotel is very skilful.
   A The chef at the Lodge Hotel is bad at his job.
   B The chef at the Lodge Hotel has a lot of expertise.
   C The chef at the Lodge Hotel is highly trained.

6 The ingredients for the recipe can be changed to ones you have available.
   A You can use different ingredients to make this dish if you can't find everything.
   B You can be flexible about what ingredients you add to this recipe.
   C You should follow the recipe strictly or it won't taste good.

7 The chef at the new restaurant is famous across the country.
   A The chef at the new restaurant is well known nationally.
   B The chef at the new restaurant is recognised across the country.
   C The chef at the new restaurant is unknown outside of his town.

8 I didn't like the soup; it was too spicy.
   A The soup had too much pepper.
   B The soup wasn't tasty.
   C The soup was a bit too hot for my taste.

10▶ Underline the words which helped you find the answers to exercise 9.

CLASSIFICATION TASKS]

Sometimes in the test you will be asked to match several pieces of information with three different options. Like with other matching exercises, you must listen for ideas, since the same word will often not be used on the recording as in the question.

The options with letters (A–C) can be used more than once. The numbered information you must find (1–5) will be in the order that you will hear it.

1 1 ▶

36

Listen to a famous TV chef talking about different countries and their cuisines. Match the statements with the correct country, A–C.

1 They use chopsticks made of several different materials.
2 You can find a lot of different types of regional cooking here.
3 This place is famous for hot, peppery food.
4 In this country people use recipes that came from different countries.
5 This country is well known for its grilled meat.

A China
B Japan
C Korea

EXAM SKILLS]

1 2 ▶

37

You are going to hear an interview with a chef about a TV programme he has made about food in China.

Choose FOUR answers from the types of food in the box and write the correct letter A–F next to questions 1–4.

Which of the foods:
1 is often enjoyed by children?
2 can be cooked in a short time by the dinner guests?
3 needs expertise to make?
4 can be adapted to your tastes?

Types of food
A Beijing duck
B kebabs
C dumplings
D noodles
E hotpot
F jellyfish

 **GO FURTHER ONLINE**

SPEAKING

IN THIS UNIT YOU WILL LEARN HOW TO

- talk about food in your country (Speaking Part 1)
- use the preparation time to collect your ideas for Part 2
- organise your talk (Speaking Part 2).

LEAD-IN

0 1 ▶ Look at the photographs of different dishes. Which ingredients do you think are used to make each one? Match the pictures with the words in the box. Some ingredients are used more than once.

beef	cabbage	carrots	cheese	chicken
egg	tomatoes	yoghurt	ginger	chillies
lamb	onions	soy sauce	rice	spices
flour	garlic			

0 2 ▶ With a partner, discuss your favourite food. What ingredients are used to make it?

Some things we eat are *countable* and some are *uncountable*. This changes some of the words we use to talk about them.

Examples:

There *are* some egg*s*.
There *is* some water.

There *aren't any* eggs.
There *isn't any* water.

There *are a lot of* eggs.
There's *a lot of* water.

There *aren't many* eggs.
There *isn't much* water.

03▶ **With a partner, describe what you can see in the fridge. Use the sentences below to help you.**

1 There _____ eggs.
2 There _____ cheese.
3 There _____ milk.
4 There _____ carrots.
5 There _____ bananas.
6 There _____ orange juice.

EXPRESSING OPINIONS ABOUT FOOD

04▶ Listen, then read Mohammed's answers to these Part 1 questions about food. Are the phrases in bold positive or negative opinions?

38

Examiner	What kind of food is popular in your country?
Mohammed	These days a lot of young people actually **enjoy** Western food like pizza and fried chicken. Our national food is often **too spicy**, especially for children and foreigners, and also it **takes too long to cook**. I think that it's **delicious** though!
Examiner	What do you think of Western food?
Mohammed	Well, I suppose Western food is **quick to make** and **is tasty** too, so everyone can eat it without too much trouble. I think that a lot of people like food to be **convenient** because they're so busy nowadays.
Examiner	Is there any kind of food you don't like?
Mohammed	Yes, I'm **not keen on** sushi at all. It's **so strange** eating something that hasn't been cooked. I know it's very **fresh** and **healthy** but I just **don't like the taste** and I **can't stand** the texture – it's **too chewy** for me.

Positive	Negative

05▶ Answer the three questions in exercise 4 with a partner. Use some of the positive and negative phrases in the box.

USING THE PREPARATION TIME IN PART 2

06▶ Look at the task card and listen to Angelica talking about a meal that is popular in her country. Then answer the questions below.

39

Describe a popular meal from your country that you like to eat.

You should say:

- what the meal is
- why it is popular in your country
- why you like it

and say why you would recommend it to a visitor to your country.

1 Did Angelica introduce what she was going to talk about?
2 What was the meal that Angelica described?
3 Why is it popular in her country?
4 Why does she like it?
5 Why would she recommend it to visitors to her country?

07 ▷ You only have one minute to make notes on the topic for Part 2, so it is a good idea to write down key words and phrases. Match the four points on the card with some key words that another student wrote down (a–d).

Describe a popular meal from your country that you like to eat.

You should say:

- what the meal is [1]
- why it is popular in your country [2]
- why you like it [3]

and say why you would recommend it to a visitor to your country. [4]

TIP 07

Remember that you need to speak for 1–2 minutes on the topic you are given, so in this case make sure you choose a meal you can talk about easily.

a *We love meat, traditional, lots of sheep!, proud of our cuisine*
b *better in Turkey than UK, different types (Shawarma, doner, etc.), most famous street food*
c *I'm busy → buy quickly, tasty, juicy, reminds me of beach holidays*
d *lamb, slowly grilled, spices, garlic – serve with rice / bread / vegetables*

08 ▷ Spend one minute writing notes to the questions about a popular meal in your country.

TIP 08

It is important to make notes and try to cover every point on the card.

09 ▷ Take it in turns with your partner to speak for two minutes. If your partner stops, think of questions to ask them.

Example   A I used to eat it at the beach in summer …
           B Who did you go to the beach with?

ORGANISING A PART 2 TALK

 When you are asked to speak on a topic for two minutes you should try and organise your talk:

- Introduction – say what you are going to talk about.
- Body – answer the questions on the card.
- Conclusion – briefly give a conclusion to your talk.

1 0 ▶ **Can you use the phrases *in italics* in an introduction (I) or a conclusion (C)?**

1 *I'm going to talk about* my favourite food, paella.

2 *I'd like to tell you about* pelmeni – it's a very famous dish in my country.

3 *So*, it is one of the most famous foods in my country for those reasons.

4 *To sum up*, I think it's popular because it is easy to cook.

5 *As you can see*, it's a tasty and healthy dish and that's why it's popular.

 You can help to structure your talk by saying why you chose the topic: *I chose this topic because …*

You can also use words like *firstly / first of all*, *secondly*, *thirdly* to help you (and the examiner) keep track of your talk.

1 1 ▶ **Work in pairs. Look at the students' notes relating to the task card below. Spend one minute thinking how you will structure your talk, then take it in turns to practise presenting the information.**

Describe your favourite food.

You should say:

- what the food is
- how often you eat it
- how the food is made

and say if you can make the meal yourself.

Student A	Student B
Pizza – delicious, easy cook, filling	*Vegetable soup – tasty, healthy, cheap*
on Fridays – late lectures, special day	*at weekends, winter – long time to cook, better in cold weather*
oven, bread, add cheese, tomato, toppings	*chop vegetables, boil, wait*
only frozen! / take-away	*yes, love cooking, relaxing, fun*
Conclusion – easy and tasty	*Conclusion – enjoy making, filling, economical*

EXAM SKILLS

1 2 ▶ **Read the task card and spend one minute preparing your talk. Take it in turns to speak. Try to speak for two minutes.**

Describe a special occasion when you had a really enjoyable meal.

You should say:

- what the occasion was
- who was at the meal
- what you ate

and explain why the meal was so enjoyable.

Remember to:
- make notes of key ideas
- introduce your talk
- structure your talk
- give it a conclusion.

TIP 1 2

It is good to use different adjectives in this part of the test. Think of different ways of saying the words and avoid words like *good* and *bad*.

GO FURTHER ONLINE

READING

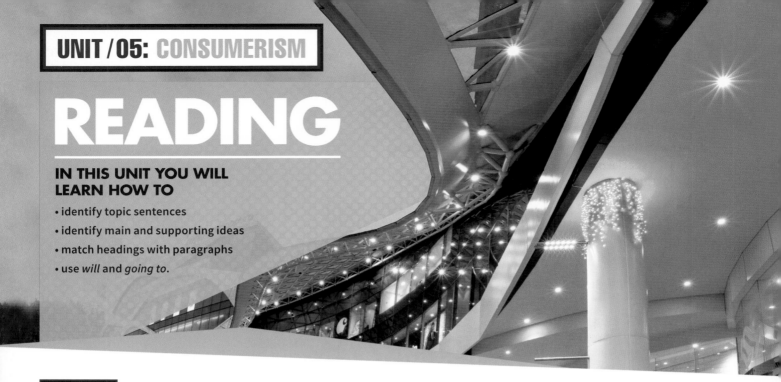

IN THIS UNIT YOU WILL LEARN HOW TO

- identify topic sentences
- identify main and supporting ideas
- match headings with paragraphs
- use *will* and *going to*.

LEAD-IN

01▶ Which of these activities can you do at a shopping mall? Which can you see in the pictures?

buy clothes	buy or rent an apartment	check your health
go climbing	go in a hot air balloon	go to the beach
have a snack	have a beauty treatment	have an expensive meal
see a film	see an art exhibition	see plants and trees
ski		

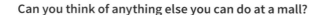
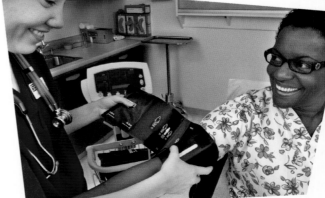

Can you think of anything else you can do at a mall?

0 2 ▶ Read the text in one minute. Answer the questions orally without looking at the text again.

1 Which of the activities in exercise 1 were mentioned?
2 Can you remember any places that were in the text?
3 Is the text mainly about the past, present or future?

THE FUTURE OF MALLS

A Shopping malls have never been just about shopping. They began in the United States after the Second World War and, for the young, they were always a place to 'hang out' and be seen. However, the world has moved on, and just providing shops and a food court is no longer enough to keep malls alive. Malls became less popular at the start of the 21st century, mainly because of online shopping. There is even a website, deadmalls.com, which shows the end of many US malls. Malls need to change to survive. So what will the mall of the future look like?

B Malls are already becoming bigger and better all over the world. Asia and not the US is now the 'mall capital' of the world and is home to the five largest malls in the world. China is home to the two largest. Some malls in the Middle East and East Asia are starting to specialise. It is predicted that this will happen more and more in the future. Some malls will only sell electrical items, for example, or only fashion for young people. Some malls will only include expensive shops or cheap shops, as already happens in Bangkok and Singapore.

C Malls are becoming 'the new downtown', with cinemas, bowling alleys, climbing walls and even concert halls. Xanadu, a mall 30 km from Madrid, is a recreation centre for a family day out as well as a shopping centre, with ski slopes, minigolf, go-karts, balloon rides, bowling and billiards. We have always been able to grab a burger at the mall, but in the future we are going to see 'fine dining' too, with more expensive restaurants based at malls, as well as spas, fitness centres and art galleries. There are also going to be more apartments and office space so that more people can live, work, shop and be entertained in one location.

D Mall owners are going to need to think of new ideas to remain in business. One growing trend is the seasonal changes in the mall. It began with having Santa Claus in December, but now there are 'pop-ups' – temporary shops, stalls and kiosks – for other seasons and events. Brent Cross in North London has an 'urban beach' in summer, and its main lobby has different promotions and events every week, from bungee jumping for kids to free health checks.

E So, we have looked at the facilities malls will need to offer. Malls will need to consider the environment too. There will be more open-air malls and more natural features. Mall designers will have to make sure people can get there by public transport. They will also need to use more natural sources of heat and light. We will see more plants, trees, grass and even waterfalls at our local malls in the future.

F The future of malls looks exciting: there will be 'virtual malls' and technology will be used within malls to help us shop, find bargains and even park our car. With all these creative innovations, the mall will go from strength to strength.

MATCHING HEADINGS

 Matching headings tests your ability to summarise and understand the main idea of a paragraph.

You are given a list of headings (more than the number of paragraphs) and you must choose a suitable heading for each paragraph.

To match headings, you need to be able to find the main idea of a paragraph. You can usually find one sentence that sums up the main idea. This is the topic sentence. This has been highlighted in paragraph A: *Malls need to change to survive.*

The sentence *Malls need to change to survive* is supported by evidence in the paragraph, including:
- *The world has moved on.*
- *Malls became less popular at the start of the 21st century, mainly because of online shopping.*
- *There is even a website, deadmalls.com, which shows the end of many US malls.*

TOPIC SENTENCES AND MAIN AND SUPPORTING IDEAS

03▶ The topic sentence in paragraph B is *Malls are already becoming bigger and better all over the world.* Write two pieces of evidence from paragraph B which support the topic sentence.

04▶ Find the topic sentences in paragraphs C, D and E.

05▶ Below is one supporting idea for each of paragraphs C, D and E. Add one more for each paragraph. Write the supporting ideas in your own words.

C Xanadu … is a recreation centre for a family day out as well as a shopping centre.

D Brent Cross … has different promotions and events every week.

E There will be more open-air malls and more natural features.

> **TIP 03**
>
> The topic sentence is often, but not always, the first sentence in a paragraph, so that is the first place to look.

PARAPHRASE

 In a 'matching headings' task, the headings you have to match will be a paraphrase of the main idea of the paragraph. Don't expect the same words to be used in the headings and the passage. The headings may contain synonyms (words which mean the same) and antonyms (words which mean the opposite) or they may use paraphrase (phrases which have a similar meaning to words in the passage).

For example, a heading for paragraph A in *The future of malls* might be 'Adapt or die'. This is a paraphrase of the main idea 'Malls need to change to survive'.

change – adapt (synonyms)   *survive – die* (antonyms)

> **TIP**
>
> As you prepare for your exam, make a list of synonyms in your notebook. Knowing different ways to say things is one of the key skills in IELTS.

0 6 ▷ In the test, there are always more headings than you need. Read these headings for paragraphs B to E (they are not in the right order).

   i Innovate and stay alive

   ii Fast food paradise

   iii Expanding and improving

   iv Malls and the natural world

   v A new city centre

0 7 ▷ Match the words and phrases 1–6 (from the headings above) with the words and phrases a–f (from the topic sentences of paragraphs B–E).

1 innovate	**a** becoming bigger
2 stay alive	**b** environment
3 expanding	**c** think of new ideas
4 improving	**d** downtown
5 natural world	**e** remain in business
6 city centre	**f** becoming better

0 8 ▷ Choose a heading from exercise 6 for paragraphs B to E. Write the correct number i–v in the gaps. There is one more heading than you need.

Paragraph B _____   Paragraph C _____

Paragraph D _____   Paragraph E _____

GRAMMAR FOCUS: FUTURE FORMS

0 9 ▷ Find examples of future forms in the passage *The future of malls*. Which two ways of talking about the future are used? Write one example of each.

 Will + infinitive and *going to* + infinitive are both used to talk about the future.

Going to is used when there is a link to the present, for example if something is already planned or a change has started:

   Mall owners **are going to need to** think of new ideas to remain in business.

We see from the text that many malls have already started thinking of new ideas.

Will + infinitive is used for prediction: something the writer believes about the future. It does not have to be based on present evidence:

   … the mall **will go** from strength to strength.

This is the writer's prediction or belief about the future.

1 0 ▷ Complete the sentences with the correct form of *will* or *going to*.

1 Look at these plans for the new mall! There _____ be a climbing wall!

2 This newspaper article says they _____ spend $25 million on the project.

3 I think it _____ be great when it is finished!

4 I agree, but I'm afraid many local businesses _____ have to close.

5 I heard there _____ be 12 different restaurants!

6 I expect most of the shops _____ be expensive ones.

EXAM SKILLS

11▶ Which paragraph in the passage *Markets around the world* contains information on the following? Write the correct letter, A–G.

1 markets put on at a particular time of year
2 markets where anyone can sell anything
3 markets selling things to eat
4 advice for people who want to dress differently from others
5 examples of markets outside Europe

12▶ The reading passage has seven paragraphs, A–G. Choose the correct heading for paragraphs B–F from the list of headings (i–vii) below. Write the correct number, i–vii. There are two headings you won't need.

> **List of headings**
> i   Local art and craft work to take home
> ii Inexpensive things to eat straight from the countryside
> iii Toys for children of all ages
> iv Invent a new style for yourself at bargain prices
> v   London has the best markets
> vi Find gifts for winter celebrations
> vii Sell what you don't need

1 Paragraph B ____
2 Paragraph C ____
3 Paragraph D ____
4 Paragraph E ____
5 Paragraph F ____

Markets around the world

A We have become so used to shopping in big supermarkets and chain stores, identical in every town, that we have forgotten about one important way to shop – markets. Markets are found in every country in the world, but wherever you go they are different and reveal the local culture – and agriculture. From farmers' markets selling fresh produce to craft and antique markets, they are the best place to find something unique at a great price.

B Food is at its cheapest and freshest in markets. Farmers often sell direct to the consumer, without all the packaging, shipping and advertising that increases costs in shops and supermarkets. You can often find unusual products and those that are not mass-produced. Food markets vary hugely according to where they are in the world. For example the Kauppatori market in Helsinki, Finland sells moose, reindeer and bear salami. Wherever you are, food will be locally produced and reasonably priced.

C Markets are also good places to buy clothes. Some sell cheap new and second-hand clothes, while others specialise in vintage or ethically made clothes and original items. The markets of London are some of the best in the world for those who want to create a unique look for themselves. Many new designers start with a market stall, so if you are looking for a totally original item of clothing, you could get something really special at a bargain price at Brick Lane, Spitalfields or Portobello Road markets.

D Another type of market is a flea market. This is a much more informal type of market, where second-hand products can be sold by anyone. If you have unwanted items at home, you could take them to a flea market and sell them yourself. There are also antiques and possibly local crafts at this kind of market. In some parts of the world there may not even be stalls; rather, vendors lay out their goods on a sheet on the ground. In other parts of the world, flea markets have developed into car boot sales, where people sell their unwanted items from their cars.

E In some places, markets are directed at visitors and tend to sell handicrafts typical of the region. For many tourists, a visit to a nearby market to buy souvenirs is an important part of their holiday. Guadalajara in Mexico has a huge range of traditional textiles, glassware, ceramics and art works and Seoul in Korea has some wonderful original designs of all kinds of products at affordable prices. Countries in the Middle East usually have beautiful hand-made rugs and carpets, and Indian markets sell colourful handloom fabrics and beautiful silk scarves.

F In Europe, December is the time when seasonal markets are held to sell decorations and gifts for the festive season. One of the most famous of these is held in Wenceslas Square in Prague in the Czech Republic. The market is made up of colourfully decorated wooden huts selling traditional handicrafts, embroidered lace, wooden toys, scented candles, Christmas tree ornaments, and puppets and dolls beautifully dressed in traditional costumes. This looks very pretty, especially in the snow.

G So, wherever you are in the world and whatever you are looking for, there is a market for you. You can get all kinds of unusual things at great prices.

GO FURTHER ONLINE

UNIT / 05: CONSUMERISM

WRITING

IN THIS UNIT YOU WILL LEARN HOW TO

- organise a Part 2 essay
- write an introduction
- write about points for and against, and give opinions
- give examples and evidence to support your views.

LEAD-IN

0 1 ▷ Put the words and phrases into the correct column.

advantages	all things considered	benefits
disadvantages	drawbacks	in my view
negative aspects	positive aspects	personally

Good points	Bad points	Opinion

02 ▶ These sentences are from an essay on the advantages and disadvantages of shopping online. Are they talking about good points (G), bad points (B) or giving an opinion (O)? Write G, B or O. The first one has been done for you.

1 A wider range of products is available online.   _G_

2 You can't try on clothes and shoes if you buy online.   ____

3 I prefer going to shops and choosing things in person.   ____

4 There is no need to carry heavy shopping to your car.   ____

5 You save money on petrol, parking or bus fares.   ____

6 Goods might be delivered when you are out.   ____

7 It isn't a good idea to give your credit card details online.   ____

8 You often have to pay a lot for postage and wait for your goods.   ____

9 I think it is better to support local shops.   ____

PART 2 QUESTION TYPES

◎ In Part 2 you have to write an essay of about 250 words. There are different types of question in Part 2, and you must write a well-organised answer considering different points of view.

The topics in Part 2 are all general and do not need special knowledge.

03 ▶ Three of the question types you might find in Part 2 are:

1 Do you agree (or disagree) that …?

2 Do the advantages/benefits of … outweigh the disadvantages/drawbacks?

3 Discuss two different views and give your opinion.

Match the question types 1–3 with what you have to do (a–c).

a Say if you think there are more good points than bad points.

b Write about both sides and say what you think.

c Give your opinion on this.

TIP 03

Read newspapers and websites to find out about current issues.

04 ▶ Look at the following question.

> Do you agree that supermarkets are a threat to small shops and local communities?

Decide on your *own* opinion. Choose from these options.

A I strongly agree. Supermarkets will force small shops to close and this will damage local communities.

B I agree to some extent. There may be a slight threat to small shops and local communities.

C I generally disagree. There is a place for both small shops and supermarkets.

D I strongly disagree. Supermarkets will not have an impact on small shops and local communities.

TIP 04

Avoid being totally neutral: even if you don't have an opinion on the topic, it is better to agree or disagree. Choose the side you can find most points for.

The same topic could be expressed as a different question type:

Do the advantages of supermarkets outweigh the disadvantages?

Are these advantages or disadvantages of supermarkets?

1 They are cheap.
2 There are many different products.
3 You often need a car to get there.
4 You don't usually meet your friends there.
5 Food is usually fresh.
6 There are sometimes queues at the checkout.
7 There is plenty of free parking.
8 Small shops lose their customers.

WRITING AN INTRODUCTION

 It is important to begin your essay with a clear introduction.

An introduction **should** contain:
• background information about the topic or a description of the present situation.
  (*Nowadays you can find a supermarket in every town.*)
• a brief plan of your essay. (*I will consider both sides of the argument and give my own view.*)

An introduction **may** also contain:
• your opinion. (*I think there are too many supermarkets.*)

An introduction **should not** contain:
• your main points for or against. (*Supermarkets give jobs to local people.*)
• supporting evidence for the points. (*In my city we have five different supermarkets.*)

0 6 ▶ **Which of these, A or B, is the better introduction for the essay topic in exercise 5? Give reasons.**

A I totally agree that the advantages of supermarkets outweigh the disadvantages. There are many benefits – cheap prices, plenty of choice, late opening hours, and only a few drawbacks. In this essay I will explain my opinion.

B Nowadays you can find a supermarket in every town. There are often several to choose from and there is strong competition between them. This clearly has many benefits, but there are some drawbacks too. I will consider both sides of the argument and give my own view.

0 7 ▶ **Study the information about introductions in the box above, and then read the following Part 2 question and a student's introduction. What are the good and bad things about this introduction?**

Some people think shopping online is better, while others prefer going to the shops. Discuss both these views and give your own opinion.

Online shopping has increased in popularity over the last few years. People now shop for a wide variety of items on websites. Other people still prefer going to the shops to buy things. There are a lot of reasons why online shopping is growing. One of them is that there is a wider choice of items. In this essay, I will consider each of these opinions and give my own view.

08 ▶ **Check the notes below. Did you find the same points?**

Online shopping has increased in popularity over the last few years. People now shop for a wide variety of items on websites. Other people still prefer going to the shops to buy things. There are a lot of reasons why online shopping is growing. One of them is that there is a wider choice of items. In this essay, I will consider each of these opinions and give my own view.

✓ Background / current situation.

✗ Uses almost the same words as the questions — should have used different words.

✗ Main point – shouldn't be in the introduction.

✓ Gives a brief plan of the essay, but no personal information.

09 ▶ **Write a three-sentence introduction to this question.**

A 'cashless society' is one where people use debit/credit cards and other forms of payment instead of cash. Do the advantages of a cashless society outweigh the disadvantages?

DEVELOPING AN ARGUMENT

10 ▶ **Match the main points (1–4) with the supporting evidence (a–d).**

⊙ To write a well-developed argument you need to include main points and examples which support them.

Main points

1 Supermarkets are often in competition with each other.
2 Supermarkets keep increasing the range of services they offer.
3 Supermarket chains also offer online grocery shopping.
4 Shopping can be an enjoyable and social experience.

Examples / evidence

a You can sometimes get free delivery on some days of the week.
b When I was a child, my mother enjoyed talking to shopkeepers and neighbours while she was shopping.
c Some supermarkets will refund money if the same goods cost less at another supermarket.
d You can now buy insurance and foreign currency at large supermarkets.

11 ▶ **Can you think of examples which support these main points?**

1 Supermarkets provide jobs for local people.
2 Large supermarkets can offer a large choice of products.
3 Some large supermarkets offer loyalty cards.

1 2 ▶ Read the essay question and answer the questions below.

Small, independent shops will have no place in the future. To what extent do you agree with this statement?

1 Do you agree or disagree?
2 Note down a few points which support your opinion.

1 3 ▶ Read the model answer. Were any of your points made?

MODEL ANSWER

Many people now do most of their shopping online or in large supermarkets. Many small, family-run shops do not have enough customers to survive. Some people believe that this is going to happen more and more in the future. However, my view is that there will always be a place for smaller shops.

There are many disadvantages to shopping online. Sometimes you have to wait for delivery for several days and sometimes the goods are not what you want. I often have to return clothes and other items because the size or colour is wrong for me. Supermarkets, too, have their drawbacks. The goods are all the same everywhere. For example, if you buy a coat from a supermarket, you will probably meet other people with exactly the same one.

Small, independent shops are more interesting places to shop. You can find unique items which other people will admire. I have a friend who collects antiques and he finds them in local shops, not supermarkets or websites. Some small shops specialise in one area, which is very useful. For instance, in music shops, the staff are very knowledgeable about music and instruments. You can get advice about what to buy. Finally, small, local shops give character to a town. In my parents' village there are a few shops selling boating equipment, which suits the place as it is near the sea.

I strongly believe that there will always be a place for small shops. However, the owners will need to make sure they sell different things from the supermarkets and keep their shops interesting.

1 4 ▷ Complete the essay plan.

PARAGRAPH 1: Introduction
Current situation
Opinion

PARAGRAPH 2
Main idea 1: There are disadvantages to shopping online
Supporting evidence: Wait for delivery, goods not what you want
Main idea 2: Supermarkets have drawbacks
Supporting evidence: a) _____

PARAGRAPH 3
Main idea 1: Small shops are interesting
Supporting evidence: b) _____
Main idea 2: Small shops specialise
Supporting evidence: c) _____
Main idea 3: d) _____
Supporting evidence: Boating equipment shops in parents' village near sea

PARAGRAPH 4: Conclusion
Briefly summarise your opinion

---

1 5 ▷ Find the following in the essay.

1 two expressions for giving opinions
2 two expressions for introducing examples
3 an expression to show it is the last point
4 two different future forms
5 two more linking expressions

[EXAM SKILLS]

 **GO FURTHER ONLINE**

1 6 ▷ Write an essay on the following topic.

In the future, the main reason for going to the shopping mall will be for entertainment, not to shop. Do you agree or disagree?

Give reasons for your answer and include any relevant examples from your own knowledge or experience.

Write at least 250 words.
You may use some of the following ideas or your own ideas.
• Most people shop online.
• People enjoy shopping at malls with friends.
• Malls have cinemas, bowling alleys, restaurants.
• Malls have plans for even more entertainment facilities.
• At the mall you can try on clothes and get advice on products from shop assistants.
• Shops and entertainment are under one roof.

Remember to:
• organise your ideas into four paragraphs
• for 'agree or disagree' questions, give your opinion in the first paragraph
• consider both sides of the argument
• use examples to provide supporting evidence
• use linking expressions
• use future forms.

LISTENING

IN THIS UNIT YOU WILL LEARN HOW TO

- answer multiple-choice questions (3 options)
- identify 'distractors'
- recognise paraphrase and synonyms.

LEAD-IN

01▷ Match the places in the box with pictures A–E.

| coffee shop | department store | outdoor market | shopping centre | supermarket |

A

B

C

D

E

02▷ Listen to three short recordings. Which place, A–E, is each speaker talking about?

40

1 _____ 2 _____ 3 _____

SECTION 2 OF THE LISTENING TEST

 Section 2 of the Listening test is a little more difficult than Section 1. You will hear a recording spoken by one speaker, or mainly one speaker, on a topic of general interest.

You have to listen for information about important details or facts on the recording, usually without the help of another speaker's questions to guide you.

You hear the recording in two parts and there are questions on each part.

IDENTIFYING DISTRACTORS

03▶

41

Listen to four short recordings and answer questions 1–4 in the table below. Write **NO MORE THAN ONE WORD AND/OR A NUMBER** for each answer.

 Distractors are words and phrases on the recording that are incorrect answers to a question. Identifying distractors helps you to choose the correct answer and shows that you have understood the recording.

Questions	Distractors	
1 The new sport shop is going to be located in the _____ of the town.	5 _____ 6 _____	
2 What does the tour guide recommend they buy? _____	7 _____ 8 _____	
3 The shopping centre opens at _____ o'clock on Sundays.	9 _____ o'clock 10 _____ o'clock 11 _____ o'clock	
4 What is the most popular product in the shop? _____	12 _____ 13 _____	

04▶

41

Listen to the recordings again. Write the distractors in the second column of the table (questions 5–13).

Can you remember the exact words which told you what the correct answer was?

RECOGNISING PARAPHRASE AND SYNONYMS

05▶ Match the words and phrases 1–6 with their synonyms or paraphrases a–f.

1 a good selection
2 at the weekend
3 shoes
4 under one roof
5 walk
6 picture

a in one building
b photograph
c on Saturday and Sunday
d footwear
e a wide choice
f go on foot

 The words the speakers use on the recording are often different to the words in the questions. Often, you will hear a *synonym* (a word with the same meaning or a similar meaning) or a *paraphrase* (a group of words with a similar meaning).

[MULTIPLE-CHOICE QUESTIONS]

In this type of task, you choose the correct answer from three options, A, B or C.

There are two types of multiple-choice question:
- a question followed by three possible options
- an unfinished statement followed by three possible endings.

You must only answer A, B or C on the answer sheet because there is only ever **one** correct answer.

0 6 ▶ **Read the question and match the <u>underlined</u> words with paraphrases 1–3.**

1 What kind of T-shirts does the man
sell most of?   *Paraphrases*
A T-shirts with a <u>picture on them</u>   1 nothing on them
B T-shirts with <u>words on them</u>   2 writing on them
C <u>plain T-shirts</u>   3 photograph on them

42 **Then listen and choose the correct answer, A, B or C.**

0 7 ▶ **Read the question and identify the key words.**
Then choose the correct paraphrase for each option A–C.

2 The writer will arrive at   *Paraphrases*
A 12.00 pm.   A midnight / noon
B 2.15 pm.   B quarter to two / quarter past two
C 3.30 pm.   C half past three / half past four

43 **Then listen and choose the correct answer, A, B or C.**

0 8 ▶ **Read the question and identify the key words. Then look at synonyms 1–3.**
Which ONE is incorrect? Why?

3 What does the woman complain
about?   *Paraphrases*
A the staff   A the customers
B the litter   B the rubbish
C the food   C the lunch

44 **Listen and choose the correct answer, A, B or C.**

Then listen again and explain why the other options are wrong.

EXAM SKILLS

09▶ **Follow the advice below and answer the questions.**

45

- First identify the key words in the questions.
- The questions follow the order of the recording, but the options A, B and C might not.
- Listen for the key words in the questions, or words with a similar meaning.
- Be aware of distractors – think about the whole meaning of the sentences you hear. Don't choose an option just because you hear words from it on the recording.

Listen and choose the correct letter, A, B or C.

1 The Shopping Tour bus is outside
 A the theatre.
 B the train station.
 C some cafés.

2 Nowadays the theatre is popular because of
 A its modern architecture.
 B its music performances.
 C the famous actors that appear there.

3 The shopping tour will begin at …
 A 9.10.
 B 9.30.
 C 9.45.

4 What can people buy in Market Place today?
 A souvenirs
 B fruit and vegetables
 C clothes

5 The main purpose of the visit to the Regional Food Centre is
 A to have a meal.
 B to buy local fruit juices.
 C to taste cheeses from the region.

6 At the Fashion Fair, how will people on the tour know which building the footwear is in?
 A It is a red building.
 B It has a green roof.
 C It has blue doors.

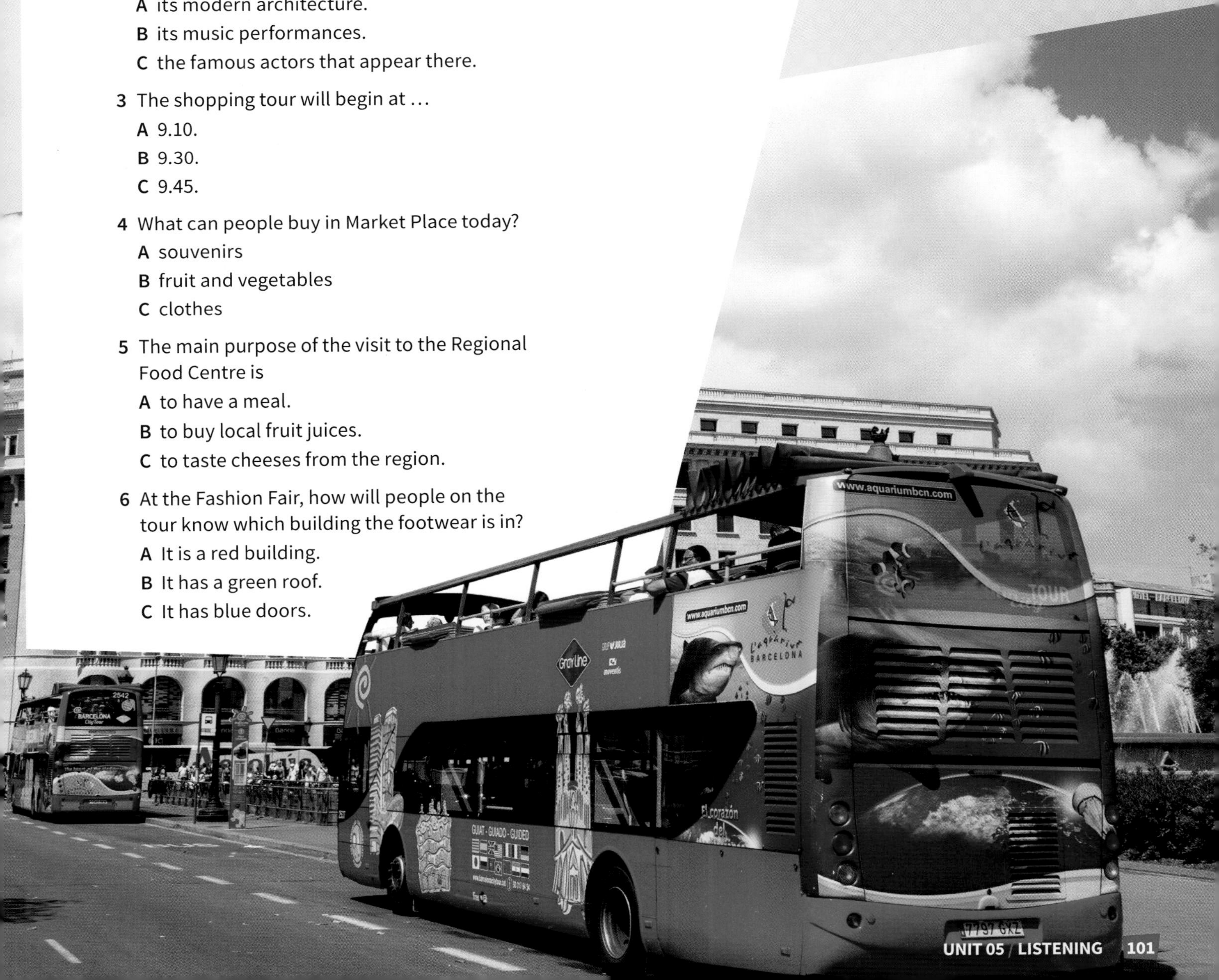

GO FURTHER ONLINE

UNIT / 05: CONSUMERISM

SPEAKING

IN THIS UNIT YOU WILL LEARN HOW TO

- talk about different experiences you might have when shopping

- plan your Part 2 talk using techniques for developing ideas

- express your feelings through intonation.

0 1 ▸ Discuss these questions with a partner.

- Where do you like to go shopping?
- What do you like to buy when you go shopping?
- How often do you go shopping?

0 2 ▸ Complete the script of Daniel talking about his choices for shopping using the words and phrases in the box.

afford	all sorts of	atmosphere	convenient	keen on	out-of-the-way
place	original	selection	traditional	trying on	reasonable

Daniel The place where I really enjoy shopping is Covent Garden Market. It's very
1 _____ because it isn't far from where I live. It isn't a
2 _____ food market, though at one time it used to sell fruit and
vegetables. Now, it's a collection of 3 _____ independent shops
and stalls. There's an amazing 4 _____ of things to buy – clothes,
jewellery, books, art and crafts. I love it because it has a great
5 _____ . There are cafés outside in the square, and often you
can see street performers. It's very lively and friendly. I avoid the big malls
because they're often 6 _____ – you need a car to get to them.

And what do I enjoy buying? Well, I'm 7 _____ fashion and like to
go clothes shopping whenever I can. I love 8 _____ clothes even
if I can't 9 _____ to buy them! And I absolutely love going to the
sales! Sometimes I manage to find great designer shoes at very
10 _____ prices. And I like shopping for really fun and
11 _____ gifts for my friends – things that nobody else has.
Covent Garden's a great 12 _____ to do that.

Listen and check.

03▶ Match words and phrases 1–6 with their opposites a–f.

1	convenient	a	local
2	traditional	b	doesn't have any atmosphere
3	amazing selection	c	modern
4	reasonable	d	inconvenient
5	has a great atmosphere	e	lack of choice / not much choice
6	out-of-the-way	f	expensive

04▶ With a partner, discuss again where you like to go shopping. Provide reasons for your answer using some of the words and phrases above.

[DEVELOPING IDEAS IN PART 2]

◉ To do a good Part 2 talk, it is important to develop ideas about the topic. You have one minute to make notes. It's important that you use this time and find a way of making notes that works for you.

05▶ Look at two types of notes about shopping, based on Daniel's talk. One uses a mindmap and the other uses bullet points. Choose the one you like best and add to the notes. Change the ones that are not true for you.

TIP 05

Don't try to write full sentences when making notes – you don't always have time for this!

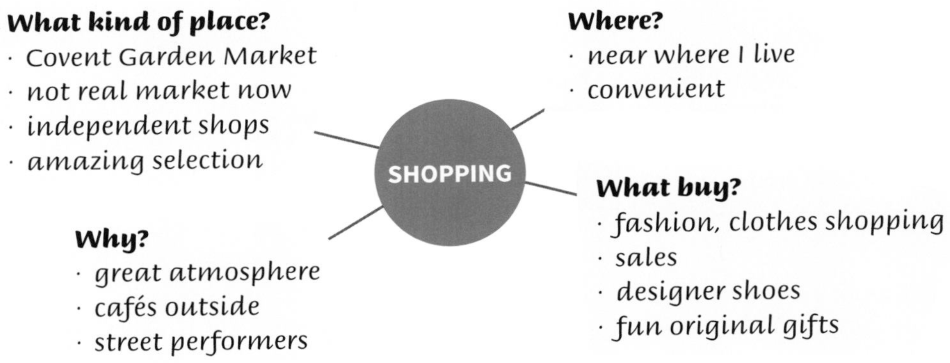

What kind of place?
· Covent Garden Market
· not real market now
· independent shops
· amazing selection

Where?
· near where I live
· convenient

SHOPPING

What buy?
· fashion, clothes shopping
· sales
· designer shoes
· fun original gifts

Why?
· great atmosphere
· cafés outside
· street performers

SHOPPING
What kind of place?
• Covent Garden Market
• not real market now
• independent shops
• amazing selection
Where?
• near where I live
• convenient

Why?
• great atmosphere
• cafés outside
• street performers
What buy?
• fashion, clothes shopping
• sales
• designer shoes
• fun original gifts

06▶ Exchange your notes with a partner and try to speak on the topic using their notes.

07▶ Read the task card. Then listen to Yunmi giving her Part 2 talk. As you listen, make notes on her talk. Choose the style of notes that suits you best.

Describe a place where you like going shopping.

You should say:

- what kind of place it is
- where it is
- what you like to do there

and explain why you like shopping there so much.

08▶ With a partner, try to recreate Yunmi's talk using the notes you have made. Talk for as long as you can using the notes.

When you have finished, read Yunmi's script on page 184. Complete the checklist below.

Could I talk for two minutes using the notes?	Yes	No
Did my notes cover all the points on the card?	Yes	No
Did my notes cover *enough* (not all) of Yunmi's talk?	Yes	No
Did I need to write notes in full sentences?	Yes	No
Do I need to change the way I write my notes?	Yes	No

If you answered YES to the final point in the checklist, discuss with your partner how you can improve your note taking.

09▶ Work in pairs. You have one minute to prepare to speak about your two questions. Spend 30 seconds on each question. Use the question words in the box to help you.

> when?   where?   why?   how much?   what?

Student A
- What do you enjoy spending money on?
- Can you remember a present you bought somebody that they really liked?

Student B
- What is the most expensive thing that you have ever bought?
- Can you remember something you bought that was very useful?

Take it in turns to answer your questions. Spend one minute on each question. If your partner stops before the minute is finished, try to help them by asking questions.

PRONUNCIATION – INTONATION

10▶ Listen to the sentences and decide if they are *positive* or *negative* in tone.

1 I love shopping at the Galleria. It's amazing!
2 I wish there were more places to go shopping where I live.
3 It's a pity that so many shops here have closed down.
4 I'm really excited that they're building a new shopping mall.

Listen again and try to copy the way the speaker shows a positive or negative feeling.

 When we speak, we can change how we say something to show the listener how we feel.

11▶ Write three reasons why you like shopping and three reasons why you don't like shopping. With a partner, say each sentence out loud twice, first by just reading it in a neutral way and then with the correct intonation.

Reasons I like shopping

1 _____

2 _____

3 _____

Reasons I don't like shopping

1 _____

2 _____

3 _____

[EXAM SKILLS]

12▶ Read the task card and then make notes for your talk. Time yourself for 60 seconds, then stop writing.

Describe a shop that you enjoy going to.

You should say:

- where it is
- what it sells
- how often you go there

and explain why you enjoy visiting this shop.

🖱 **GO FURTHER ONLINE**

Talk about the topic with a partner. Try to talk for two minutes.

Then listen to your partner's talk. Make notes of any interesting vocabulary or ideas.

Then, give your talk again to your partner.

READING

IN THIS UNIT YOU WILL LEARN HOW TO

- scan a text to find information quickly
- answer *True / False / Not Given* questions
- complete a summary of a text.

LEAD-IN

0 1 ▶ Can you name these sports?

0 2 ▶ Match the sports 1–9 with the descriptions a–l in the box. Each sport matches several descriptions.

1 hockey	4 football	7 table tennis
2 tennis	5 rugby	8 martial arts
3 volleyball	6 baseball	9 basketball

a It's a team sport.	**e** You hit the ball over a net.	**i** It's played with a ball.
b You score goals.	**f** You hit the ball with a bat.	**j** You tackle other players.
c There's a goalkeeper.	**g** You can play singles or doubles.	**k** You use a racket.
d You earn coloured belts.	**h** You mustn't run with the ball.	**l** You play on grass.

0 3 ▶ Which of these sports have you played or watched? Which would you like to try?

TRUE / FALSE / NOT GIVEN

In this type of task you have to say if a statement is *True* (it agrees with the information in the passage), *False* (it does not agree with the information in the passage – it says the opposite, or something different) or whether the information in the statement is *Not Given* in the passage (there is nothing in the passage to indicate if it is true or false). You must give your answer only according to what is in the passage – you must not use your own knowledge about the topic.

The questions are in the same order as the information in the text.

04 ▶ Read the text in ONE MINUTE.

Tell your partner anything you can remember. Don't worry about giving exact information. You could use these expressions.

There was something about …
I don't remember the details, but it involved …
There's a game which is a bit like …

UNUSUAL SPORTS

A Do you ever get bored with the same old sports? If you're tired of tennis, fed up with football or bored of basketball, don't worry. There are plenty of new and unusual sports out there for you to try. Many of these are a mix of existing sports, sometimes with a local element added. Bossaball, for example, is a mix of football and volleyball, played on an inflatable pitch with a trampoline in the middle. To make it more exciting, it also has elements of Brazilian martial arts!

B If you are very good at horse riding, you could try the national sport of Afghanistan, buzkashi. Many versions have been played in the Central Asian region for hundreds of years. The game involves players on horseback trying to get hold of a dead goat. The Afghan Buzkashi Federation wants the game to spread throughout the world and has finally written down the rules because they hope to get Olympic status for the sport.

C A sport that is more likely to become famous is kabaddi. It is popular in India and other parts of South Asia. It is similar in some ways to the game called 'tag' or 'it' which schoolchildren play. One person is 'it' and has to catch the others. In kabaddi, a 'raider' from one team tries to tag a player from the other team and then return to their own half of the field without getting caught. In some versions of the game, the raider must chant the word 'kabaddi' as he returns to his place. Kabaddi is good fun, good exercise and doesn't need any equipment. It is played at the Asian Games.

D There is an unusual sport which describes itself as a 'classic mix of brains and brawn'. The game, called 'chess boxing', involves a round of chess and then a round of boxing, then another of chess, and so on. There is one minute between rounds. The first chess boxing world championship took place in 2003 in Amsterdam and was won by a Dutchman, Iepe Rubingh. Since then, it has become more popular, particularly in Germany, the UK, India and Russia. It is a difficult sport, as players need to be very good at two very different activities and be able to switch quickly between the two.

E Finally, an unusual sport that will be familiar to most of us is roshambo, which began in China about 2000 years ago and spread gradually to the rest of the world. Played by young and old, in the UK it is known as 'rock-paper-scissors'. It is surprising that it is called a sport and taken so seriously: there's a World Rock Paper Scissors Society and a league which holds championships every year. So, whatever kinds of sport you like, there is something new and interesting for you to try.

0 5 ▶ Quickly scan the text to find the paragraph which contains information about these sports *as quickly as you can.*

1 a sport which is trying to get into the Olympic games
2 a sport which has been played for more than a thousand years and is based on an activity most of us know
3 a sport influenced by two very popular sports
4 a sport which may involve repeating a word
5 a sport which involves two activities which are very unlike each other

TIP 0 5

When answering *True / False / Not Given* questions you must scan the text to find the information as quickly as possible, as you also need time to read a few sentences in detail.

0 6 ▶ The following questions relate to the sections you just found. Decide if they are *True* or *False* according to the text.

1 Players of chess boxing only need to reach a high level in one of the activities.
2 Buzkashi got written rules long after the game first started.
3 Roshambo can be played by anyone, even children and the elderly.
4 Bossaball is played on grass.
5 It could be quite expensive to play kabaddi.

0 7 ▶ Does this statement agree with the information in the passage? Write *True, False* or *Not Given.*

1 Kabaddi is only played by men.
Hint: You ONLY need to read the paragraph about kabaddi, which is paragraph C. You will already know from your initial skim reading that information about kabaddi is not found anywhere else in the text.

TIP 0 7

Don't waste time going through the whole passage to find the information. *Not Given* answers will relate to one part of the text. Once you have read the relevant part in detail, if you can't find the information, choose *Not Given.*

0 8 ▶ Read only the relevant paragraphs. Is this information True (write T) or Not Given (write NG)?

1 Bossaball is only played in Brazil.
2 Buzkashi is sometimes played with a sheep instead of a goat.
3 There are different versions of the game kabaddi.
4 Chess boxing is played in several different countries.
5 The roshambo world champion is from China.

0 9 ▶ Answer *True, False* or *Not Given* to these questions about the text.

1 People play bossaball on a soft surface.
2 Buzkashi is an Olympic sport.
3 Kabaddi is often played in schools.
4 Iepe Rubingh invented chess boxing.
5 Iepe Rubingh is from Germany.
6 People consider roshambo a serious sport.

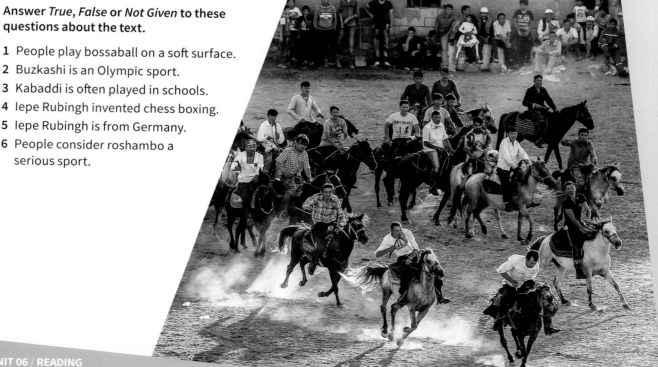

SUMMARY COMPLETION

 In this type of task you have to choose words to complete a summary of the text, or part of the text.

Sometimes the instructions tell you to choose words from the passage to fill the gaps.

Sometimes you are given words in a box and you have to choose the correct ones. Not all the words in the box will be needed.

1 0 ▷ **In the task below you have to fill the gaps by choosing words from the box. Look at gap 1 and follow the steps in the example. Then complete gaps 2–6.**

 Example

Notice that gap 1 is followed by an adjective (*new*) and a noun (*sports*).

This tells you that the word you need could be an adverb or an adjective.

There are adjectives in the box, but no adverbs.

The adjectives are *boring* and *strange*.

A writer is unlikely to suggest *boring* sports.

The answer is *strange*. This matches what the text says.

Complete the summary using the list of words A–L below.

If you have had enough of the ordinary sports people play, you can try a number of 1 __K__ new sports. Some of these were created when people 2 ____ two well-known sports. Sometimes they added a 3 ____ from the part of the world where they live. Bossaball is an example of this. It takes volleyball and football, adds a trampoline and some Brazilian martial arts.

Buzkashi, a sport from Afghanistan, is played on 4 ____ and uses a dead goat instead of a ball! People in Afghanistan would like this sport to become international.

Chess boxing is a sport where you need to 5 ____ rapidly from one type of activity to another. You need to be 6 ____ and also fit. It is becoming more and more popular and now holds world championships.

A boring	B change	C clever	D feature	E horses	F join
G mixed	H moving	I serious	J sport	K strange	L trampolines

GRAMMAR FOCUS: COMPARATIVES

1 1 ▷ **Complete these comparative sentences with your opinions on the sports in the text.**

1 ____Kabaddi____ is faster than ____roshambo____ .
2 _____ is more dangerous than _____ .
3 _____ is more exciting than _____ .
4 _____ is harder than _____ .
5 _____ is not as unusual as _____ .

 Kabaddi is a sport that is *more likely* to become famous.

Since then it has become *more popular* …

1 2 ▶ Skim read the text for one minute before moving on to answer the questions on the next page.

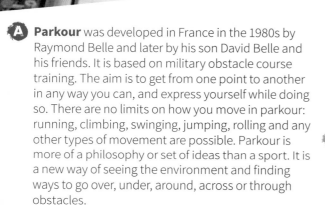

PARKOUR

A **Parkour** was developed in France in the 1980s by Raymond Belle and later by his son David Belle and his friends. It is based on military obstacle course training. The aim is to get from one point to another in any way you can, and express yourself while doing so. There are no limits on how you move in parkour: running, climbing, swinging, jumping, rolling and any other types of movement are possible. Parkour is more of a philosophy or set of ideas than a sport. It is a new way of seeing the environment and finding ways to go over, under, around, across or through obstacles.

B **Parkour** can be done alone or in groups. The most famous group of traceurs (people who do parkour) were the Yamakasi, a group made up of David Belle and his friends and cousins. They formed in the late 1980s and became popular during the 1990s and 2000s after appearing in several films, documentaries and advertisements. In the Yamakasi, there were strict rules. Members had to arrive on time and they were not allowed to complain or make excuses. They valued humility, so they were not allowed to show off or compete with other members.

C **Parkour** is a 'state of mind'. It is about getting over mental as well as physical barriers. It teaches people to touch the world and interact with it. It is about understanding what it means to be human. The organisation Parkour.net believes that parkour can never be a competitive sport. It is an art and is concerned with self-development. They say you can't ask, 'Who is the best at parkour?' Raymond Belle's advice is: 'If two roads open up before you, always take the more difficult one. Because you know you can travel the easy one.'

D **There** are some gyms and camps where you can practise and learn parkour. However, many traceurs do not like the idea of special places for their activity. The idea behind parkour is to adapt to any environment and be creative about how you get through it. It is about freedom and self-expression. The founder of parkour refused to teach people how to do moves or get over obstacles. The whole point is to learn your own technique and way of moving. So the idea of having classes or a limited space to practise in conflicts with the values of parkour.

E **Parkour** is also known as freerunning. Sometimes freerunning refers to another form of parkour developed by Sebastien Foucan, which has more focus on the individual. The term freerunning came out of the film *Jump London* (2003). It told the story of three French traceurs practising parkour around the famous monuments of London. Freerunning was the English translation of parkour. There are more similarities than differences between the two activities, and the Parkour UK website uses the two terms to refer to the same activity.

Questions 1–8

Do the following statements agree with the information in the text?

Write

TRUE   *if the statement agrees with the information*
FALSE   *if the statement contradicts the information*
NOT GIVEN *if there is no information on this*

1   You have to use a limited number of moves in parkour.
2   Parkour is mainly done in the countryside.
3   Parkour began in the twentieth century.
4   The Yamakasi did not allow latecomers.
5   When doing parkour, Raymond Belle recommends that you always choose the easy route.
6   There are many gyms in France where you can do parkour.
7   The founder of parkour was a very good teacher of parkour.
8   Freerunning and parkour are similar.

TIP 1 2

Be careful of words like *some, often, occasionally* that change the meaning of a sentence. For example, *some sports* does not mean the same as *many sports*.

Questions 9–15

Complete the summary of the text using the list of words A–M below.

Parkour is an activity that involves **9** _____ in many different ways through different environments. People who practise parkour are called **10** _____ . They believe that parkour is not a sport and can never be part of a **11** _____ . The values of parkour are adaptability, **12** _____ and freedom. Parkour should not be taught because it is about discovering your own way of moving and overcoming **13** _____ . Although there are gyms and other places where you can learn and practise parkour, many feel that this **14** _____ with the values of the discipline. Freerunning is a type of parkour. However, it is more about **15** _____ development than parkour, which is often, but not always, done as part of a group.

A agrees	**B** barriers	**C** competition	**D** conflicts	**E** creativity
F latecomers	**G** move	**H** moving	**I** personal	**J** respect
K team	**L** tournaments	**M** traceurs		

Use the strategies you have learnt:

- Read the whole summary first.
- Decide what type of word is needed for each gap.
- Make a prediction before looking at the words given.
- Remember that there are more words than gaps.
- Read the sentence, checking for grammar and meaning.

GO FURTHER ONLINE

WRITING

IN THIS UNIT YOU WILL LEARN HOW TO

- organise and write a Part 2 essay
- compare two different time periods
- link and signpost your ideas.

LEAD-IN

0 1 ▶ Choose the correct option(s). In each case, either one or two are correct.

1 go running / go for a run / go for running
2 go to the cinema / go to cinema / go for the cinema
3 see a film / look at a film / watch a film
4 visit to friends / visit friends / visit some friends
5 play the sports / play sport / play sports
6 join to a club / join a club / join for a club
7 go walking / go to a walk / go for a walk
8 go gym / go to the gym / go for the gym

Which of the activities do you enjoy doing?

EVALUATING A PART 2 ESSAY

02 ▷ Read a student's essay on the following topic. (Ignore the highlighting for now.) What are the *good* things about it?

People nowadays spend their free time less actively than in the past.
Do you agree or disagree?

SAMPLE ANSWER

Some people are saying that people are less active than they were in the past. There are points for and against this idea, but overall I agree with the statement. In this essay I explained why.

In my opinion, the main reason why people less active is computers. Several years ago we go to speak to our colleagues. We walked to their desk or office. Now we send an email without getting up from our seat. Even our free time is less active because we playing computer games and go on social media. Before, people were walking to a café to meet their friends or they went to their house. Nowadays, though, we chat online at home. In the twentieth century, children do many activities. In today's world, parents are scared for their children's safety, so they prefer to keep them at home. For many, it is easier to stay at home than to go out.

On the other hand, some physical activities are become more popular. There are more gyms than there used to be and it is fashionable to go running or to the gym. In my view, though, only some people do these things. Most people join a gym but they are not going regularly. However, they never stop playing computer games and watching TV! Also, these days everyone took their driving test as soon as possible and starts driving. In the past, young people walked and went by bus.

To sum up, I am agree that people are less active in their free time compared with the past. Now people are lazier and less fit than they were before. (273 words)

03 ▷ Answer these questions about the essay.

1 Does it have the right number of paragraphs?
2 Is every paragraph clear?
3 Are linking expressions used?
4 Is the writer's opinion given clearly?
5 Has the writer looked at both sides (*for* and *against*)?
6 Are tenses used correctly?
7 Are there any grammatical mistakes?

04 ▷ The teacher has highlighted the student's errors. Can you correct them?

GRAMMAR FOCUS: COMPARING PAST AND PRESENT

05 ▷ In the essay, the student is comparing the situation now with the situation in the past. Complete the expressions she uses to refer to the present or the past.

TIP 05

Try to use different phrases to compare past and present or present and future. Make a list of them, as this kind of question is quite frequent.

Present	Past
n _ w	b _ _ o _ e
n _ _ _ d _ _ s	_ _ the p _ _ _
i _ t _ _ _ _'s w _ _ _ _ d	s _ _ _ ral years _ _ _
th _ _ _ days	t _ _ r _ u _ _ d to b _

06 **Look at the following sentences from the essay:**

People are *less active*.
Some physical activities are becoming *more popular*.
People are *lazier* and *less fit*.
It is *easier* to stay at home.

Choose the correct form to make some more comparisons between the past and present.

1 Joining a gym is **expensiver / more expensive** than it used to be.
2 It is **more hard / harder** to find the time to do exercise.
3 Most people eat **healthier / more healthier** food than they did before.
4 It is **dangerous / more dangerous** for children to play outside.
5 The pace of life is **faster / more faster** than it used to be.

LINKING IDEAS

07 **Find the following expressions in the essay.**

1 two expressions used to give an opinion _____ _____
2 two expressions used to introduce the opposite view _____

_____

3 an expression to show there are two sides to the argument _____
4 an expression to introduce the conclusion _____
5 an expression to show that a point is the most important _____

08 **Read this Writing Part 2 question and then, before you read the essay in exercise 9, think of some advantages and disadvantages.**

Some children spend most of their free time taking part in clubs and other planned activities. Do the advantages of this outweigh the disadvantages?

09 ▷ Fill in the gaps in the essay with the linking expressions in the box.

My own view is	Unfortunately	Firstly	also
my own opinion	One reason is that	Thirdly	In addition

Many parents think that their children should have many free-time activities, such as joining sports clubs and having music lessons. Children often have no time which can really be called free time. In this essay I will look at the advantages and disadvantages of this and give **1** _____ .

2 _____ , if we think of all the great artists, musicians and sportsmen and women in the world, they all started by doing their activity as a hobby. They found they had a talent and developed their skills to become world class. Secondly, children usually enjoy their activities, make friends and become well-developed people.
3 _____ , parents think that being busy will stop the children getting into trouble. Their parents know what they are doing at all times.

4 _____ , this is not always a positive trend. **5** _____ children can become stressed when they have to run from activity to activity.
6 _____ , they need time to play freely and use their imaginations. They can get to know themselves and their likes and dislikes during this time. It is
7 _____ important to give them time to relax, watch TV, read and be with their parents, grandparents and siblings.

8 _____ that we need to have a balance. Children should choose one or two activities they really like, and have free time to just be themselves the rest of the time.

[EXAM SKILLS]

1 0 ▶ Read the following essay question and then write Agree (A) or Disagree (D) next to each point 1–6 below.

Children are now less active in their free time than in the past. Therefore, sports lessons must be compulsory in schools. To what extent do you agree or disagree? Give reasons for your answer and include any relevant examples from your own knowledge or experience.

Write at least 250 words.

1 If people are unfit, the government will have to spend a lot of money on medical care in the future.
2 Physical activity improves children's mental well-being.
3 Sports lessons are a waste of valuable study time.
4 Schools need to spend a lot of money on sports facilities.
5 Sports help children learn discipline and working with others as a team.
6 Some young people do not enjoy sports.

 **GO FURTHER ONLINE**

1 1 ▶ Write your essay using the following plan:

Paragraph 1 Introduction – a general opening sentence (a paraphrase of the question)
I agree or *I disagree – in this essay I will give reasons*

Paragraph 2 Summarise the opposite view: *Some people believe …*
Say why you disagree with them – give your main point

Paragraph 3 Give your view – at least two more points, with supporting evidence

Paragraph 4 Conclusion – state your view again and give a brief summary of your main arguments

1 2 ▶ Check your essay using this checklist.

• Are my paragraphs clearly shown? (leave a line or indent)
• Have I used linking words and expressions?
• Have I used phrases to introduce my opinion?
• Are my tenses correct (mostly present and future)?
• Have I checked my spelling, grammar and punctuation?

TIP 1 2

In the exam, leave a few minutes at the end to read through your essay with a checklist like this one in your mind.

UNIT /06: LEISURE TIME

LISTENING

IN THIS UNIT YOU WILL LEARN HOW TO

- understand a description of a place
- follow directions
- label a map
- recognise distractors.

01 ▶ Each picture illustrates a word or phrase used to give directions. Match the pictures with the words in the box.

 A common task in the Listening test is labelling a map. In order to complete this type of question, it is important that you are familiar with words and phrases for giving directions.

| behind | go past | go straight ahead / straight on |
| in front of | next to | opposite | turn left | turn right |

Useful verbs

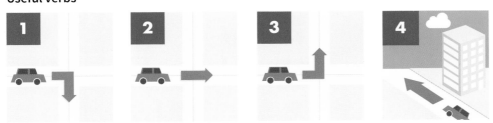

Useful prepositions of place

Check with a partner. Did you get the same answers?

Can you think of any more useful words for giving directions?

02 ▶ Describe a route you often take to a partner.

To walk to my local shop, I have to turn left outside my house and then turn right onto a main road. I then walk straight ahead until I get to a mini-roundabout …

[LABELLING A MAP]

UNDERSTANDING THE MAP AND THE QUESTION

- You listen and identify where places are on a map by choosing the correct letter.
- You listen and choose the correct label for places on a map from the list of words provided. There will be more words than you need.
- You listen and label places on a map by writing up to three words.

03▶ Study the map. What does it show?

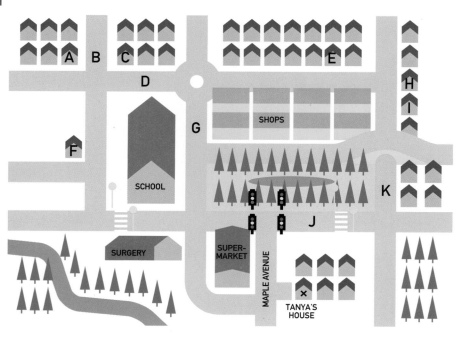

TIP 03

First read the question and try to understand what the map shows and what you have to do. Then study the map carefully and try to predict the type of language you might hear.

Match the places that appear on the map (the words in the box) with the pictures.

bridge	crossroads
park	traffic lights
river	roundabout
pond	zebra crossing

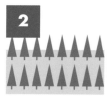

Can you think of any other places or features in a town that might be useful when you are giving someone directions?

FINDING PLACES ON A MAP

TIP 04

Once you have understood the map, you are in a much better position to complete the listening task. Note that the questions are in the order in which you will hear the answers on the recording.

04▶
🎵
49

Look at the map and find Tanya's house. Then listen to the phone message. Tanya has offered to give Melissa a lift to a concert. Listen to Melissa giving Tanya directions to her house and label the map. Write the correct letter, A–K, next to questions 1 and 2.

Then listen again and find Melissa's house. Write the correct letter, A–K, next to question 3.

1 Main Street _____   **2** Silver Street _____   **3** Melissa's house _____

05▶ Now listen to Melissa's second message. She wants Tanya to pick up another friend, Sarah, on the way. Listen and label the map. Write the correct letter, A–K, next to questions 4–6.

4 New Road _____   5 Sarah's house _____   6 Oak Avenue _____

Listen again and check your answers.

RECOGNISING DISTRACTORS

06▶ Read the extracts below from Melissa's messages, and underline any words and phrases which may distract you from choosing the correct answer.

You need to listen carefully because in this type of listening task you will often hear 'distractors' (information which you think might help you find the answer, but in fact does not).

(Question 1) *Then, you need to turn left at the traffic lights and then take a sharp right onto Main Street. You can also go straight on here, past the surgery, but I usually drive down Main Street.*

(Question 4) *Again, you need to turn right onto Maple Avenue, and up to the lights. Instead of turning left here, turn right, with the park on your left.*

(Question 5) *Drive along New Road until you reach the bridge. Sarah's house is the second house after the bridge. That's on the right; there are shops on the left.*

MAP OF A BUILDING

07▶ Listen to Tanya's message to another friend, arranging to meet before the concert.

Listen to Tanya's description and label the map. Choose the correct letter A–H and write the answers next to questions 1–4.

In this type of task, you could also be given a map of a building.

A art gallery   E restaurants   1 _____
B cinema   F exhibition centre   2 _____
C live music   G Arena   3 _____
D car park   H shopping centre   4 _____

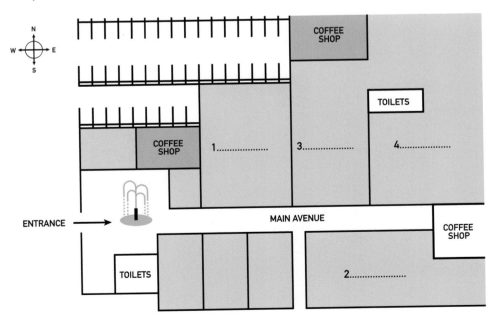

MAP OF A PARK

08▶ Look at the map with a partner and discuss the different things you can see on the map.

Another type of map you might find in a map-labelling task is a map of a park. The illustration below is a map of an activity camp.

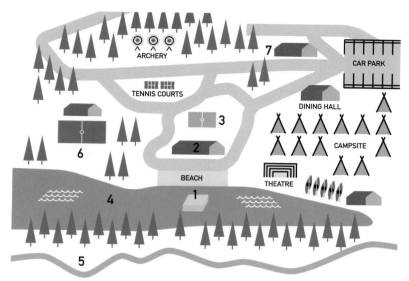

09▶
52
Listen to the manager giving a tour of the activity camp to a group of teenagers. Label the map with which activity they can do in each place. Use no more than TWO WORDS for each activity.

1 _____

2 _____

3 _____

4 _____

5 _____

6 _____

7 _____

[EXAM SKILLS]

GO FURTHER ONLINE

10▶
53
You will hear someone giving a talk about plans for a new forest centre.

Label the map. Choose the correct letter A–M and write the answers next to questions 1–8.

Pine Woods Centre

1 tickets on sale here _____

2 picnic field _____

3 barbecue area _____

4 Tree Tops Challenge _____

5 playground for young children _____

6 indoor play area _____

7 sheep _____

8 goats _____

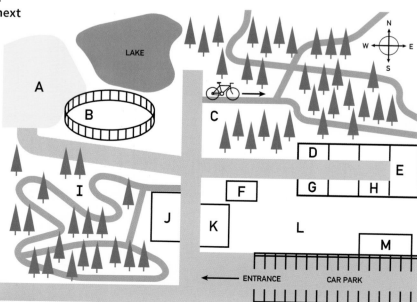

UNIT / 06: LEISURE TIME

SPEAKING

IN THIS UNIT YOU WILL LEARN HOW TO

- use positive and negative adjectives to talk about free-time activities
- recognise and use linking words in your talk (Speaking Part 2)
- pronounce weak forms of words
- give a complete talk and assess your own performance (Speaking Part 2).

In the first part of the Speaking test you may have to answer simple questions about how you spend your free time.

LEAD-IN

 01 ▶ **Ask and answer these questions with a partner.**

1 Do you do any of the activities in the pictures?
2 Which of these activities do you like or dislike?
3 Are there any other things you do in your free time?

A

B

TIP 01

It is useful to know which verbs go with different sports and activities. Common verbs used with leisure and sports activities include *play*, *do* and *go*.

play soccer ✔   *do soccer* ✗

C

D

E

02 ▶ With a partner, use the positive adjectives in the box to say how you feel about various free-time activities.

amusing	great	enjoyable	excellent	exciting
brilliant	healthy	peaceful	relaxing	

Examples: *Yoga is a very **peaceful** and **relaxing** activity.*
*I am **excellent** at taekwondo.*

03 ▶ With a different partner, use the negative adjectives in the box to talk about free-time activities.

Examples: *I feel **miserable** when I play football in the rain.*
*Boxing can be an **exhausting** sport – you need to be fit and strong.*

dangerous	exhausting	tiring	harmful	hopeless
miserable	frightening	useless	stressful	

EXTENDING YOUR TALK]

 It is important to use a variety of language in your talk. It is useful to use linking words such as *and*, *or*, *but*, *also*, *so*, *in fact*, *for example*, and *because*. These will make your talk flow better and will help you to give extra information.

04 ▶ **Listen to a candidate called Serena giving her talk.**

54

I'm going to talk about a hobby I'd like to take up in the future. I really want to learn ballroom dancing. This is because I love Latin music and I love the way the dancers move and shake. I also want to give myself a challenge and learn something new. Watching ballroom dancing always makes me feel excited. I don't think it'll be too difficult for me, because I already do ballet and tap dancing. I like learning new steps. For example, I really want to learn the tango or the samba because these are exciting and look good to people watching. I've tried Flamenco dancing but I'm not very good. I'm also worried about finding the right dance partner, because I'll be a little slow to learn in the beginning. So I might fall over sometimes. In fact I'll probably fall over quite a lot!

05 ▶ **The words Serena uses to connect her ideas are in bold. Match phrases 1–7 with the connecting words and phrases A–G.**

1 This is because I love Latin music
2 I love the way the dancers move and shake.
3 I like learning new steps
4 I really want to learn the tango
5 I've tried Flamenco dancing
6 I'm also worried about finding the right dance partner
7 I might fall over sometimes.

A **In fact**, I'll probably fall over quite a lot!
B **For example**, I really want to learn the tango
C **or** the samba
D **I also** want to give myself a challenge
E **but** I'm not very good.
F **and** I love the way the dancers move and shake.
G **because** I'll be a little slow to learn in the beginning.

 Listen again and check your answers.

54

06 ▶ **Complete the sentences with your own ideas. You can use the activities in the box, or you can choose your own. Practise saying them with a partner.**

baseball	going on social media	dancing	watching TV
hiking	playing computer games	travelling	sewing
sport	making jewellery		

1 I like [*activity*] **and** …
   I like table tennis and I'm a member of my college team.
2 I like [*activity*] **because** …
3 I love [*activity*], **but** …
4 I'm not keen on [*activity*] – **in fact** …
5 I love all kinds of [*activity*]. **For example**, …
6 A lot of people in my country [*activity*]. **They also** …
7 At weekends I enjoy [*activity*] or [*activity*] with my friends.

07 ▶ Now, read the script of Marco giving a talk about a leisure activity he would like to do in the future. Choose the correct linking words.

I'm going to tell you about a leisure activity I'd like to do in the future. I'd really like to learn how to play the acoustic guitar. This is (1) **because / so** I love music (2) **and / but** I love the beautiful sound this kind of guitar makes. I (3) **and / also** want to give myself a challenge (4) **so / and** learn something new. I don't think it'll be too difficult for me (5) **but / because** I already know how to read music. I play the piano (6) **but / so** I'm not very good. I think playing the guitar will be easier. I (7) **for example / also** like the fact that you can carry a guitar round easily and play it anywhere. (8) **For example / Because** I can play it in the park (9) **but / or** on the beach.

I can't think about learning it at the moment (10) **and / because** I'm too busy. I need to focus on my studies (11) **and / or** prepare for my exams. I think that I'd like to take up the guitar next year. All my exams will be over by then, (12) **so / but** I'll have more time, and more money too. (13) **In fact, / Because** I'll need money to pay for lessons! I think that learning the guitar would change my life in a positive way. If I learn to play it really well, I'll start my own band. I'd love to perform live on stage at a concert. I think that would be fantastic!

 Listen and check your answers.

[FOLLOW-UP QUESTIONS]

 After you have given your Part 2 talk, the examiner may ask you one or two questions related to the topic you talked about.

08 ▶ Listen to students answering the following questions.
After listening, practise asking and answering the questions with a partner.

1 Do you generally enjoy trying new things?
2 Is there any other activity you would like to try one day?

Share your ideas with a partner.

TIP 08

If the examiner asks you a question at the end of Part 2 you should answer with two or three sentences.

PRONUNCIATION – STRONG AND WEAK FORMS

09 ▶ Listen to the following words pronounced (a) when they are stressed and (b) how they might sound in a sentence.

	stressed	weak form
to	/tuː/	/tə/
and	/ænd/	/ənd/ or /ən/
a	/æ/	/ə/
of	/ɒv/	/əv/
some	/sʌm/	/səm/
for	/fɔːr/	/fəʳ/
from	/frɒm/	/frəm/

 When we speak English, we pronounce the key words in a sentence more clearly than the other words. These are usually nouns, verbs, adjectives. We say the little 'grammar' words (*and, some, to, for, of*, etc.) quickly and don't give them their full pronunciation. We call these 'weak forms'.

10 ▶ Look at the sentences. Underline the words that you think will NOT be stressed.

1 I want to learn to play the guitar.
2 I enjoy playing football and baseball.
3 I bought a new golf club.
4 I would like to learn to play chess.
5 I need some driving lessons.
6 I played drums in a band for a long time.
7 I plan to cycle from the north of Africa to the south.

58 Listen and check your answers.

Practise saying the sentences with a partner.

[EXAM SKILLS]

11 ▶ Make your own notes for this task card. Use the key words to help you.

Talk about a new sport or hobby you would like to take up.

You should say:

- what it is
- how you would start it
- why you have not started it yet

and explain what help you would need.

12 ▶ Use your notes to complete the task with a partner. You should try to talk for two minutes.

Listen to your partner talk on the same topic. Make notes of any interesting vocabulary or phrases they use. Complete the checklist.

	YES	NO
Did your partner talk for two minutes?		
Did your partner cover all four points on the task card?		
Did your partner link their ideas together well?		

Finally, both complete the task again.

GO FURTHER ONLINE

READING

IN THIS UNIT YOU WILL LEARN HOW TO

- match features of the passage
- identify the writer's views
- write first conditional sentences.

LEAD-IN

 01 ▷ How much do you know about the internet?

1 Name two search engines.
2 Name two news websites.
3 Name two social media sites.
4 Name a website that has factual information on many topics.

02 ▷ What do you use the internet for?

SKIM READING

 03 ▷ Skim read the passage in ONE MINUTE.

What is the purpose of the passage?

A to give the advantages and disadvantages of the internet

B to advise people how to become famous on the internet

C to explain how beginners can start to use the internet

BECOME

RICH AND FAMOUS

THROUGH THE INTERNET

In the past, to become famous you needed a talent: singing, playing an instrument, dancing or writing books. Nowadays, it is much easier to become famous. This is because of the internet. All you need is a camera or webcam, computer, internet connection and a bit of creativity.

First of all, you need to decide what you are going to write or speak about: hair and makeup, comedy, sport, news and current affairs, raising money for a charity or something specialist like keeping tropical fish. Then choose a site to post on. Some sites are international and some may be particular to one country, such as Weibo in China. YouTube is a good site to choose if you make your own videos. It is easy to upload your short films, and many people use it.

If you want to become famous on YouTube, you should make lots of videos and release one every day. YouTubers who become popular are often those who present tips, advice, 'how to' guides and opinions on entertainment or stories in the news. If you allow advertisements in your videos, you will make money when people view the adverts. Facebook is a good platform for those who want to make money, but not for those who want to be famous. To earn money through Facebook, you need a very original and/or funny page, with interesting photos which can get you a few hundred thousand 'likes'. If you achieve fame on Facebook, it probably won't last.

Twitter is a social media site where people can communicate through short messages. It works well for those who want to be well-known but are not so interested in making money. If you want to become known on Twitter, you will need to post lots of entertaining content. Instagram is a site where people mainly put up photos and videos. It is a site which can make you well-known, particularly if you want to become a famous photographer.

MATCHING FEATURES

Read the task instructions and statements (1–6) and the list of websites (A–E). Then follow the steps in the box below and complete the task.

Choose the correct website (A–E) for each statement. You may choose any website more than once.

1 You want to be rich and become famous.
2 You want to take photographs as a career.
3 You want people to know you but don't care about money.
4 You want to make money but not be famous.
5 You can post a new film daily.
6 You want to show people how to do something.

A YouTube
B Facebook
C Twitter
D Instagram
E your own blog

- Scan the text for the websites A to E. If possible, underline them.
- Find the key words in sentences 1 to 6 and underline them.
- Find every time 'YouTube' is mentioned in the passage. Read all the information about it.
- Which of sentences 1 to 6 refers to YouTube? Write A next to that sentence.
- Do the same for websites B to E.

In this type of task you get a list of people, places or things and a list of sentences. You need to match each sentence with a person/place/thing.

TIP 04

In this task type the questions will not be in the same order as the passage but the options e.g. people/places *will* be in text order. You will need to 'jump around' the passage a bit rather than reading it from beginning to end.

TIP 04

Only use information from the passage to answer the question, even if you think some information in the passage is incorrect.

Creating your own blog is possibly the best way to become internet famous and make money, through advertising, especially once you have become known on one of the sites above. You need to be aware of the topics and issues that are 'trending' (that are popular right now) and post about those ideas. Learn to create 'vines' (a series of short extracts from videos put together in a creative way) and become an expert on photo editing. With these few easily learnt skills and some imagination, you can achieve the fame you've always dreamed of – online at least.

IDENTIFYING THE WRITER'S VIEWS

0 5 ▸ **Look at statements A to C. All of them give information about social media. Only one of them contains the writer's personal view. Which one?**

◎ This task tests your ability to decide if statements represent the writer's views. The views will not be stated directly.

A 'Weibo' is the Twitter of China, but actually has twice as many users as Twitter.
B In the United States, over 70% of the population have a social media account.
C Over 1.5 billion people waste their time on Facebook.

Does the writer directly state his/her opinion? How can you identify his/her opinion?

0 6 ▸ **Read this short text about what it is like to be famous. Then answer the questions below.**

Being famous is not as much fun as it sounds. I am only a little bit famous. About two or three times a day people stop me to ask me to sign a piece of paper or to have their photo taken with me. For me, it is not at all enjoyable, as it often makes me late. However, I feel I should be polite to the person and have a chat with them. Sometimes I wonder how it would feel to be very famous. You wouldn't be able to get a quick coffee with a friend or go to a movie. I don't think life would be very easy.

Do the following statements agree with the claims of the writer? Write

> **YES** *if the statement agrees with the claims of the writer*
> **NO** *if the statement contradicts the claims of the writer*
> **NOT GIVEN** *if it is impossible to say what the writer thinks about this*

1 The writer considers herself to be very well known.
2 It is inconvenient for her to be stopped by people she doesn't know.
3 She would like to drink more coffee.
4 Being very famous would be enjoyable.

07 ▶ Read the task instructions and statements and look at the passage 'Become rich and famous through the internet' again. Then follow the steps in the box below and complete the task.

Do the following statements agree with the claims of the writer of the passage 'Become rich and famous through the internet'? Write

YES   *if the statement agrees with the claims of the writer*

NO   *if the statement contradicts the claims of the writer*

NOT GIVEN *if it is impossible to say what the writer thinks about this*

1 Before the internet, you didn't need any special skills to become famous.

2 If you choose a specialist subject, you are more likely to get known.

3 Having your own blog is an excellent way to find fame.

- Read each statement carefully. The statements come in the order of the text.
- Sometimes you will need to read the whole passage quickly to decide; for other statements you only need to read a sentence or two.
- Remember the statement might not use exactly the same words as in the passage.

TIP 07

When you have found the part of the text which contains the answer, read every word carefully. Sometimes a small word can change the meaning completely. For example, if the writer says people are 'too friendly', the positive adjective 'friendly' becomes negative.

08 ▶ Check your answers, and the reasons for them, in the notes below.

1 The answer is at the beginning of the text: *In the past, to become famous you needed a 'talent'*, another way of saying 'special skills'. The text states that it is now easier to become famous 'because of the internet'. So the answer is No.

2 Specialist subjects are mentioned in the second paragraph, along with other possible things to write about. The writer does not say if writing about a specialist subject is more likely to make you famous than writing about the other topics mentioned (comedy, sport, etc.), so the answer is Not Given.

3 To answer this, you only need to read the last paragraph, about blogs. The writer states that blogs are *possibly the best way to become internet famous*. This is the same as saying that blogs are an excellent way to become famous, so the answer is Yes.

TIP 08

You should be able to tell from the statement which part of the text to read in order to find the answer. If you can't answer Yes or No for that part of the text, the answer is Not Given. You do not need to continue searching in the rest of the text.

09 ▶ Now follow the same steps for statements 4 to 6.

4 You can get famous easily through Facebook.

5 It is not worth the effort needed to get famous through Twitter.

6 Learning to make 'vines' could help you, if you are aiming to become famous.

GRAMMAR FOCUS: FIRST CONDITIONAL

Look at this sentence from the passage 'Become rich and famous through the internet'.

*If you **want** to become known on Twitter, you **will need** to post lots of entertaining content.*
This is called a first conditional. It has two clauses, an '*If*' clause and a result clause. The '*If*' clause is in the present tense. The result clause has '*will / won't* + infinitive'.

10 ▶ Find three more sentences from the passage which begin with 'If'. Complete the table.

	If clause	Result clause
1		
2		
3		

What is used instead of *will / won't* in one of the result clauses?

11 ▶ **Read the passage and answer the questions below.**

Famous animals

A Like people, animals each have their own personality and talents. And like some people, some animals achieve fame. Some of them become famous through films, TV or advertisements, and others through their work, for example rescuing people or playing a role in a war. Still others have done something special or been the first to do something.

B There have been many famous dogs in history. One of them is Hachiko, a dog remembered for his loyalty to his owner. Hachiko was born in Japan in 1923 and was owned by Hidesaburō Ueno, a professor at Tokyo University. Every day, Hachiko waited for Ueno at Shibuya station and the pair walked home together. One day in May 1925, Ueno died suddenly while he was at work. For the next nine years, nine months and 15 days, his faithful dog continued to meet the train his owner used to take every day. At first the station staff did not welcome him, but gradually people understood his loyalty and began giving him food and treats. Hachiko did not stop waiting for Ueno until his own death in 1935. There have been films and books about Hachiko, and every year there is a ceremony to commemorate him at the railway station in Tokyo, where he waited so faithfully.

Questions 1–7

Choose the correct animal (A–C) for each question. You may choose any animal more than once.

Which animal …

1 never forgot their human friend?

2 lived part of their life in the wild?

3 made large profits for the humans who cared for them?

4 was not wanted by their parent?

5 has had valuable work done in their memory?

6 is formally remembered at regular times?

7 had souvenirs of them made?

A Hachiko

B Knut

C Elsa

C One animal that achieved fame in the twenty-first century is Knut the polar bear. Knut was born in Berlin Zoo in December 2006. Sadly, Knut was rejected by his mother, Tosca, and was raised by zookeepers. Knut was extremely popular with the public, not only in Germany, but across the world. Knut's story increased attendance at the zoo by about 30% and increased the zoo's revenue by five million euros. The zoo made substantial amounts of money by selling Knut toys, candy and other products. There were even songs written about him. By the time he was a year old, Knut weighed almost 100 kg and it was too dangerous for him to be handled by humans. Poor Knut missed his favourite keeper. Knut suffered in his short life without his mother, and later without human contact. He died of a virus at the age of four.

D Even some wild animals have become famous. One of them is Elsa the lioness, born in 1956. Elsa's mother was killed by a game warden, a person whose job it was to protect wild animals. The warden, George Adamson, had killed the lioness to defend himself, but he felt guilty about the orphaned cubs. He and his wife, Joy, took them home and brought them up. They trained Elsa, one of the cubs, to live in the wild. During her adult life in the wild, she had three cubs and took them to visit her human foster parents. Joy Adamson told Elsa's story in a book called *Born Free*. *Born Free* was made into a film, which was popular with both adults and children. In 1984, the actors who had starred in the film started the Born Free Foundation, an organisation that protects wildlife in many ways. The Foundation's important work includes improving conditions in zoos and circuses, stopping hunting for 'sport' and working against the killing of elephants for ivory.

E Many of us enjoy learning about famous animals. They can inspire us with their characters and stories, just as human celebrities can. Some of them are remembered for years through books, films, toys and other items created in their memory. But in the end, it is humans and not the animals themselves who benefit from that fame.

Questions 8–16

Do the following statements agree with the claims of the writer in the reading passage?

Write

YES	*if the statement agrees with the claims of the writer*
NO	*if the statement contradicts the claims of the writer*
NOT GIVEN	*if it is impossible to say what the writer thinks about this*

8 All animals are very much the same.

9 There are many different reasons why animals might be remembered.

10 Ueno died after a long illness.

11 After some time, the people who worked at the railway station were kind to Hachiko.

12 The songs written about Knut were very popular.

13 Knut had a happy life because of his fame.

14 The Adamsons made money from Elsa.

15 The Born Free Foundation does useful work.

16 Famous animals get many advantages from their fame.

GO FURTHER ONLINE

UNIT /07: FAME AND THE MEDIA

WRITING

IN THIS UNIT YOU WILL LEARN HOW TO

- avoid repeating words in your Part 2 essay
- develop a paragraph
- provide specific support for your main points.

LEAD-IN

01▶ Put the words into the correct column.

celebrity	blogger	famous	fan	paparazzi	media
newspaper	model	fortune	star	photographer	popular
reporter	talented	wealthy	website	well-known	

Nouns (things)	Nouns (people)	Adjectives

WRITING PART 2: PARAGRAPHS

0 2 ▶ **Look at this essay title.**

Does being famous have more advantages or more disadvantages?

Read this second paragraph (the paragraph after the introduction) from a student's essay on this topic. What are the good and bad things about it?

There are many advantages of being famous. If you are famous, you might also be wealthy. You can buy a big house and an expensive car. Another advantage is that you have fans. They take photographs of you and send you letters. One more advantage is if you are famous you don't have to wait in queues. You can go to the front. The last advantage of being famous is you can use your fame and money to help good causes. If you give money to charity, others will do so too. In this way, you can make a real difference in the world.

0 3 ▶ **The paragraph gives four advantages of being famous. Each point is supported by evidence. Complete the table. The first point has been done for you.**

	Point	Evidence
1	you might be wealthy	you can buy a big house and an expensive car
2		
3		
4		

0 4 ▶ **Rewrite the paragraph. Instead of always using *famous* and *advantages*, try to use some of these words:**

famous: *(have) fame, well-known, someone that everyone knows*
advantages: *benefits, good points, positive aspects*

0 5 ▶ **Read the student's next paragraph and answer the questions.**

There are also disadvantages of being famous. The main one is that you do not have a private life. Reporters follow you everywhere. Even if you are tired or sick, they take photographs of you. *The second drawback of being well-known is that people say bad things about you. They even tell lies about you. The third negative aspect of fame is your family may also suffer. Even your children may have paparazzi following them. A final problem is that it can be very stressful. Some actors or singers are badly affected by the pressure.

1 How does the student avoid repeating the words *disadvantages* and *famous*?
2 What are the student's FOUR main points?
3 What evidence does the student provide for each point?

GIVING SPECIFIC EXAMPLES

 It is also good to give <u>specific examples</u> for some of your points.

For example, 'Many celebrities have got into trouble after getting angry with reporters and photographers who were following them' could be added at * to support the first point in the student's second paragraph.

06▷ **Where in the paragraph could you add these sentences?**

1 Even people like Bill Gates, who gives most of his money to charity, are criticised!

2 Many famous people have become ill due to overwork and always being in public view.

3 For example, everyone has seen pictures of Harper, the daughter of David and Victoria Beckham.

07▷ **Add specific support to these points. The person or situation can be from your own country.**

Famous people are often rich.

You might have a lot of fans.

You will be able to use your fame and money to help others.

GRAMMAR FOCUS: PRONOUNS

TIP 07

You will get more marks if you give specific examples to support your points. It can be something that happened to you or a friend, something you read or something that happens in your country. Make sure it provides evidence of the point you are making.

 Using pronouns is a way of avoiding repetition.

Examples

Lionel Messi is a famous footballer. ~~Lionel Messi~~ / He plays for Barcelona and Argentina.
I can think of many drawbacks. The first ~~drawback~~ / one is the cost.

08▷ **Replace the repeated words with pronouns.**

1 Fan Bingbing is a popular actress in China. Fan Bingbing starred in *My Fair Princess*.

2 Benedict Cumberbatch is one of my heroes. I met Benedict Cumberbatch when I was in London.

3 Our country has laws that protect people from paparazzi. Some countries' laws are not as strict as our laws.

4 There are some reasons for my opinion. The first reason for my opinion is it is difficult to be famous.

09 ▶ Read the essay title. Which of the statements a–d below best matches your opinion on the essay topic?

There should be strict laws banning people from taking photographs of people under 18 in order to protect young celebrities and the children of celebrities. To what extent do you agree or disagree?

TIP 09

'To what extent do you agree or disagree?' means 'How strongly do you agree or disagree?' Use phrases like *I strongly agree*, or *I tend to disagree*.

a I strongly agree. Laws must be very strict to protect children.

b I tend to agree. It is probably not a good idea to allow photos of children.

c I tend to disagree. I think people are interested in seeing photos of famous children.

d I strongly disagree. People have the right to take pictures of whoever they want.

10 ▶ Read the essay and answer the questions about it that follow.

1 What is the writer's opinion?

2 What three pieces of specific support does the writer give?

3 Does the writer consider the opposite opinion?

4 These are all possible plans for this essay. Which one has the writer used?

Plan 1
Opinion
Opposing argument + why I disagree
Opposing argument + why I disagree
Restate opinion

Plan 2
Opinion
My main arguments
Opposing arguments
Restate opinion

Plan 3
General introduction
(no opinion)
Arguments for
Arguments against
My opinion (given for the first time)

MODEL ANSWER

All children have the right to a normal childhood. On the other hand, everyone is interested in child stars and the children of celebrities. Overall, I agree that it is more important to protect children, so we should not allow people to take photographs of people under 18.

It is true that people are interested in seeing photos of famous children. They want to see if they look like their celebrity parents. The Beckham children, for example, are often in the newspapers. People think the Beckham boys should play football like their father. The little girl has to be perfectly dressed like her mother. In my opinion, this is not fair on the children. Another problem is that people believe they have the right to see pictures of famous children, particularly important ones like those of the British royal family. Prince William is working hard to make sure his children, Prince George, Princess Charlotte and Prince Louis, can grow up with their privacy protected.

People say that 'fame has a price'. They think that if photographers take pictures of well-known people, that is part of the price. I disagree with children 'paying for fame'. They didn't choose to be famous. They have the right to be badly dressed or have a bad day like everyone else. I once saw a website called 'Celebrities with ugly kids'. How will those children feel when they see that website one day?

In conclusion, I understand that photos of famous children sell newspapers. However, I think such photos should be banned to protect the children.

[EXAM SKILLS]

 11▸ Write an essay answering the following question. Use the advice in the box. You may use the ideas below if you wish.

Do you agree or disagree that celebrities are paid far too much money?

Give reasons for your answer and include any relevant examples from your own knowledge or experience.

Write at least 250 words.

- Write a brief plan.
- Give your opinion clearly.
- Make sure each main point has supporting evidence.
- Briefly consider the opposite opinion.
- Leave a few minutes to check your essay.

 **GO FURTHER ONLINE**

Agree
- Essential workers such as nurses and teachers often receive low salaries.
- Celebrities are often born with their talent for singing or acting. They have not spent years at university like doctors and engineers.
- Most of them waste their money on expensive houses, cars and parties.

Disagree
- Celebrities do not have a private life and work very hard.
- Very few people reach the top levels of music, acting or sport – we should reward those that do.
- It is a case of supply and demand. We create demand by going to see their concerts and buying their music.

LISTENING

IN THIS UNIT YOU WILL LEARN HOW TO

- complete a flow-chart
- predict what information is missing in a flow-chart
- deal with technical or scientific flow-charts.

LEAD-IN

01► Do you know who this famous person is and what he does?
Do you know how he became famous?

02► You will hear a journalist talk about how this artist became famous. Complete the flow-chart below. Write NO MORE THAN TWO WORDS for each answer.

59

[FLOW-CHART COMPLETION]

◉ Flow-chart completion tasks are similar to other completion tasks. Either:
- you are given a list of words to choose from, or
- you complete the chart by using words from the recording.

The instructions will tell you how many words you can use.
The answers come in the same order as the recording.

He learnt how to play a variety of instruments: **1** _____ , guitar, drums and trumpet.

↓

He entered talent **2** _____ in his home town and his mother posted some videos on YouTube.

↓

The YouTube clips brought him a lot of **3** _____ .

↓

He was discovered by a **4** _____ .

↓

He signed a recording **5** _____ and became a **6** _____ .

03▶ Think about how you completed the flow-chart in exercise 2 and answer the questions.

1 Were the words in the recording exactly the same as the words in the flow-chart?
2 Was there extra information in the listening which you didn't need to use and which might have led you to give the wrong answer?

PREDICTING THE ANSWER

04▶ Read the opinions below on being famous and complete these tasks:

- Underline the key words in each sentence.
- Read the word before and after the gap.
- Make a note of the possible grammatical forms of the missing word, i.e. adjective, noun, verb, etc.
- Try to guess the missing word, or some possible words.

TIP 04

In the exam it is unlikely that you will be able to guess the actual missing word. However, it will help you a lot if you think about the type of word you are listening for.

A: I wouldn't like to be famous. I would hate people to **1** _____ me all the time. You would always be followed by **2** _____ and never able to have a private life. Being followed on a good day, when you've been to the hairdresser and are wearing your best jeans, is perhaps **3** _____ , but can you imagine how it would make you feel on a bad day?

B: I would love to be famous. I would adore all the **4** _____ and the special treatment. Everywhere I went, people would know my name and I wouldn't need to **5** _____ any more. The best part, though, would be meeting other famous people. I can imagine that would be so **6** _____ . They would come to my **7** _____ yacht and I would **8** _____ their mansions.

Compare your answers with a partner. Were some of your guesses the same?

05▶ Listen and fill the gaps in exercise 4.

60

0|6|▶ Now read the flow-chart below. Using the technique in the previous exercise, predict the grammatical form of the missing words. Try also to think about the possible meaning.

Complete the flow-chart below. Write NO MORE THAN TWO WORDS for each answer.

How to become famous

Find something you like doing and **1** _____ at becoming the best in that particular skill.

↓

Study **2** _____ and try to learn as much as possible.

↓

Create **3** _____ and market yourself. You need to be able to sell yourself. Social media is a great way to do this these days.

↓

Don't worry if sometimes you **4** _____ . You can learn from the experience.

0|7|▶ Listen and fill the gaps in exercise 6.

61

TECHNICAL / SCIENTIFIC FLOW-CHARTS

⊙ The subject matter for this type of task can vary. It is possible to be presented with a flow-chart which is technical or scientific. The language used, therefore, can often seem challenging at first.

One approach to handling this type of flow-chart is this:
• Underline the key words you *do* understand.
• Decide which type of word is missing from each gap: adjective, noun, verb, etc. (make a note).
• Try to work out the overall meaning of each stage of the chart.

08▷ Read the flow-chart below, which uses a lot of technical language, and follow the advice on the previous page.

TIP 08

Try not to panic when you see technical or scientific words you don't recognise. Focus on the words you *do* understand.

> ### Getting the best from your camcorder
>
> Most camcorders can perform all necessary tasks using automatic functions. But for a more professional result, you must also learn how to use the **1** _____ controls.

↓

> The **Focus** function on the camera is very **2** _____ . You need to turn the focus ring one way or the other, depending on whether the object you want to film is **3** _____ or further away.

↓

> The **Iris** is an adjustable opening (aperture) which controls the amount of **4** _____ coming through the lens (the exposure). As you open the iris, more light comes in and the picture appears **5** _____ .

↓

> Finally, the **Zoom** is a very **6** _____ manual function and therefore often over-used. This feature moves your shot closer or further away from the subject. For **7** _____ zooms a tripod is recommended.

09▷ Look at the options in the box. Discuss with a partner which are possible for each gap.

A bigger	**B** brighter	**C** closer	**D** important	**E** light
F long	**G** manual	**H** popular	**I** short	**J** useful

10▷ You will hear a talk on how to get the best from your camcorder. Choose SEVEN answers from the list and write the correct letter, A–J, next to questions 1–7 in exercise 8.

62

TIP 10

Listen carefully, as some of the options in the box are distractors.

[EXAM SKILLS]

1 1 ▷ You will hear a lecture on how to make a short film. Complete the flow-chart below. Write **NO MORE THAN TWO WORDS** for each answer.

63

Making a short film

When deciding which type of film to make, use the **1** _____ you have among you.

↓

Make the plot of your film **2** _____ .

↓

Have a **3** _____ with you at all times.

↓

Write the screenplay: a description of the scene, the location, the actors' words, the **4** _____ and directions for the actors about what they should do.

↓

Prepare a storyboard. This is a bit like a **5** _____ .

↓

Choose a director. He or she is in control of the **6** _____ elements of the film.

↓

Cast your film. One way to find actors might be to **7** _____ .

GO FURTHER ONLINE

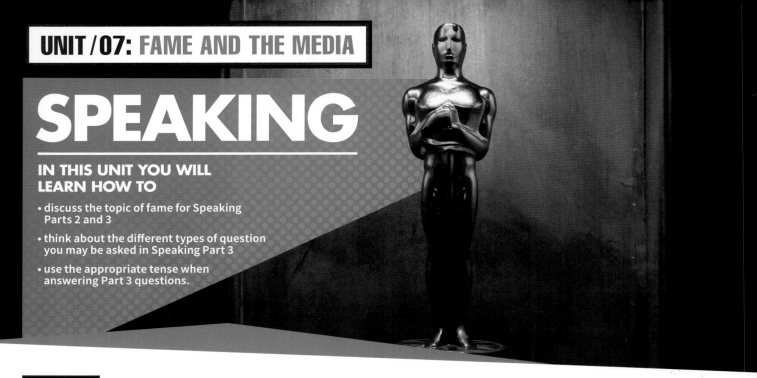

UNIT /07: FAME AND THE MEDIA

SPEAKING

IN THIS UNIT YOU WILL LEARN HOW TO

- discuss the topic of fame for Speaking Parts 2 and 3
- think about the different types of question you may be asked in Speaking Part 3
- use the appropriate tense when answering Part 3 questions.

01▷ What are these people famous for?

What words would you use to describe them? Match the words below with each person. There can be more than one answer.

If you can't match the words with these people, think of a famous person they could describe.

active	brave	brilliant	charming	professional	talented
cruel	expert	powerful	generous	experienced	honest

A **B** **C**

SPEAKING PART 2]

02▶
64

Listen to a candidate talking about a famous person. The task is shown here. Then answer questions 1–5 below.

Describe a famous person who you like or admire.

You should say:

- who they are
- why they are famous
- where and when you saw them

and explain why you like this person.

1 Who was the famous person?
2 What does the famous person do?
3 Where did the candidate see this person?
4 When did the candidate see this person?
5 Why does the candidate like this person? (Give three reasons.)

Reason 1: _____

Reason 2: _____

Reason 3: _____

03▶
65

Listen to another candidate doing the same task. As you listen, complete the script using the connecting words in the box. One of them can be used more than once.

TIP **03**

Use these words to make longer, connected answers for Speaking Parts 2 and 3.

and	because	but	in spite of	so	when	who	whose	why

Well, the famous person I'm going to describe is David Beckham. He was a footballer **1** _____ played for Manchester United, **2** _____ he also played for England. I first saw him play for United **3** _____ I was only seven, **4** _____ that was probably in about 2002. I remember it as one of the most exciting days in my life!

David Beckham became famous **5** _____ he was a very talented footballer. His speciality was scoring amazing goals from free kicks. **6** _____ he wasn't well-known only for his football skills. He became even more famous when he married a pop star – Victoria, one of the Spice Girls. And another reason for his fame was his good looks and his style. I think almost every boy in the world wanted to have a David Beckham haircut! I know I did.

I adored him as a boy **7** _____ I was mad about football and he was my hero. The reason **8** _____ I still like him is that **9** _____ his fame he behaves like a normal guy. I heard a story from someone **10** _____ car was broken down in the middle of the countryside. And then a car stopped and a man got out and asked him if he needed a push. It was David Beckham!

04 ▷ Now, it is your turn to do the Part 2 task. Read the card again and complete the set of notes below. Try to do this in 60 seconds.

Describe a famous person who you like or admire.

You should say:

- who they are
- why they are famous
- where and when you saw them

and explain why you like this person.

Notes	
Who?	
Why famous?	
Where?	
When?	
Why like? Reasons	
1	
2	
3	

05 ▷ Using your notes, do the Part 2 task with a partner. You should each try to talk for two minutes. When your partner is speaking, listen to your partner's talk and make notes of any useful phrases you hear.

[PART 3 QUESTIONS]

 In Speaking Part 3, the examiner will ask you some general questions about the topic you have been speaking about. These might ask you to do certain things, for example *explain* something or *compare* something.

06▶ **Match the questions (1–5) with what each question is asking you to do (a–e).**

1 Do you think people are too interested in the lives of famous people?
2 How can people use their fame to do good?
3 Are there any differences between famous people now and in the past?
4 What will people be famous for in the next few years?
5 What would be the advantages and disadvantages of being famous?

a make a *suggestion* about a topic
b *explain* about the details of a topic
c *compare* two different things about a topic
d *predict* what will happen in the future
e *give an opinion* about a topic

TIP **06**

It is important to listen carefully to the examiner's questions so that you understand what he/she is asking you to do.

07▶ **Now match questions 1–5 above with answers A–E below.**

A I think that people used to be famous more for what they did rather than who they were or what they looked like.
B Charity work seems like it could be a good idea. Most famous people earn a lot of money and it would be great if they could give some of that money to help others.
C I think we will see more normal people like you or me becoming famous over the internet. Anyone can upload a video now and get millions of views.
D If you are famous you can make a lot of money and be given a lot of free things to advertise. On the other hand, it might be difficult to do normal things, like go shopping in the supermarket.
E Well, I think that there are maybe too many celebrity TV shows and magazines these days, so that might be true.

[EXAM SKILLS]

08▶ **Think of your own answers to the Part 3 questions from exercise 6 with a partner.**

If possible, record yourselves and listen to the recordings together.

Make notes of which tenses your partner uses, and also any interesting phrases, then try to answer the questions one more time.

 **GO FURTHER ONLINE**

UNIT / 08: NATURAL WORLD

READING

IN THIS UNIT YOU WILL LEARN HOW TO

- complete notes with words from the text
- match sentence endings with their beginnings
- use modals of possibility and ability.

POD OF DOLPHINS

LEAD-IN

0 1 ▶ Do the two underlined words in each sentence have a similar meaning or the opposite meaning? Use a dictionary if necessary.

1 A <u>predator</u> catches and eats its <u>prey</u>.
2 A <u>group</u> of dolphins is called a <u>pod</u>.
3 Environmentalists work for the <u>conservation</u> and <u>protection</u> of the planet.
4 Only a few baby turtles <u>survived</u>; all the others <u>died</u>.
5 Mothers have an <u>automatic</u> desire to protect their babies; keeping them safe is <u>instinctive</u> behaviour.

SKIM READING

0 2 ▶ Skim read the text in ONE minute and check your answers to exercise 1.

SHARKS

OUR FRIENDS AND PROTECTORS

A When asked about their favourite animals, many people answer 'dolphins'. They are known as friendly, intelligent creatures that have a special relationship with humans. For example, dolphins can tell when a woman is pregnant. They can also tell when someone is in trouble. No one is really sure why this is the case. Experts think they may understand that humans are similar to them and try to protect them from predators and other dangers. Dolphins' protection of humans might not be just automatic or instinctive: they may actively decide to help in certain situations.

ORCA (KILLER WHALE)

B There are many stories about dolphins protecting humans from sharks. Wildlife filmmaker Hardy Jones was filming a group of dolphins, when a large shark swam towards him ready to attack. Four dolphins came to his rescue and drove the shark away. Perhaps they could tell he was a person who cared very much about dolphins. In fact, Jones was a well-known campaigner against the killing of dolphins. In another incident, in 2004, in New Zealand, four people were saved from a great white shark by a pod of dolphins. The dolphins herded the swimmers into a group and formed a protective ring around them. As they had not yet seen the shark, one of them tried to swim away. He couldn't get away, because every time he tried, he was pushed back inside the ring by the dolphins.

C Dolphins don't only save humans from sharks, but protect them in other situations too. A scuba diver was hit by a boat near the Channel Islands (between England and France) in 2006. The man was unconscious, but survived 56 hours in the water, watched over by a pod of about 150 dolphins. In 2014, dolphins again came to the help of a human. Joey Trevino was losing hope. He had been in the sea for 24 hours after his boat sank in the Gulf of Mexico. He felt he couldn't keep going any more. A friendly dolphin approached him and gently pushed him, as if to say 'don't give up'. That moral support and encouragement may have saved Trevino's life.

D Dolphins have also been known to help other species. In New Zealand, two pygmy sperm whales were in difficulty next to a sand bank. People were trying their best to get them back out to sea, but the whales couldn't find their way past the sand bank. After several hours of failed attempts, they were ready to give up. Along came 'Moko', a bottlenose dolphin, who seemed to communicate with the whales and led them to a channel which took them back to the ocean.

E Whales have also been known to protect both humans and other mammals. In California, in 2012, a BBC Planet Earth film crew filmed a group of humpback whales who were protecting migrating grey whales from attacks by orcas (killer whales) over a period of at least seven hours. In China, Yang Yun applied for a job training whales at Polar Land in the city of Harbin. For the 'interview' she had to dive down as far as possible in the seven-metre deep pool. When she was about five metres down, Yang Yun found she couldn't move her legs due to the freezing temperatures. Two beluga whales, Mila and Nicola, sensed that she was in trouble. Mila gripped Yang Yun's leg in her mouth and pushed Yun to the surface, saving her life.

BOTTLENOSE DOLPHIN

F Stories of marine mammals helping humans – and each other – date back to Ancient Greece. Although we may never be sure why they help us, many people feel that it is a good reason for us to do whatever we can to protect them.

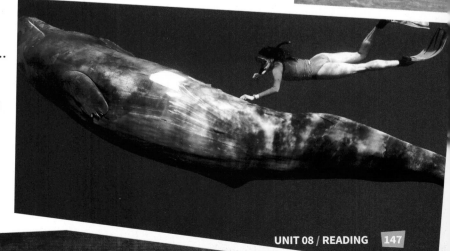

[NOTES COMPLETION]

03 ▶ One question type in the Reading paper is 'notes completion'.
Read the advice in the box and study the example below.

- Read the instructions carefully. Check how many words you can use. Do the words need to come from the passage or from a box of words that you are given?
- Read the notes carefully.
- Think of similar words to the key words in the notes.
- Decide what kind of word is needed in the gap. Use words like prepositions (*in, from*) and articles (*a, an, the*).
- Find the relevant part of the passage. Look out for the similar words you noted earlier.
- Find a word or words that seem to fit.
- Read the notes carefully with your words added.
- Make sure that the completed notes match the meaning of the passage and that your words match the grammar of the sentences.

TIP 03

The notes usually only relate to one part of the passage. Find the correct part and read it in detail. The information in the notes may not be in the same order as in the passage.

Example

Look at the gapped sentence and read paragraph F.

Stories of (whales and dolphins) (assisting people) (were first heard of) (in) _____ .

| = marine mammals | = helping humans | = date back to | 'in' tells us the answer is likely to be a year or a place |

The answer is ___Ancient Greece___ .

04 ▶ Read paragraph B in detail. Then match the words and phrases 1–5 from paragraph B with words and phrases a–e which have similar meanings.

1 filming   a saved the life of
2 came to his rescue   b famous
3 well-known   c videoing
4 against the killing of   d group (of dolphins)
5 pod   e for the protection of

05 ▶ Complete the notes below. Write NO MORE THAN TWO WORDS from the passage.

A pod of dolphins saved the life of a man called **1** _____ , while he was videoing them.
The man was a famous **2** _____ for the protection of dolphins.

Which paragraph did you need to read in detail to complete the notes above? Did you need to read the whole paragraph?

06 ▶ Complete the notes below. Write NO MORE THAN THREE WORDS from the passage.

Orcas were trying to catch and hurt a group of **1** _____ who were travelling from one place to another. The migrating whales were helped by **2** _____ . The whole incident lasted more than **3** _____ .
Beluga whales helped a diver who couldn't get to the surface. Because of the icy waters she was unable to **4** _____ . One of the whales saved her life by taking hold of her **5** _____ and giving her a push upwards.

Which paragraph did you need to read?

MATCHING SENTENCE ENDINGS

In this question type you are given the first part of some sentences. You have to choose the correct ending from a list. There are more sentence endings than you need.

- Read the sentence beginning carefully.
- Find the key words and think of some similar words for them.
- Find the part of the text where the answer is.
- Read the sentences carefully, looking out for the key words or similar words.
- Remember the information may be presented in a different order from the question.
- Try to complete the sentence in your own words.
- Check the list and find an ending that is similar to yours.
- Check that the completed sentence is grammatical and that the meaning matches the text.
- If the answer is a noun, check that you have used the correct form: singular or plural.

07▶ Which paragraph do you need to read to find the ending to this sentence?

Moko 'spoke' to the beached whales …

Write your own ending.

08▶ Choose one of these endings for the sentence above.

A because her first attempts had failed.
B to help them return to the deep water.
C because she led them to safety.

TIP 08

Don't be tricked by endings that have words and phrases from the text in them. It doesn't mean the ending is correct.

09▶ Read the explanations below and check your answer to exercise 8.

A The words 'attempts' and 'failed' are in the text, but they were not Moko's attempts; they were the people's attempts.
B In the text the words 'led them to a channel which took them back to the ocean' are similar to 'help them return to the deep water'. This is the right ending.
C Moko led them to safety but that is not the *reason* she spoke to the whales.

10▶ Complete each sentence with the correct ending a–h.

1 Dolphins may protect humans
2 Dolphins swam towards Hardy Jones
3 The swimmer tried to leave the protective ring of dolphins
4 A dolphin nudged Joey Trevino
5 Dolphins and whales help us

a so we should protect them.
b to encourage him not to lose hope.
c because there were so many dolphins.
d because they recognise that humans are similar to them.
e because they sometimes actively decide to help.
f because he had not seen the shark.
g because a shark was about to attack him.
h because he was a campaigner for dolphin protection.

GRAMMAR FOCUS: MODALS OF POSSIBILITY AND ABILITY

11▶ Find two more examples of modals of possibility (look in paragraphs A and F).

12▶ Find more examples of modals of ability in paragraph B.

Modal verbs *may*, *might* and *could* are used when something is **possible** but not certain:

*Experts think dolphins **may understand** that humans are similar to them.*

The modals *can* and *could* are used to talk about **ability** in the present and past.

*Dolphins **can tell** when a woman is pregnant.*
*Yang Yun found she **couldn't move** her legs due to the freezing temperatures.*

1 3 ▶ Read the passage and answer the questions opposite.

THE MODERN ZOO

The first zoo is believed to have been in Egypt in around 3500 BC. Early collections of animals on display often belonged to royalty. King Henry I of England had lions, leopards and camels. He had received them as gifts. Until the late twentieth century, the main purpose of zoos was for entertainment. They existed to give people the chance to see animals they could not see in the wild. In 1959, famous wildlife expert Gerald Durrell opened the first zoo which put conservation of animals first.

Nowadays zoos' aims are: conservation, education, entertainment, in that order. Modern zoos try to get a balance between providing safe, comfortable homes for the animals and opportunities for visitors to see animals in natural surroundings. Zoos now share their knowledge and support each other. The World Association for Zoos and Aquariums (WAZA) works to educate people about animal welfare and conservation. It also helps to coordinate breeding programmes.

From the 1990s, zoos began to see their main role as saving the most threatened species. Each zoo focuses on a small number of species. The Siberian tiger and the orangutan are two species that have been saved through breeding programmes run by zoos. For example, in 2005 there were between 331 and 393 Siberian tigers in the Russian Far East. By 2015, there were 562. The tigers were helped to breed under the Species Survival Plan of the Association of Zoos and Aquariums (AZA). Often the aim is to reintroduce endangered species into their natural habitats. In Indonesia, Borneo Orangutan Rescue teaches orangutans how to live in the wild. When they are ready, they are taken to protected forests to live naturally.

Now that we have a better understanding of animals, zoos try to recreate natural habitats of animals as accurately as possible. For example, polar bears live in a plain, white open space. Zoos try to provide 'enrichment' for the animals to improve their wellbeing. This includes climbing frames, feeding puzzles, unusual objects and different types of food. It allows animals to

Questions 1–6
Complete the notes below.
*Choose **NO MORE THAN TWO WORDS** from the passage for each answer.*

Before the 1990s, zoos existed mainly for **1** _____ .

The first zoo to focus on protecting animals was started by **2** _____ .

Since the 1990s a number of zoos have introduced programmes which aim to breed threatened animals and return them to their **3** _____ . But first the animals have to learn how to survive in the **4** _____ .

Zoos offer animals **5** _____ by making it challenging for them to find their food, providing them with climbing equipment, and even mixing them with other species.

6 _____ enable the public to view zoo animals from their homes.

Questions 7–11
Complete each sentence with the correct ending, A–H.

7 The first zoo
8 The World Association for Zoos and Aquariums (WAZA)
9 Borneo Orangutan Rescue
10 Colchester Zoo
11 Indianapolis Zoo

A has created an environment that copies the animals' natural habitat.
B was started by Gerald Durrell.
C has webcams in all the enclosures.
D prepares one species to return to their own environment.
E does not always separate different types of animal.
F is part of the AZA.
G is involved in teaching about how to better care for animals and protect them and in helping zoos work together.
H was a private collection of animals.

GO FURTHER ONLINE

behave in a normal way, such as scratching, climbing, digging and solving problems. Another type of enrichment is mixing up types of animal that would naturally mix in the wild. Colchester Zoo in England has a 'kingdom of the wild' paddock where several species live together. They have found positive changes to the behaviour of these animals as a result.

Different types of technology are used to help create natural environments for animals. In Indianapolis Zoo, in the United States, for example, there is a 'functional forest' called the Hutan Trail, a series of towers and cables 20 metres above the ground. This allows the orangutans to swing around the zoo as they would swing around the forest in their native Indonesia. The cables are strong enough to give them a safe and comfortable trip around

the zoo. They have access to three oases, where they can go when they want to be apart from the group.

Likewise, technology has been used to engage the public more with the animals. In many zoos there are webcams in some enclosures so visitors can keep up with their favourite animals between visits to the zoo.

Zoos have moved on over the last few decades. They now play an important role in protecting animals and in making people more aware of the importance of animals. Zoos have made people aware that animals should not be over-hunted and that they play an important role in the ecology of the planet and in helping to maintain the balance of nature.

WRITING

IN THIS UNIT YOU WILL LEARN HOW TO

- deal with two-part questions
- link different parts of the essay
- write a conclusion.

LEAD-IN

01 ▷ **Match the words to make some common word pairs.**

1 endangered		**a** fuels
2 air		**b** warming
3 renewable		**c** pollution
4 natural		**d** species
5 global		**e** habitats
6 fossil		**f** energy

02 ▷ **Fill in the gaps with the word pairs above to make sentences you could use in a conclusion.**

1 In conclusion, _____ is already causing sea temperatures to rise.

2 In my opinion, loss of _____ is a continuing threat to wild animals.

3 To sum up, _____ is having a serious effect on people who live in cities.

4 If we don't take action now, the number of _____ will continue to increase.

5 I suggest governments stop using _____ and start using clean sources of energy.

6 Finally, I believe that _____ can offer us hope to save our planet.

WRITING A CONCLUSION

03 ▷ **Which of these *may* be included in your conclusion?**

a a concluding phrase

b a prediction (what will/might happen in the future)

c supporting evidence

d your opinion

e an idea you haven't mentioned before

f plenty of detail

g a summary of your main ideas

h what you hope (or fear) might happen in future

i your recommendations

j your answer to the question

k at least four sentences

TIP 03

The conclusion is a very important part of your essay. It is the last thing the examiner reads, so it must be good!

Which of them *should* be included?

04 ▷ **Match examples 1–6 with the features a–k in exercise 3.**

1 In short, all types of pollution are increasing.

2 So, in conclusion, we can say that …

3 Personally, I feel that there is a limit to what we can do.

4 I think there will be very few wild animals left in 25 years' time.

5 I hope people will work hard to protect our beautiful planet.

6 Governments should use the law, education and clean energy to improve the situation.

05 ▷ **Which paragraph, A or B, is a better conclusion to the essay title? Why?**

The individual has an important role to play in protecting the environment. To what extent do you agree with this statement?

A To conclude, my view is that everyone can help protect the environment. We can recycle as much as possible, maintain our vehicles properly and ask our Member of Parliament to support laws that prevent damage to the environment. If we all do this, we can ensure the planet is in good condition for future generations.

B Another issue is how we use our vehicles. We should walk or use public transport whenever possible and only have one car per family. The main reason public transport in my home town is not very good is because it is not used enough. We must get our cars serviced regularly to make sure we don't pollute the air. So this is another reason why I say, in conclusion, that people can help protect the environment.

LINKING THE MAIN IDEAS AND CONCLUSION

0 6 ▷ Phrases 1–7 are useful in an essay. What can you use them for? Match the phrases 1–7 with their function a–g.

1 In this essay I will …
2 In my view, …
3 Another reason for …
4 On the other hand, …
5 For instance, …
6 It is clear that …
7 To conclude, …

a to introduce the opposite view
b to introduce a main point
c to begin your final paragraph
d to introduce an opinion
e to introduce an example
f to explain your plan
g to introduce a similar point

0 7 ▷ Read this essay title and spend two minutes noting down any ideas you have on the topic.

Many wild animals have become endangered. Why has this happened? What can governments do to stop this from continuing to happen?

0 8 ▷ Read the essay and answer the questions below.

MODEL ANSWER

TIP 0 8

Some questions have two parts to them. Your essay *must* answer both parts. Your two main paragraphs should answer one part of the question each.

Many species of wild animal are now endangered. For example, the number of black rhinos has declined from over 65,000 in the 1960s to just 2,500 today. Sea animals like some types of whale are also at risk. In this essay I will look at some of the causes of this situation. I will then move on to consider what governments can do to deal with this problem.

It is clear that animals are dying out because of human activity. People have hunted animals for sport or for their fur, horns or other body parts. For instance, they hunted tigers for their bones, which were used for medicines. Another reason for species to become extinct is that humans have destroyed their natural habitats. One example of this is gorillas in the rainforests, which are now endangered. Finally, pollution from industry has created problems for many sea creatures.

Governments can help in several ways. First of all they need to make strong laws and give punishments to those who hunt illegally. Next, they need education programmes in schools and on television to help everyone understand the problem. Finally, governments should invest in renewable and clean energy sources such as solar and wind power.

So, in conclusion, we can say that hunting and damage to the environment are the main threats that animals face. Governments should use the law, education and clean energy to improve the situation. Everyone must work together to save endangered animals.

1 Complete the chart with the main points of the essay.

	The causes	Government actions
1	hunting for sport or body parts	laws/punishments
2		
3		

2 Tick the causes and government actions that are mentioned in the conclusion.

3 Complete the sentence by choosing the correct option.
   The conclusion ends with a *prediction/hope/fear/recommendation*.

GRAMMAR FOCUS: PRESENT PERFECT AND PAST SIMPLE

09▶ According to the model essay on Page 154, how <u>have</u> past human actions <u>affected</u> animals today? Complete the list.

1 People <u>have hunted</u> animals for sport or for their body parts.

2 _____

3 _____

TIP 09

One use of the present perfect tense is to talk about actions that happened in the past which have results in the present.

10▶ Find the present perfect sentence in the introduction to the model essay on Page 154.

◎ Introductions often contain a sentence or two in the present perfect tense. Showing how the past has affected the present is often a good way to introduce the topic.

EXAM SKILLS

11▶ Read the essay title. How would you organise this essay? What ideas do you have for this topic?

Global warming is one of the biggest threats to our environment. What causes global warming? What solutions are there to this problem?

Give reasons for your answer and include any relevant examples from your own knowledge or experience.

Write at least 250 words.

12▶ Read a student's plan for this essay.

> **Paragraph 1 – Introduction**
> • Definition of global warming: increasing temperatures due to air pollution (climate change)
> • Plan of essay: causes/solutions
>
> **Paragraph 2 – Causes**
> • Cutting down trees (e.g. due to population growth)
> • Burning fossil fuels (cars, power stations, factories)
> • Using too much electricity (computers, TV, lights)
>
> **Paragraph 2 – Solutions**
> • Renewable energy (solar, wind)
> • Manage the rainforests (less cutting, more planting)
> • Transport solutions (share cars, use public transport)
>
> **Paragraph 4 – Conclusion**
> • Summarise causes and solutions
> • Recommendation: we can all try to be more 'green'

TIP 11

Make sure your answers to two-part questions are balanced. Don't spend too much time on one part so that you don't develop the other.

Write the essay in full, following the advice in the box.

◎
• Give examples to support your ideas.
• Use linking expressions.
• Refer back to the main points of the essay in the conclusion.
• Use phrases such as 'in conclusion' or 'to conclude' for the final paragraph.
• Don't introduce any new points in the conclusion.
• In your last sentence, suggest what should happen in the future.

 **GO FURTHER ONLINE**

UNIT / 08: NATURAL WORLD

LISTENING

IN THIS UNIT YOU WILL LEARN HOW TO

- listen to people talking about a topic related to the natural world
- complete notes in a task
- use headings in the notes to guide you through what the speaker is saying
- use the speaker's 'signposting' words to help you follow notes.

01▶ Match photographs A–D with the names of the animals.

Arabian leopard   blue ring octopus   mountain gorilla   Pere David's deer

02▶ Listen to the four short extracts. Which animal in exercise 1 is each speaker describing?

66

1 _____   3 _____

2 _____   4 _____

NOTE COMPLETION

 In this type of task you complete a set of notes by writing up to three words, or two words and/or a number, in each gap. The instructions tell you how many words you are allowed to write.

You must complete the notes with the **words you hear on the recording**.

USING HEADINGS TO HELP YOU

03▶ **Match the headings 1–5 with the questions a–e.**

1 Country of origin
2 Dangers
3 Diet
4 Habitat
5 Physical description

a What does it eat?
b Where does it come from?
c Where does it live?
d What does it look like?
e What threats does it face?

TIP 03
The notes often have headings to guide you. They can help you follow what the speaker(s) are saying.

04▶ **Look at the notes about the animals. Match the headings 1–5 in exercise 3 with the notes below. There is an example to help you.**

a People are using its land for cows and sheep _____
b Mainly eats grass _____
c Has long arms _____
d Lives on wet lands _____
e Comes from Africa _____1_____

TIP 04
Notes often do not follow grammatical rules or layout. For example, there may be auxiliary verbs or articles missing. The notes may also be lists with bullet points.

'SIGNPOSTING' WORDS

05▶ **Look at the signposting phrases 1–6 below. They signal different kinds of information. Match them with the meanings a–e. One meaning can be used twice.**

1 So, now I'm going to talk a little about …
2 Let's have a look at two reasons why …
3 So, I'll move on to talk about …
4 Firstly … Secondly …
5 I'd like to conclude by talking about …
6 In other words …

THIS WAY

a The speaker is going to talk about a new topic and this will be the last thing he/she talks about (might be the last heading on the Notes).
b The speaker is going to talk about a new topic – which might be a new heading on the Notes.
c The speaker is going to say the same thing using different words.
d The speaker is going to give two reasons – listen carefully for both.
e Here is the first (reason) … and here is the second (reason).

 'Signposting' words are words and phrases that speakers use to help their listeners follow their talk.

06 ▶ Read the notes about the mountain gorilla.

THE MOUNTAIN GORILLA

Country of origin
Comes from Central Africa

Habitat
Lives in mountain forests
Builds a nest on the
1 _____

Physical description
Has a thick coat of fur
Older males have a
2 _____ coloured coat
Younger males are called
3 _____

Diet
Eats plants, including leaves, fruit
and flowers
Plants provide the
4 _____ they require

Dangers for gorillas
• People are destroying the
  environment where the gorillas live
• 5 _____

07 ▶ Look at the gaps 1–5 in the notes in exercise 6. What kind of word do you have to
listen for? Match gaps 1–5 with a–e below.

1 _e_   **a** a colour
2 ____   **b** something gorillas need to eat or drink
3 ____   **c** something bad for gorillas
4 ____   **d** a name
5 ____   **e** the name of a place

08 ▶ Listen to a talk about mountain gorillas and tick the
signposting phrases in exercise 5 when you hear them.
67

09 ▶ Listen again and complete the notes. Write NO MORE THAN
TWO WORDS for each answer.
67

TIP 09

The speaker will mention some possible
answers but only one is correct in each case.
It is important to listen carefully for the
information you need for each space.
Use the headings and the notes to help you.

10 ▶ Read the notes about the American bullfrog.
Match gaps 1–6 in the notes with the questions a–f.

THE AMERICAN BULLFROG

Origin
- East United States
- was introduced into the UK at the beginning of the
  1 _____ century

Physical description
- female weighs up to **2** _____ grams
- has a green and brown body
- has a flat **3** _____
- male frog has a **4** _____ coloured throat

Reasons for unpopularity
- breeds rapidly, so numbers are increasing
- eats the food of native British frogs – insects, fish,
  birds and animals including **5** _____ –
  and also eats the frogs themselves!
- carries a disease that can kill other frogs
- financial cost – a total of £ **6** _____
  already spent on research into American bullfrogs

TIP

It can be useful to rephrase the notes to form a question in your own words. This will help you know what kind of information to listen for.

a How much does it weigh?
b What colour is the throat of the male?
c What part of its body is flat?
d When did it come to Britain?
e What kind of animals does it eat?
f How much money has been spent on control measures?

11 ▶ Listen and complete the notes in exercise 10. Write ONE WORD AND/OR A NUMBER for each answer.

68

12 ▶ Check your answers carefully.
- Did you spell your words correctly?
- Did you write numbers as digits?
- Did you write a singular noun or plural noun for question 5?

1 3 ▶ Complete the notes below. Write ONE WORD AND/OR A NUMBER for each answer.

69

THE BOX JELLYFISH

Habitat

In warm seas, not far from the coast

Most dangerous box jellyfish found in the sea near **1** _____

Appearance

Shaped like a box

Light blue in colour

Tentacles grow up to

  2 _____ metres in length

Has **3** _____ eyes

How the box jellyfish stings

- cells on tentacles can produce a powerful poison
- when tentacles touch a human or a fish, they **4** _____ to them and deliver a strong sting

Dangers to people

The sting can result in death

- by causing a heart attack
- if a swimmer can't swim back to the shore because the sting has caused such great
  5 _____

What to do if someone has been stung

- heart attack – try to revive them
- pour vinegar over the tentacles
- if vinegar not available, put
  6 _____ on the skin

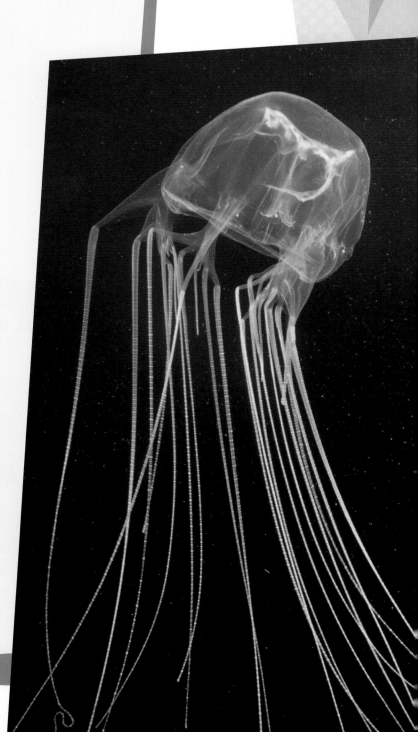

 **GO FURTHER ONLINE**

SPEAKING

IN THIS UNIT YOU WILL LEARN HOW TO

- extend your knowledge of vocabulary related to animals and their habitat
- talk at length about animals and pets for Speaking Parts 2 and 3
- develop your answers in Part 3.

LEAD-IN

01▷ Match pictures A–D with a word or phrase from each box.

Animals
camel   deer   dolphin   eagle

Characteristics
hard antlers   big claws   long fin   round hump

Habitat
desert   forest   nest   underwater

02▷ Take turns to describe one of the animals in the pictures to your partner. Talk about what the animal is, anything special about the animal (its *characteristics*) and about where the animal lives (its *habitat*).

SPEAKING PART 2

03▶ Read the Part 2 task card and complete the notes opposite. Here are some words you might find useful.

plains	ears	thick coat
fur	horn	mountains
jungle	trunk	ocean
long/short tail		sharp teeth
brightly coloured feathers		

Describe a wild animal from your country.

You should say:

- what the animal is and what it looks like
- what it eats
- where it lives

and explain how people feel about this animal.

Animal

What it looks like

1 _____

2 _____

3 _____

What it eats _____

Where it lives _____

How you feel about the animal

1 _____

2 _____

3 _____

04▶ Now, complete the Part 2 task with your partner. Talk for two minutes each. When your partner has finished, think of one or two further questions to ask them about their animal.

[PART 3 QUESTIONS]

 In Part 3 of the Speaking test the examiner will ask you some questions about the topic in Part 2. They will be questions which require you to think. For example you might be asked for your opinion, or for ideas, solutions to problems or for an explanation about why something happens.

05▶ Read the Part 3 questions 1–4 on the topic of animals and match them with the beginning of some students' responses a–d.

1 What can governments do to prevent illegal hunting?
2 Should the government provide more money for zoos?
3 How might we be able to protect wildlife in the future?
4 Is there any difference in how children learn about wildlife now than in the past?

a They definitely should. It seems to me that …
b There are two things X can do. The first is …
c There's a big difference, I think. In the past, we …
d Well, in the future, it might be a good idea to …

70 Listen and check.

06▶ Answer the questions 1–4 in exercise 5 with a partner, using the sentence beginnings to start your answer.

TIP 05

Listen for key words. You must always answer the question the examiner asks you. You will lose marks if you talk about the topic without answering the question. So you must listen carefully to the question and then begin your answer in an appropriate way.

TIP 06

Don't always use *I think* …. It's good to learn some other phrases such as *I feel* … , *I believe* … , *it seems to me that* …

DEVELOPING YOUR ANSWERS FOR PART 3

 After making sure you have answered the question, you need to develop your answer further with reasons or examples.

Giving examples	Giving reasons
For example, we could …	The reason why I think that is …
For instance, the government should …	One reason for this is that …
By way of example, maybe we would …	A good reason for X is that …

TIP 07

In Part 3 of the Speaking test try to think of real-life examples or relate the examples to your experience. But if you can't, consider inventing a fictional example to help you develop your answer. You might say, 'For example, *I heard that* …' or 'For instance, *I read that* …'

07▶ Listen to a candidate answering some Part 3 questions. Complete the table.

71

	Answer	Example	Reason
1 What should be done to people caught hunting illegally?			
2 Is there anything we as individuals can do to prevent hunting?			
3 Will there be more or less hunting in the future?			

08 ▶ Using the formula in exercise 7 for developing your answer, make a similar table with your own ideas, then practise answering the questions with a partner.

09 ▶ Look at the words and phrases below and check that you understand them.

A responsibility, trust, patience

B unnatural, risky, unique, challenging

C interesting, friendship, relaxing **but** expensive, inconvenient

D gadgets, robots replace?

E breed, release, monitor in wild

F cages not good for animals, but educational

G better conditions and animal welfare now

H important to help animals, but people will prefer other entertainment

TIP 08

You do not have to give examples first, then reasons. Feel free to change the order if it will help your answer make more sense.

10 ▶ Match the words and phrases in A–D with the Pets table and those in E–H with the Zoos table.

Pets	
1 advantages and disadvantages of owning pets	
2 keeping dangerous animals as pets	
3 children learning from keeping pets	
4 popularity of pets in the future	

Zoos	
1 differences between zoos in the past and today	
2 zoos a good idea	
3 protecting endangered animals in zoos	
4 zoos in the future	

EXAM SKILLS

11 ▶ Ask and answer these Part 3 questions with a partner. Use the tables and ideas in Exercise 10 to help you or use your own ideas.

[*Topic: pets*]

1 What are some of the advantages and disadvantages of keeping a pet?
2 Do you think that dangerous animals should be kept as pets?
3 What can children learn from looking after pets?
4 Do you think it will be popular for people to keep pets in the future?

[*Topic: zoos*]

1 Are there any differences between zoos in the past and zoos today?
2 Do you think zoos are a good idea?
3 How can we protect endangered animals in zoos?
4 Will zoos continue to be important in the future?

GO FURTHER ONLINE

ANSWER KEY

Unit 1 RELATIONSHIPS

READING

1 My brother is my parents' son.
My cousin is my aunt or uncle's son or daughter.
My father-in-law is my husband or wife's father.
My grandfather is my mother or father's father.
My uncle is my mother or father's brother.
My aunt is my mother or father's sister.
My nephew is my brother or sister's son.
My niece is my brother or sister's daughter.
My great-aunt is my grandmother or grandfather's sister.
My grandmother is my mother or father's mother.

2 2, 3, 4 and 5 are mentioned in the text.

3 1 h 2 g 3 a 4 b 5 f 6 c 7 e 8 d

4 grandparents' stories (paragraph D)
cousin's wedding (A)
young adults (E)
extended families (B)
come and go (G)
Italian proverb (F)
To find information quickly, don't read every word. Don't try to say the words. Move your eyes quickly across and down the text. Use your finger if you find it useful.

5 1 percentage / children / extended families / Asia, the Middle East, South America, Sub-Saharan Africa
2 grandparents / less busy / stressed / parents
3 young adults / think / living alone

6 1 over 40% 2 They are often retired.
3 (They think it will be) exciting.

7 1 b 2 d 3 a 4 c

8 1 almost 70% 2 grandparents' stories 3 lonely
4 your grandmother

9 1 present simple 2 b

10 1 always 2 often 3 often; (not) always 4 usually 5 Sometimes

11 The frequency adverb is usually between the subject and the verb. (*I often cook*). When the verb is 'to be', the adverb comes after the verb. (*It is always cold.*) Some frequency adverbs can also start a sentence. (*Sometimes I watch TV.*)

12 1 social media 2 geographically mobile 3 less security
4 convenience 5 mental health problems

WRITING

2 1 B 2 A 3 C

3 **Materials:** plastic, metal, wood, cloth
Parts: handles, base, tray
Shapes: round, square, triangle, rectangular

4 1 c 2 b 3 f 4 a 5 d 6 e

5 1 are picked 2 are used 3 is needed 4 is grown

6 1 First 2 After 3 Then / Next 4 The next stage 5 Next / Then
6 Finally

7 a overview b introduction

8 a and d are not overviews

9 1 The diagram demonstrates the process of preparing stringhoppers, a kind of noodle dish.
2 There are six main stages in the process, beginning with grinding the rice and making a dough and ending with using a steamer to cook the stringhoppers.
3 First, Next, After that, then, The final stage is
4 is put, is mixed, (is) formed, is put, is pushed, are placed, are ... cooked

5 a metal piece of equipment with two handles and holes in it; round baskets made of thin pieces of wood
6 grind, rice, dough, steamer, grinder, flour, stringhopper press, stringhopper mats, cook, serve, spicy, curries

10 1 spread; shaken 2 collected; transported 3 removed
4 washed 5 taken 6 cooked; added 7 checked 8 put
9 stuck

11 *Sample answer*

The pictures show the stages in the production of cherry jam. There are a number of processes involved, from picking the fruit from the tree to putting it into jars ready to sell.

First, a sheet is spread on the ground under the tree and the tree is shaken by a mechanical arm to get the cherries down from the tree. Then, the cherries are collected and transported by lorry to the processing plant. There, the leaves and the stems are removed and then the stone is taken out with a metal spike. Next, sugar, lemon juice and pectin are added to the cherries and the jam is cooked. After that, the quality of the jam is checked and then the jam is put into jars. A lid is put on top of the jars to keep the jam fresh. Finally, a label is added and the jam is ready to be sold in the shops.

LISTENING

1 C, D

2 Conversation 1: D Conversation 2: C

3 1 M 2 F 3 F 4 M

4 5 A 6 B

5 a 3rd b $10.50 c 6th d 70 e 19 f 62 g £110 h 27th

6 1 B 2 C

7 1 17th 2 20

8 B

9 1 B 2 B

10 1 30 / thirty 2 20 / twenty 3 10 / ten

11 1 c 2 e 3 d 4 a 5 b

12 1 The relationship between the people 2 The type of event
3 Colour 4 The meaning of something 5 Food 6 Presents

13 1 A 2 A 3 C 4 B 5 C 6 B

SPEAKING

2 (not) a large family, a small family, a typical family, 'the baby of the family'? a close, happy family

3 You can't say 'a best family'.

4 1 once a week
2 on Saturdays or Sundays / at weekends
3 to the beach
4 They usually go for a long walk.
5 His cousin sometimes comes with them.

6 1 d 2 c 3 b 4 a

7 2 close 3 eating 4 cook 5 married 6/7 niece/nephew

8 1 Student B 2 Student A 3 Student C

9 *Sample answers, but many others are possible*
1 ... because they are the most important people in my life.
2 ... but we still get along very well.
3 ... and she is going to move to a different city with her husband.
4 ... so I don't spend as much time with him as I want to.
5 ... even though he is quite a bit older.

10 /s/ asks, keeps, talks, wants
/z/ enjoys, plays
/ɪz/ chooses, watches

Unit 2 PLACES AND BUILDINGS

READING

3 A treehouse B shipping container homes
C igloo D houseboat

4 b

6 exercise 5 – scanning; exercise 4 – skimming

7 1 c 2 e 3 a 4 f 5 b 6 d

8 1 B 2 A 3 B

9 1 suit everyone 2 draw attention 3 reindeer skins 4 busy lives

10 1 c 2 a present simple b present simple c past simple
d past simple

11 1 live 2 have 3 moved 4 spends 5 preferred

12 1 shares 2 lived 3 stayed 4 has 5 moved

13 1 (roast) chicken 2 homesick and sad 3 her parents
4 Ping and Pong 5 forest 6 feel at home / feel welcome

WRITING

1 All of the places listed may be on a campus.

2 The following are shown on the campus maps:
bus stop, Students' Union, recreation area, cafés, car parks, library,
laboratories, squash courts, gym, halls of residence, tennis courts,
football pitch, table tennis tables

3 Sentences 1, 2, 5 and 7 are true.

4 1 next to 2 of 3 between 4 opposite 5 on 6 in 7 to/on
8 of

5 *Sample answers*
1 The halls of residence are on the left side of the campus.
2 The laboratories are opposite the Founder's Building.
3 The bus stop is in the top right-hand corner.
4 The recreation area is next to the laboratories (and the
Scott Library).
5 The table tennis tables are in front of / next to the Scott Library.
6 The Students' Union is between the gym and the bus stop.

7 1 b Introductory sentence: *The two maps show changes to the
campus of Sunnyhills University between 1995 and today.*
2 c Concluding sentence: *So, it is clear that the university changed
and expanded during this period.*
3 a Overview: *We can see that the university made many changes
during this period, including new buildings and recreation facilities.*

8 1 was relocated, increased, were moved, was built,
demolished, created, developed, changed, expanded
2 in front of, to the right, in the top left-hand corner, the far left of
(the campus), opposite

9 1 in addition, what is more 2 whereas, however 3 during this
period, in the past 4 we can see, it is clear

10 1 relocated 2 created, developed, built 3 demolished
4 expanded, increased (in size)

11 *Made, was* and *built* are irregular. The infinitives are:
expanded – expand changed – change created – create
made – make built – build increased – increase
developed – develop moved – move was – be

12 1 cut 2 became 3 caught 4 needed 5 put 6 were 7 dug
8 planted
Needed and *planted* are regular.

13 1 passive 2 active 3 active 4 passive

14 2 Trees were planted in the recreation area.
3 The bus stop was moved. 4 A new main reception was built.

15 *Sample answer*
The maps show the changes to Colwick Arts Centre between 2005
and the present day. We can see that the Centre expanded and new
facilities were added during this period.
One of the major changes is that the outside area was developed. In
2005 there was an empty area of land outside the Centre. Trees were
planted there and an outdoor exhibition area was made. The café was
moved to the front of the Arts Centre and tables were added outside.

Inside, a central exhibition area was created. In the past there were
two galleries but now there is only one; however, a drama studio was
built. In 2005 the concert hall and cinema were in the same space,
whereas now they are separate. In addition, an extra meeting room
was constructed. The toilets moved to the opposite side of the
Centre.
So, it is clear that Colwick Arts Centre is more attractive today and
has better facilities than in 2005.

LISTENING

1 A sports centre B museum C bank
D railway station E bus stop F restaurant G harbour

2 Travel and transport: bus stop, railway station
Sports and leisure: sports centre, restaurant
Arts and culture: museum
Money: bank

3 1 sports centre 2 bank

4 1 A 2 Clarke 3 2 Waddington

5 1 all one word 2 with 3 end 4 double

6 2 How much did each person pay for their meal?
3 What time is the bus due?
4 Where is the bus stop?
5 How long did the course last?
6 Which TWO things did the speaker do on the course?
7 What is the date of the next course?
8 Who will lead the course?

7 a date – 7   a meal or a kind of food – 1
a price – 2   a name of a person – 8
a period of time – 5   the names of activities or skills – 6
a time – 3   a place – 4

8 Questions 2, 3, 5, 7

9 1 steak 2 20

10 'Shoes' is correct – 'he bought shoes' is three words, and the question
asked for 'no more than one word and/or a number'.

11 1 7.50 is the correct answer; seven fifty is incorrect because it is spelt
wrong; 7.15 / seven fifteen is not the correct time.
2 Blythe Road

12 1 two / 2 days 2 safety rules
3 1st (of) September / 1 September 4 Jon Galloway

13 You need to write a number only for questions 3 and 5.

14 1 What kind of tour did the woman do?
2 How did she find out about the tour?
3 How many people were on the tour?
4 What is the address of the hire shop?
5 How much did each student in the group pay?
6–7 Which TWO items were included in the cost of the hire?
8 What is the website address of the hire shop?

15 1 bike/cycle/cycling (tour)
2 (by) email
3 8/eight
4 22 Barkway Street
5 15/fifteen (dollars)
6 helmet/lock
7 lock/helmet
8 tradelectric.com

SPEAKING

1 1 B 2 C 3 A

3 A cinema B art gallery C shopping mall D harbour
E stadium F swimming pool G library H town hall

5 2 Opinion 3 Climate 4 Areas 5 Buildings

6 **Location:** in the south, indoor
Opinion: colourful, incredible, magnificent, polluted
Climate: cool
Areas: tourist
Buildings: ancient, narrow, enormous, high-rise, huge

7 1 tall and high-rise 2 hot and humid 3 cool and mild
  4 dirty and polluted 5 lively and exciting

8 *Possible adjectives*
  1 huge, incredible, magnificent, busy, crowded, exciting
  2 ancient, flat, outdoor, narrow, historic, quiet
  3 hot, humid, crowded, narrow, flat, exciting, lively, colourful

9 1 past simple 2 present simple 3 present perfect

10 1 was 2 is 3 was 4 grew up 5 is 6 has changed
  7 didn't have 8 wasn't 9 is 10 used to 11 was 12 went

12 /t/ bought, built, developed, used to
  /d/ called, changed, designed, discovered, said
  /ɪd/ situated, located, started

14 Speaker 1 – b Speaker 2 – a Speaker 3 – d Speaker 4 – c

Unit 3 EDUCATION AND EMPLOYMENT

READING

1 **Work**: business, employers, job, office, retirement
  Studies: academic, blended learning, degree, qualification,
  primary education, lifelong learning, seminars

2 All the words except *office* are in the text.

3 The text is more positive than negative.

4 1 C (Para A) You only need to read part of the paragraph (*studying
  partly in a traditional way in the classroom and partly online or via
  email*).
  2 D (Paras B and C) You need to read the whole of paragraph B and
  the beginning of C. The elite having most of the opportunities is not a
  benefit.

5 1 overseas 2 advantages 3 disrupting 4 attending 5 enrich
  6 valuable 7 offices

6 Sentences 1, 3, 4, 6. The main ideas can usually be found in the first
  sentence of the paragraph.

7 1 B 2 A 3 C

8 1 The sentences all relate to the present and the past.
    a They benefitted in the past and they still benefit from the
      results in the present.
    b They were not educated in the past, which affects their present.
    c They became businesses in the past and they are still businesses.
  2 b
  3 a

9 1 B 2 C 3 D 4 A

WRITING

1 1 line graph 2 pie chart 3 bar chart 4 table
  1 and 4 describe changes to numbers over time.

2

↑	↓
growth (N)	decline (V, N)
increase (V, N)	decrease (V, N)
rise (V, N)	drop (V, N)
	fall (V, N)

3

infinitive	past simple	past participle
fall	fell	fallen
increase	increased	increased
drop	dropped	dropped
decrease	decreased	decreased
decline	declined	declined
rise	rose	risen
grow	grew	grown

4 1 rose 2 fall / drop / decline / decrease
  3 rise / growth / increase 4 declined / decreased / fell / dropped
  OR have declined / have decreased / have fallen / have dropped

5 B is better because it gives an overview and summarises the data
  with an example. A is just a list of all the data.

6 1 Sentences 2 and 7 should not be included.
  2 Sentences 1, 6, 8 and 9 are probably the most important. (To some
  extent this is a matter of opinion, but the answer should include the
  highest and lowest numbers, for example.)

7 1 of 2 of 3 from, to 4 by 5 Between 6 in

8 1 The line graph shows the number of unemployed recent graduates
    and non-graduates in the population of 21 to 30-year-olds in the
    years between 1990 and 2015.
  2 Overall, the numbers have not changed much: we can see a fall,
    followed by a rise, in both groups. The non-graduates are a larger
    number than the recent graduates at all points.
  3 (*sample answer*) There is a small change in the middle period. /
    The number of non-graduates dropped and then grew during that
    period.
  4 Over the five years from 2010 to 2015, the numbers of both non-
    graduates and recent graduates returned almost to their 1990
    figures of 14% and 10%.
  5 was, dropped, grew, returned
  6 Overall, the numbers **have not changed** much
  The past simple is used more because most of the verbs refer to
  actions completed in the past. The one example of the present
  perfect is used because it refers up to the present. (The text was
  written in 2015.)

9 1 USA 2 UK 3 New Zealand 4 Canada 5 Australia 6 USA
  7 UK 8 New Zealand

10 1 green – male, purple – female
  2 vertical – percentage of people who are literate; horizontal –
    region of the world
  3 Central Asia, Central/Eastern Europe
  4 five
  5 South and West Asia
  6 male – about 70%, female – about 59% (Sub-Saharan Africa)
  7 male – about 30%, female – about 41%

11 *Sample answer*
  The data shows the literacy rate for both males and females in seven
  different regions of the world. The horizontal axis lists the regions
  and the vertical axis shows percentage. In all regions except two,
  there is a difference in the literacy rates of men and women.
  Central Asia and Central/Eastern Europe have the highest percentage
  of citizens who can read and write. Almost 100% of men and women
  are literate in those regions. The lowest literacy rates are in Sub-
  Saharan Africa.
  In five out of the seven regions, there are different literacy rates for
  men and women. The greatest difference between men and women is
  found in South and West Asia. In this region, about 80% of men are
  able to read and write, but only about 60% of women. Overall, the
  difference between the most literate area and the least literate is
  about 30% for men and just over 40% for women.
  In conclusion, literacy rates vary between regions, with males having
  higher levels than females in most regions. (171 words)

LISTENING

1 A construction B sports and leisure C retail
  D hotel and catering E health F art and design G information
  technology

2 chef J building engineering C badminton coach J
  computing C doctor J fitness training C food technology C
  graphic designer J medicine C shop management C
  store assistant J web designer J textiles C

3 1 graphic designer … textiles
  2 architect … building engineering
  3 doctor … medicine
  4 chef … food technology
  5 web designer … computing
  6 store assistant … shop management
  7 badminton coach … fitness training

4 1 computing, food technology   2 chef, doctor
  3 architect, store assistant   4 fitness training, textiles
5 Conversation 1: J   Conversation 2: C
6 1 Anna has got a <u>job</u> as a _____ .
  2 She has recently completed a <u>course</u> in _____ .
  3 The <u>new name</u> of the <u>department</u> which sells <u>computers</u> and
    <u>phones</u> is _____ .
  4 The <u>Food Photography</u> course <u>takes place on the</u> _____
    of September .
  5 There is a <u>total of</u> _____ places available on the course.
7 an area of study – 2
  a type of job – 1
  a number only – 5
  a name of a place – 3
  a date – 4
8 1 store assistant   2 information technology
  3 Moving Images
9 1 store assistant (it can't be *assistant* because the word before is 'a'
    not 'an')
  2 information technology (*informations* is incorrect because it is a
    plural form – the word *information* is uncountable)
  3 Moving Images (The Moving Images consists of three words and
    the instructions tell you to use no more than two words. Moving
    Image is incorrect because it is singular, and the speaker uses the
    plural.)
10 1 19 / 19th / nineteenth
   2 12 / twelve
11 The correct answers are: 19, 19th,
12 a the price of the course – 6
   b the location of the course – 5
   c the name of the course – 1
   d the starting time of the course – 2
   e the purpose of the course – 4
   f the duration of the course – 3
13 1 h   2 i   3 f   4 e   5 d   6 c   7 b   8 a   9 g
14 1 Food Photography   2 9.30 / nine thirty   3 7 / seven   4 camera
   angles   5 hotel   6 $55 / fifty-five dollars
15 1 title – it's called   2 starts – begins   3 lasts – goes on   4 teach
   – train; different a range of   5 part – some; nearby – local   6 total
   cost – full fee

SPEAKING
1 A emergency services*   B travel and transport   C farming
  D education   E tourism   F science research and development
  G entertainment
  * the organisations that deal with accidents and urgent problems such
  as fire, illness or crime
2 tired, boring, embarrassed, not very exciting (challenging)
3 tired F   boring E   embarrassed F   challenging E   fascinated F
  great F, E   thrilled F   not very exciting E   interesting E   amazed F
4

I feel / I felt …	It is / It was …
thrilled	thrilling
bored	boring
challenged	challenging
fascinated	fascinating
not very excited	not very exciting
tired	tiring
embarrassed	embarrassing
interested	interesting
great	great

5 1 thrilled   2 interesting   3 embarrassed   4 bored   5 tiring
  6 amazing

7 Photograph D; she's a student
8 What job she would like to do in the future 6
  How many hours a week she studies/works 3
  What she does 1
  What she would like to learn in the future 5
  What she thinks about her studies/work 4
  Where she studies/works 2
13 Topics 2, 3, 4 are possible Part 2 topics.
14 The order is: E, C, D, A, B, F
15

Describe a time when you learnt something new
You should say:
· <u>what</u> you <u>learnt</u>
· <u>how</u> you <u>learnt</u> it
· <u>what</u> the <u>result</u> was
and <u>explain how you felt</u> about learning <u>something new</u>.

16 What?   learnt to fly a small plane
   How?   had lessons at a flying club
   Result?   got my pilot's licence
   How I felt?   thrilled and proud of myself
18 1 d   2 a   3 c   4 b

Unit 4 FOOD AND DRINK
READING
1 1 curry, rice   2 cereal   3 mashed potato   4 fish, chips
  5 noodles, vegetables, chicken   6 chicken, salad   7 toast
  8 burger
  Countable: burger, chips, noodle, vegetable
  Uncountable: cereal, chicken, curry, fish, mashed potato, rice, salad,
  toast
4 1 daal   2 chicken   3 China   4 burgers / fizzy drink   5 India
  6 burgers
5 1 f   2 d   3 a   4 e   5 b   6 c
6 1 repeat   2 identity   3 palm(s)   4 prosperity   5 Asia
7 1 Fresh fruit **is** healthy and we should eat **it** every day.
  2 Chips cooked in the oven **are** healthier than fried chips.
  3 Burgers and pizza are the cheapest foods you can buy.
  4 In India it is easy to find vegetarian food.
  5 My favourite food is chicken.
8 1 some   2 many   3 much   4 any/much   5 some   6 much
9 1 F   2 B   3 A   4 E   5 G   6 F   7 D
10 1 C   2 E   3 B   4 A   5 F   6 D   7 E

WRITING
2 Diagram 1: 1, 2, 5, 6
  Diagram 2: 3, 4, 7
3 1 pie   2 bar   3 1960   4 2015   5 Chinese   6 increased/rose/grew
4 1 c   34% – just over a third
  2 b   26% – about a quarter
  3 d   10% – one in ten
  4 a   1% – a tiny proportion
5 1 most   2 least   3 more   4 less   5 More   6 Fewer
6 1 uncountable   2 countable
7 **Countable**: restaurant, country, farm, home, language, person, animal
  Uncountable: coffee, land*, meat, oil, sand
  * When land means 'country', it is countable.
8 1 more   2 less   3 fewer   4 more
9 1 **The** number of Indian restaurants in **the** UK has risen.
  2 Chinese food is the most popular.
  3 **The** second most popular food is Indian.
  4 There was **a** small drop in the number of Indian restaurants in 2011.
  5 There were about **a** thousand Indian restaurants in 1970.

10 1 c 2 f 3 e 4 a 5 b 6 d
11 1 just under / a little under; just over / a little over
   2 just under / a little under
   3 between
   4 approximately / around / about
   5 approximately / around / about
12 The sentences that should not be included are:
   It is not surprising that people in the UK like British food as fish and chips is the national dish.
   Even my village has an Indian restaurant!
13 1 We can see that Chinese and Indian takeaways are the favourites, and that the number of Indian restaurants in the UK rose steadily during this period.
   2 The pie chart shows us that Indian food is popular and the bar chart shows how its popularity grew. The introductory sentence [*The pie chart shows which type of takeaway food is the most popular in the UK, while the bar chart shows how many Indian restaurants existed in the UK between 1960 and 2015.*] also mentions the two charts, though it doesn't interpret the information to make a clear link between them.
   3 Chinese and Indian takeaways are much more popular than all the others.
   4 were only chosen by 1% of people
   5 the 1990s
   6 has remained stable
   7 from about 5000 … to almost 8000
14 1 The percentage of overweight or obese adults is increasing.
   2 the period between 1985 and 1995
   3 There was a similar, slightly larger increase.
   4 The pie chart looks at the number of overweight and obese people in a single year and gives information about how obese they are.
   5 6%
   6 The largest group was people who were obese, but apart from the severely obese group, the groups were very similar in size.
15 *Sample answer*
   The bar chart shows the percentage of the adult population who were overweight or obese between 1965 and 2015, while the pie chart shows the percentage of people who were a healthy weight, overweight, obese and severely obese in 2015. The rise in the number of people who are too heavy was gradual from 1965 to 1985. The first significant increase occurred between 1985 and 1995, from around 48% to almost 60%. In the next ten-year period there was a similar large rise. By 2005, approximately 70% of people weighed too much. The upward trend continued into the 21st century but at a slightly lower rate.
   The pie chart confirms that in 2015 over 70% of adults were too heavy, and it also gives more detail about how much they were overweight. Only 6% of people were so overweight that their health was seriously at risk, i.e. severely obese. The remaining people were divided more or less equally between the other groups.

LISTENING

1 A boil B fry C bake D grill
2 **Meat dishes:** beef, steak, burger, lamb
  Vegetables: potatoes, carrots, cucumbers, peas
  Fruits: apples, strawberries, pears, bananas
  Sweets: biscuits, cake, chocolate, pastries
3 1 c 2 a 3 b They are going to prepare salad and roast chicken.
4 A is the correct answer. Frying the potatoes won't be healthy, and they don't have enough oil baking the potatoes will take too long.
5 1 C 2 A 3 B Option D was mentioned, but it didn't match any of the shops.
6 1 E 2 C 3 D

7 1 The interviewer asks if Adam's is a French restaurant (F) or a steakhouse (B), but Chris says it *sells food from all over the world,* so E is the correct answer.
  2 Vegetarian (A) dishes are mentioned when Chris talks about The Duke, but *it's the fish dishes that make it famous* and so it can't be a vegetarian restaurant.
  3 Chris says that The Tower isn't a fast food restaurant (G) and *it specialises in all different types of food from Italy* so D is the correct answer.
8 1 busy 2 tasty 3 low-cost 4 fashionable 5 reasonable
9 1 C 2 B 3 A 4 C 5 A 6 C 7 C 8 B
10 1 cheap – reasonable, budget
   2 tasty – delicious, mouth-watering
   3 old-fashioned – traditional, historic
   4 street – outdoors, from stalls in the streets
   5 skilful – expertise, highly trained
   6 can be changed – use different ingredients, flexible
   7 famous – well known, recognised
   8 too spicy – too much pepper, too hot
11 1 B 2 A 3 C 4 B 5 C
12 1 B 2 E 3 D 4 C

SPEAKING

1 *Suggested answers*
  1 **Arabian Kabsa:** lamb, onions, garlic, spices, carrots, ginger, rice
  2 **Pizza:** flour, cheese, tomatoes (and other toppings)
  3 **Egg noodles and Chinese dumplings:** egg, flour, beef, onions, cabbage, soy sauce, chillies
3 1 are a lot of / are some 2 isn't much / is some 3 is a lot of / is some 4 are some 5 aren't any 6 is some
4 **Positive:** enjoy, delicious, quick to make, is tasty, convenient, fresh, healthy
  Negative: too spicy, takes too long to cook, not keen on, so strange, don't like the taste, can't stand, too chewy
6 1 Yes 2 risotto 3 a lot of rice is produced there, simple to cook, you can use different ingredients 4 It reminds her of home. It makes her feel cheerful. It's a good meal to make for friends. It is tasty. 5 Because it is special and tastes different to risotto in other countries.
7 1 d 2 a 3 c 4 b
10 1 I 2 I 3 C 4 C 5 C

Unit 5 CONSUMERISM

READING

1 According to the text, all these activities can be done at a mall.
  The pictures show a climbing wall, a beauty treatment, skiing, a health check and having an expensive meal.
2 1 All of the activities are mentioned.
  2 The text mentions the US, Asia, China, the Middle East, East Asia, Bangkok, Singapore, Madrid, (North) London.
  3 It is mainly about the present and future.
3 (1) Asia and not the US is now the 'mall capital' of the world and is home to the five largest malls in the world. (2) China is home to the two largest.
4 C Malls are becoming 'the new downtown', with cinemas, bowling alleys and even concert halls.
  D Mall owners are going to need to think of new ideas to remain in business.
  E Malls will need to consider the environment too.
5 *Possible answers*
  C There will be more fine dining / There will be spas, fitness centres and art galleries / There will be more apartments and office space.
  D There are 'pop-up' shops, stalls and kiosks at different times of the year.
  E Malls will have to make sure people can reach them by public transport / Malls will have to use natural sources of heat and light / There will be more plants, trees, grass and waterfalls.

7 1 c   2 e   3 a   4 f   5 b   6 d

8 B iii   C v   D i   E iv

9 *will* – So what **will** the mall of the future **look** like? / It is predicted that this **will happen** more and more in the future. / Some malls **will** only **sell** electrical items / Some malls **will** only **include** expensive shops / the facilities malls **will need to** offer / Malls **will need to** consider the environment too. / There **will be** more open-air malls / designers **will have to** make sure / They **will also need to** use more natural sources of heat and light / We **will see** more plants, trees / there **will be** 'virtual malls' / technology **will be used** within malls / the mall **will go** from strength to strength

going to – in the future we **are going to see** 'fine dining' too / There **are also going to be** more apartments / Mall owners **are going to need to** think of new ideas

10 1 is going to   2 are going to   3 will   4 will / are going to
5 are going to   6 will

11 1 F   2 D   3 B   4 C   5 E

12 1 B ii   2 C iv   3 D vii   4 E i   5 F vi

WRITING

1 **Good points:** advantages, benefits, positive aspects
Bad points: disadvantages, drawbacks, negative aspects
Opinion: all things considered, in my view, personally

2 2 B   3 O   4 G   5 G   6 B   7 O   8 B   9 O

3 1 c   2 a   3 b

5 *Suggested answers*
Advantages: 1, 2, 5, 7
Disadvantages: 3, 4, 6, 8

6 Introduction B is better because the writer's opinion is not given in the introduction. In an 'advantages/disadvantages' essay it is better to give views on both sides before you give your own opinion. Introduction A gives some of the main points in favour of supermarkets, which is not appropriate in an introduction.

7 See exercise 8.

9 *Sample introduction*
More and more people are relying on debit and credit cards and also on their phones to pay for things in shops and online. If this trend continues, we might become a 'cashless society'. There are both advantages and disadvantages to this, as I will outline in this essay.

10 1 c   2 d   3 a   4 b

11 *Sample answers*
1 In my local town the employment offered by the shops is essential as there are not many other jobs.
2 You can get expensive, mid-price and cheap versions of many products.
3 By shopping at the same supermarket you can earn points which save you money.

14 a goods are all the same
b They have unique items, e.g. antiques.
c Music shops have staff who know about music.
d Small shops give character to a town.

15 1 my view is, I strongly believe
2 for example, for instance
3 Finally
4 Some people believe that *this is going to happen* …; there *will always be* a place for smaller shops
5 too, however

16 *Sample answer*
In some countries a mall is known as a shopping centre. The main purpose of a mall was to shop. This is beginning to change and I believe that in the future, the main purpose of a mall will be for entertainment.

More and more of us enjoy shopping online. It is safer than ever and much more convenient. Many websites offer free next-day delivery. On sites like eBay and Amazon, there is far more choice and there are also many discounts and special offers. Obviously, this means that fewer shops will be needed. However, people still want to go out, meet their friends and have fun. A mall is a place which offers space to do that. If people have done their shopping online, the mall will have to offer other facilities to attract visitors.

Some malls already have cinemas and places to eat. However, as well as cheaper cafés and fast food chains, malls are beginning to offer better restaurants and places to eat. I believe this trend will continue. In addition, malls will offer all kinds of leisure facilities such as gyms, swimming pools, children's play areas, spas, and so on. There will be more live shows, including music, theatre and dance, and a range of exhibitions and special events.

I believe malls have an important role in future society but they will have a different purpose from today. There will still be a few shops but most people will go to the mall to relax and enjoy themselves with their family and friends.

5 LISTENING

1 A supermarket   B shopping centre   C outdoor market
D department store   E coffee shop

2 1 D department store   2 C outdoor market   3 B shopping centre

3 1 east   2 tea   3 11 / eleven   4 trousers

4 5/6 south, north   7/8 souvenirs, cameras   9/10/11 9 / nine, 6 / six, 5 / five   12/13 shirts, jackets

5 1 e   2 c   3 d   4 a   5 f   6 b

6 A – 3   B – 2   C – 1
Listening: The correct answer is C.

7 The key words are 'writer' and 'arrive'.
A noon   B quarter past two   C half past three
Listening: The correct answer is B.

8 Paraphrase A is wrong. The staff are the people who serve the customers.
Listening: The correct answer is B.

9 1 A   2 C   3 B   4 A   5 A   6 B

SPEAKING

2 1 convenient   2 traditional   3 all sorts of   4 selection
5 atmosphere   6 out-of-the-way   7 keen on   8 trying on
9 afford   10 reasonable   11 original   12 place

3 1 d   2 c   3 e   4 f   5 b   6 a

7 *Sample notes*
What kind of place? department store – 100 years old, famous, 4 floors, 30 departments
Where? centre of town – near car park, station
What I like: jewellery department – rings, necklaces, gold
Why I like it: atmosphere – traditional, assistants friendly, helpful

10 1 positive   2 negative   3 negative   4 positive

Unit 6 LEISURE TIME

READING

1 A baseball   B martial arts (Wu Shu)   C hockey   D table tennis
E rugby

2 1 hockey: a, b, c, i, j, l
2 tennis: e, g, i, k
3 volleyball: a, e, h, i
4 football: a, b, c, i, j, l
5 rugby: a, i, j, l
6 baseball: a, f, i
7 table tennis: e, f, g, i
8 martial arts: d
9 basketball: a, b, i

5 1 B 2 E 3 A 4 C 5 D
6 1 False 2 True 3 True 4 False 5 False
7 Not Given
8 1 NG 2 NG 3 T 4 T 5 NG
9 1 True 2 False 3 Not Given 4 Not Given 5 False 6 True
10 2 **G** (mixed) 3 **D** (feature) 4 **E** (horses)
   5 **B** (change) 6 **C** (clever)
11 *Students' own answers*
12 1 False 2 Not Given 3 True 4 True 5 False 6 Not Given
   7 False 8 True
   9 **H** (moving) 10 **M** (traceurs) 11 **C** (competition)
   12 **E** (creativity) 13 **B** (barriers) 14 **D** (conflicts) 15 **I** (personal)

WRITING

1 1 (go running / go for a run 2 go to the cinema
   3 see a film / watch a film 4 visit friends / visit some friends
   5 play sport / play sports 6 join a club
   7 go walking / go for a walk (*slight difference in meaning*)
   8 go to the gym
2 The essay is well organised with an introduction, two main
   paragraphs and a conclusion. It is clear and easy to follow.
3 1 Yes 2 Yes 3 Yes 4 Yes 5 Yes 6 Not always 7 Yes
4 *are saying* – say *explained* – will explain
   people less active – people are less active *go* – went / used to go
   we playing – we play *were walking* – walked / used to walk
   do – did / used to do *are become* – are becoming
   are not going – don't go *took* – takes *I am agree* – I agree
5
Present	Past
now	before
nowadays	in the past
in today's world	several years ago
these days	there used to be
6 1 more expensive 2 harder 3 healthier
   4 more dangerous 5 faster
7 1 I agree with, in my opinion, in my view, I agree that
   2 on the other hand, however
   3 There are points for and against this idea
   4 To sum up
   5 the main reason
9 1 my own opinion 2 Firstly 3 Thirdly 4 Unfortunately
   5 One reason is that 6 In addition 7 also 8 My own view is
11 *Sample answer*

Nowadays young people often spend their free time at home
watching TV or playing computer games. Very few do sports outside
of school. This means that if they don't do exercise during school
time, they will be unfit and suffer from health problems. I agree that
children should do sports lessons at school. In this essay I will
explain why.

Some people say that sports lessons are a waste of time. Students
have to prepare for exams and should spend all their time on
academic work. This is what many people think in my country. In my
opinion they are wrong. A healthy mind needs a healthy body. Doing
exercise every day makes you happy and relaxed. Studying all the
time can make you stressed.

Another reason for my opinion is that having an unfit generation will
cause many problems for society. When today's children get older,
unfortunately they may suffer from illnesses like heart disease. The
government will have to spend a lot of money on doctors and
hospitals. It is much better to create a fit and healthy adult
population by getting children to do sports when they are still at
school. In addition, sports teach people discipline and working as a
team. This will help them in their future life.

In conclusion, I can say that prevention is better than cure. Children
who do sports will be healthier, happier adults. They are more likely
to continue with their active lifestyle when they grow up. In this way
we can make a better society for the future. (263 words)

LISTENING

1 1 turn right 2 go straight ahead / straight on
   3 turn left 4 go past 5 next to 6 opposite
   7 in front of 8 behind
   Examples of other words and phrases: go over/across (the bridge),
   drive along, pass, come to / get to / reach, on the other side of
3 The map shows the streets and places in a small town.
   1 roundabout 2 park 3 traffic lights 4 pond
   5 zebra crossing 6 crossroads 7 river 8 bridge
   Examples of other useful places: railway station, bus stop, cinema,
   statue, fountain
4 1 G 2 D 3 C
5 4 K 5 I 6 B
6 The distractors are:
   (Question 1) *You can also go straight on here*
   (Question 4) *Instead of turning left here*
   (Question 5) *there are shops on the left.*
7 1 F 2 A 3 H 4 G
9 1 diving 2 badminton 3 basketball 4 swimming 5 cycling
   6 football 7 table tennis
10 1 J 2 L 3 M 4 I 5 B 6 F 7 G 8 E

SPEAKING

5 1 F 2 D 3 B 4 C 5 E 6 G 7 A
7 1 because 2 and 3 also 4 and 5 because 6 but 7 also
   8 For example 9 or 10 because 11 and 12 so 13 In fact,
10 1 I want <u>to</u> learn <u>to</u> play <u>the</u> guitar.
   2 I enjoy playing football <u>and</u> baseball.
   3 I bought <u>a</u> new golf club.
   4 I would like <u>to</u> learn <u>to</u> play chess.
   5 I need <u>some</u> driving lessons.
   6 I played drums <u>in a</u> band <u>for a</u> long time.
   7 I plan <u>to</u> cycle <u>from the</u> north <u>of</u> Africa <u>to the</u> south.

Unit 7 FAME AND THE MEDIA

READING

1 *Sample answers*
   1 Google, Yahoo, Bing, MSN
   2 BBC, CNN, New York Times, Yahoo News
   3 Facebook, Twitter, Instagram, China: Weibo
   4 Wikipedia, Britannica.com, Encyclopedia.com
2 *Students' own answers*
3 B
4 1 E 2 D 3 C 4 B 5 A 6 A
5 C The opinion is not stated directly, but the phrase 'waste their time'
   shows the writer doesn't like Facebook.
6 1 No 2 Yes 3 Not Given 4 No
7 See exercise 8.
9 4 No 5 Not Given 6 Yes
10 **If clause** If you want to become famous on YouTube,
   Result clause you should make lots of videos and release one
   every day.
   If clause If you allow advertisements in your videos,
   Result clause you will make money …
   If clause If you achieve fame on Facebook,
   Result clause it probably won't last.
   Should is used instead of *will / won't* in one of the result clauses.
11 1 A 2 C 3 B 4 B 5 C 6 A 7 B
   8 No 9 Yes 10 No 11 Yes 12 Not Given
   13 No 14 Not Given 15 Yes 16 No

WRITING

1 **Nouns (things):** media, newspaper, fortune, website
   Nouns (people): reporter, photographer, celebrity, fan, model, paparazzi, blogger, star
   Adjectives: wealthy, popular, talented, famous, well-known

2 **Good things:** well organised, main points are clear, supporting evidence is given
   Bad things: repetition of key words

3 **Point 2:** you have fans
   Evidence: they take photos of you, send you letters
   Point 3: you don't have to wait in queues
   Evidence: you can go to the front
   Point 4: you can help good causes
   Evidence: others might also give to charity

4 *Fame* has many advantages. If you are *well-known* you might also be wealthy. You can buy a big house and an expensive car. Another *benefit* is that you have fans. They take photographs of you and send you letters. One more *good point* is if you are *someone that everyone knows*, you don't have to wait in queues. You can go to the front. The last *positive aspect* of being famous is you can use your fame and money to help good causes. If you give money to charity, others will do so too. In this way, you can make a real difference in the world.

5 1 Disadvantages: uses pronouns (the main one) and similar words (drawback, negative aspect, problem)
   Famous: uses similar words (well-known, fame) and avoids using 'being famous' when it is not necessary (the main one, a final problem …)

   2 1 You don't have a private life.
     2 People say bad things about you.
     3 Your family may suffer.
     4 It is stressful.

   3 1 Reporters follow you everywhere and take photos of you.
     2 They even tell lies about you.
     3 Your children may have paparazzi following them.
     4 Some actors or singers are badly affected by the pressure.

6 There are also disadvantages of being famous. The main one is that you do not have a private life. Reporters follow you everywhere. Even if you are tired or sick, they take photographs of you. Many celebrities have got into trouble after getting angry with reporters and photographers who were following them. The second drawback of being well-known is that people say bad things about you. They even tell lies about you. Even people like Bill Gates, who gives most of his money to charity, are criticised! The third negative aspect of fame is your family may also suffer. Even your children may have paparazzi following them. For example, everyone has seen pictures of Harper, the daughter of David and Victoria Beckham. A final problem is that it can be very stressful. Some actors or singers are badly affected by the pressure. Many famous people have become ill due to overwork and always being in public view.

7 *Sample answers*
   Famous people are often rich. Jackie Chan is worth $350 million.
   You might have a lot of fans. Taylor Swift gets thousands of fan letters a week.
   You can use your fame and money to help others. Bill Gates donates most of his money.

8 1 Fan Bingbing is a popular actress in China. She starred in *My Fair Princess*. (Also accept: Fan Bingbing is a popular Chinese actress who starred in *My Fair Princess*.)
   2 Benedict Cumberbatch is one of my heroes. I met him when I was in London.
   3 Our country has laws that protect people from paparazzi. Some countries' laws are not as strict as ours.
   4 There are some reasons for my opinion. The first one is it is difficult to be famous.

10 1 The writer agrees that taking photographs of under 18s should be banned.
   2 The Beckham children, Prince William and his children, the 'Celebrities with ugly kids' website

3 Yes. The writer understands that people are interested in seeing photos of celebrities and acknowledges (but rejects) the point of view 'fame has a price'.

4 Plan 1

11 *Sample essay*
Every year a list of the highest paid celebrities is published. Some stars are paid hundreds of millions of dollars every year. Some people think they deserve this money for their talent and hard work. I personally disagree. I don't believe anyone should have such excessive amounts of money. In this essay I will explain the reasons for my view.

Some people argue that the highest earning celebrities are special. They have a talent that few of us possess and they have worked incredibly hard to become the best. My view is that we all have our own skills and abilities and most of us work hard. Just because someone's talent is for making things or teaching, why should they get paid so much less?

It is true that we create the demand for celebrities that lets them become so wealthy. However, I think we are all paying too much for tickets to concerts and sporting events. This is unfair because people with low incomes don't have the opportunity to see these events in person. If celebrities earned less, more people would be able to afford to buy music and go to concerts.

In addition, I think that it is bad for society that only singers, actors and sportsmen are valued. Children no longer want to grow up to be train drivers, carpenters, plumbers or even teachers because they want a 'celebrity lifestyle' of expensive houses and private jets.

To conclude, I strongly agree that famous people should have a lifestyle which is more similar to that of ordinary people.

(261 words)

LISTENING

1 1 He is Justin Bieber, a famous singer and songwriter.
  2 The answer is found in the recording for exercise 2.

2 1 piano 2 competitions 3 fans 4 music executive 5 contract 6 (global) superstar

3 1 No 2 Yes

4 1 verb 2 noun 3 adjective 4 noun 5 verb 6 adjective 7 adjective 8 verb

5 1 recognise 2 journalists 3 acceptable 4 attention 5 queue 6 interesting 7 private 8 visit

6 1 verb 2 noun or adverb 3 noun 4 verb

7 1 work (hard) 2 (the) experts 3 opportunities 4 fail

8 1 adjective 2 adjective 3 adjective 4 noun 5 adjective /adverb 6 adjective 7 adjective

10 1 **G** manual 2 **J** useful 3 **C** closer 4 **E** light 5 **B** brighter 6 **H** popular 7 **F** long

11 1 talents 2 simple 3 notebook 4 camera movements 5 comic book 6 creative 7 advertise

SPEAKING

1 *Sample answers*
  A Angelina Jolie (actor, famous for her humanitarian work) – active, charming, talented, generous
  B Paul McCartney (singer and songwriter, member of The Beatles) – brilliant, talented, experienced
  C Bill Gates (started the company Microsoft) – active, brilliant, professional, powerful, generous

2 1 Bill Gates 2 computer programmer, creator of Microsoft 3 on television 4 2001, when Windows XP came out
  5.1: He is responsible for bringing computers into family homes.
  5.2: He was the world's youngest self-made billionaire.
  5.3: He gives a lot of his money to charity.

3 1 who 2 and 3 when 4 so 5 because 6 But 7 because 8 why 9 in spite of 10 whose

6 1 e 2 a 3 c 4 d 5 b

7 1 E 2 B 3 A 4 C 5 D

Unit 8 NATURAL WORLD

READING

1 1 opposite   2 similar   3 similar   4 opposite   5 similar

4 1 c   2 a   3 b   4 e   5 d

5 1 Hardy Jones   2 campaigner
   The information was in paragraph B. No.

6 1 grey whales   2 humpback whales   3 seven/7 hours   4 move
   her legs   5 leg
   The information was in paragraph E.

7 D

8 See exercise 9.

10 1 d   2 g   3 f   4 b   5 a

11 (in A) Dolphins' protection of humans might not be just automatic or
    instinctive: they may actively decide to help in certain situations.
    (in F) Although we may never be sure why they help us …

12 they could tell, he couldn't get away

13 1 entertainment   2 Gerald Durrell   3 natural habitats   4 wild
    5 enrichment   6 Webcams
    7 H   8 G   9 D   10 E   11 A

WRITING

1 1 d   2 c   3 f   4 e   5 b   6 a

2 1 global warming   2 natural habitats   3 air pollution
   4 endangered species   5 fossil fuels   6 renewable energy

3 a, b, d, g, h, i and j **may** be included
   a, d, g and j **should** ideally be included

4 1 g   2 a   3 d   4 b   5 h   6 i

5 Paragraph A is better because it includes the points in exercise 3.
   Paragraph B adds new information and supporting evidence, which
   are not appropriate for a conclusion, though B does also give the
   writer's opinion and answer to the question.

6 1 f   2 d   3 g   4 a   5 e   6 b   7 c

8 **The causes**   **Government actions**
   habitats destroyed   education programmes
   pollution   invest in clean energy
   2 All of them are mentioned in the conclusion.
   3 The conclusion ends with a *recommendation.*

9 2 Humans have destroyed their natural habitats.
   3 Pollution has created problems for many sea creatures.

10 For example, the number of black rhinos has declined from over
    65,000 in the 1960s to just 2,500 today.

12 *Sample answer*
    Global warming, also known as climate change, is the rising of
    temperatures all over the world because of human activity. In this
    essay I will explain the main causes of global warming and also
    suggest some solutions.
    The earth's temperature is rising due to greenhouse gases, such as
    carbon dioxide, which get stuck in the air. One major cause is the
    increase in air pollution from burning fossil fuels like coal in factories
    and power stations. As the population grows, more energy is being
    used. Also, nowadays everyone owns several devices, such as
    computers, tablets and phones. These have to be charged every day.
    Another major problem is cutting down trees. Trees use carbon
    dioxide and release oxygen so we need a lot of them. People have cut
    down trees to use the wood for different purposes.

Although global warming is a major problem, there are some
solutions. One of these is to use clean or renewable energy sources.
For instance, solar power uses the sun to generate energy; we can
also use the power of the wind and waves instead of fossil fuels. We
need to protect the rainforests. For every tree that is cut down we
need to plant a new tree. We can all help in different ways. One of
them is to use public transport when possible and only have one car
per family.
To sum up, humans have created the problem of global warming.
Therefore, humans must also try to solve the problem. We can all try
to live a 'green' lifestyle by saving electricity and not buying things we
don't need. (267 words)

LISTENING

1 A mountain gorilla   B blue ring octopus
   C Pere David's deer   D Arabian leopard

2 1 mountain gorilla   2 blue ring octopus
   3 Arabian leopard   4 Pere David's deer

3 1 b   2 e   3 a   4 c   5 d

4 a 2   b 3   c 5   d 4

5 1 b   2 d   3 b   4 e   5 a   6 c

7 2 a   3 d   4 b   5 c

9 1 ground   2 grey   3 blackbacks / black backs   4 water
   5 Hunting

10 1 d   2 a   3 c   4 b   5 e   6 f

11 1 19th / nineteenth   2 750   3 head   4 yellow   5 snakes
    6 100,000

13 1 Australia   2 3 / three   3 24 / twenty-four   4 stick   5 pain
    6 (sea)water

SPEAKING

1 A eagle: big claws, nest   B dolphin: long fin, underwater
   C camel: round hump, desert   D deer: hard antlers, forest

5 1 b   2 a   3 d   4 c

7 1 **Question**: What should be done to people caught hunting illegally?
   Answer: They should have their money given to animal charities and
   the same for people buying the animal products.
   Example: The government in Kenya took money from people who
   were caught buying animal furs.
   Reason: This will help those charities better protect wild animals.

   2 **Question**: Is there anything we as individuals can do to prevent
   hunting?
   Answer: We can stop buying things made from animals.
   Example: Many fashion designers no longer use real fur, they use
   fake fur instead.
   Reason: The demand for things made from animals will drop, and so
   will demand for hunting.

   3 **Question**: Will there be more or less hunting in the future?
   Answer: I think there will be less hunting in the future.
   Reason: Many of our animals are already close to becoming extinct.
   Example: There are almost no white rhinos left.

10 *Suggested answers*
    Pets: 1 C   2 B   3 A   4 D
    Zoos: 1 G   2 F   3 E   4 H

LISTENING SCRIPTS

Unit 1 RELATIONSHIPS

LISTENING

2 🎚 02

Conversation 1

Manager: Good evening, Willowtree Hotel. How can I help?

Customer: Hello, I'd like to make a reservation in your restaurant for next Saturday evening.

Manager: Next Saturday? If you hold on, I'll just check … So … for how many people?

Customer: I need a table for 12 – it's my husband's 30th birthday, so we're having a dinner to celebrate.

Conversation 2

Sales assistant: Good afternoon, can I help you?

Customer: Yes, I'm looking for a gift for my sister. She's going to be 18 next week. So I thought a piece of jewellery would be nice.

Sales assistant: Good idea! Do you have anything particular in mind – a necklace, perhaps?

Customer: Mm, she has so many necklaces. I was thinking of a pair of earrings, possibly.

Sales assistant: Does she have a favourite colour?

Customer: Mm, she likes blue ….

5 🎚 03

a the 3rd   **b** $10.50   **c** the 6th   **d** 70   **e** 19   **f** 62   **g** £110
h the 27th

6 🎚 04

Customer: I need a table for 12 – it's my husband's 30th birthday, so we're having a dinner to celebrate.

Manager: So that's 12 people for the 16th.

Customer: No, no, it's the day after – the 17th – Saturday the 17th, at eight o'clock.

Manager: Ah, yes, of course. A party of 12 for the Saturday … Oh, I'm sorry, but I'm afraid our main restaurant is fully booked that evening, but we do have a small room available for private hire. It can seat up to 20 people, so there would be plenty of space for 12 of you.

Customer: That sounds perfect.

8 🎚 05

Customer: That sounds perfect.

Manager: Excellent. Now we offer a set three-course menu for £23 per person and we can also supply you with a birthday cake at no extra charge. How does that sound?

Customer: That sounds good. So how much would that cost in total?

Manager: Let me see – for the food and the room, that will come to £318.

Customer: Did you say three hundred and eighty pounds?

Manager: No, three hundred and eighteen.

Customer: OK, I think I'd like to go ahead and make a booking.

Manager: OK, I'll just take your details.

9 🎚 06

Sales assistant: Good afternoon, can I help you?

Customer: Yes, I'm looking for a gift for my sister. She's going to be 18 next week, so I thought a piece of jewellery would be nice.

Sales assistant: Good idea! Do you have anything particular in mind – a necklace, perhaps?

Customer: Mm, she has so many necklaces. I was thinking of a pair of earrings, possibly.

Sales assistant: Does she have a favourite colour?

Customer: Mm, she likes blue …

Sales assistant: What about this pair? They have some beautiful little blue stones.

Customer: Mm … They're quite nice, I suppose.

Sales assistant: They're silver, and they're handmade, so you won't find anything like them anywhere else.

Customer: Oh, really? So, how much are they?

Sales assistant: Well, they *were* £30, but actually we've got a sale on at the moment, so they're a little cheaper – only £20. So you can save £10!

Customer: Great. I'll take them.

Sales assistant: And would you like me to giftwrap them for you?

Customer: How much do you charge for that?

Sales assistant: For £4 we give you a pretty box and your own choice of wrapping paper. Or for £5 you can have our luxury wrapping service, which includes a silver box and silver ribbon. And if you would like a card to write your own personal message, that will be £2 extra.

Customer: Well, it's a special birthday so I'll take the luxury option. But I already have a card, thank you.

Sales assistant: That's fine. I'll do that for you now. And how would you like to pay – cash or card?

10 🎚 07

Customer: Oh, really? So, how much are they?

Sales assistant: Well they *were* £30, but actually we've got a sale on at the moment, so they're a little cheaper – only £20. So you can save £10!

13 🎚 08

Mark: Hi there, Nam! You aren't *still* working on your history assignment, are you?

Nam: Hi, Victor! No, I'm taking a break. I'm looking at some photos, actually – a family celebration. Do you want to see them?

Mark: So, who's the cute baby in this picture here?

Nam: She's my niece – my brother's daughter. Her name's Tae-Hee. She's one year old in this picture. It's a very important birthday in Korea – we call it 'Dol' or Doljanchi. It's a very special celebration – in fact, I think it's probably more important than a wedding or a graduation! And we invite all our family and friends and sometimes our neighbours. Here's a picture of the restaurant where we celebrated Tae-Hee's big day.

Mark: What a lovely place – and a beautiful garden, too.

Nam: Yes, it's a perfect location for taking photographs. Can you see me just there next to the trees?

Mark: Ah yes, I like your hat! And I like the red and silver hat Tae-Hee's wearing too. It's really pretty.

Nam: Yes, it's a traditional hat for a girl. Baby boys wear a different one – all black. It looks very serious!

Mark: That's a bit boring. Black and silver would be more interesting. What's Tae-Hee wearing round her skirt?

Nam: That's a little purse. Boy babies wear this too. It's made of silk and it means good luck in our culture. And she's wearing a belt too. Look – do you see? The belt means she will have a long life!

Mark: And what's this on the table there? It's very colourful.

Nam: It's rice cakes.

Mark: I've never seen anything like that before. It looks like a rainbow!

Nam: We always eat rice cakes at a baby's party. There are usually 12 different types of them on the table. Look – this rice cake is completely orange in colour and this one here is bright green!

Mark: It looks like a vegetable!

Nam: Now, look – this is me with my brother's wife, Mi-Cha. We get on really well together.

Mark: What are you holding?

Nam: Oh, it's a little bag. All the guests get a gift bag at the end of the party. And inside there's a present from the baby's parents. It's really fun to open it because you don't know what you'll get. So it could be a candle, or some chocolates. Guess what I got? You can see it in this next photo.

Mark: It looks like a box of tea. But shouldn't it be the other way round – the baby gets the presents?

Nam: Well, the baby receives money from the guests, so in a way you're right! And actually, I've got my present right here. So, why don't we open the box right now and have a cup of tea? Then we can try to finish our assignments.

Mark: Sounds good to me!

SPEAKING

2 〓 09

Examiner: Let's talk about family. So, tell me about your family.

Hoi Chin: My family? Well, my family isn't a large family. It's quite a small family, in fact – and quite a typical family for my country. Just my parents, my older brother and me. So, I'm the baby of the family! I think we're a close, happy family. We do a lot of things together, particularly preparing food – and eating it of course!

4 〓 10

Examiner: How often do you go out with your family?

Candidate: Sorry? Can you repeat that?

Examiner: How often do you go out with your family?

Candidate: Well … we're a close family, we like spending a lot of time together. We try to go out once a week – usually at weekends – on Saturdays or Sundays. We all really like being in the fresh air so we often go for a long walk along the beach. We enjoy going early in the morning when it's quiet. We never go when it's crowded! We live near a big park, so we sometimes go there. We usually go for a long walk and sometimes have a barbecue by the lake. Sometimes our cousin comes along too. He loves running around in the sunshine. He even enjoys swimming in the lake, so it's a good day out for him too!

7 〓 11

Hoi Chin: My family? Well, my family isn't a large family. It's quite a small family in fact – and quite a typical family for my country. Just my parents, my older brother and me. So, I'm the baby of the family! I think we're a close, happy family. We do a lot of things together, particularly preparing food – and eating it of course! Yes, we spend a lot of time in the kitchen. My father's a very good cook – he's much better than my mother.

My brother's getting married next year, so I'm really looking forward to having a sister-in-law! And who knows? Perhaps our family will get bigger in the future! I'd love to have a niece or a little nephew to take to the park one day. Yes, I really want to be an aunt!

8 〓 12

Student A: I get own really well with both of my sisters. The older one's at university in Australia, so I don't see her very often any more. The younger one still lives at home though, and we spend all of our free time together.

Student B: I'm a lot like my father. We look similar and have the same interests.

Student C: Most people say that I'm similar to my father because we both have green eyes and black hair. However, I think that I'm more similar to my mother in character. We're both easy-going and calm, so I think it's a mixture of both.

10 〓 13

asks, chooses, enjoys, keeps, plays, talks, wants, watches

11 〓 14

Examiner: Is there anyone in your family who annoys you sometimes?

A: My father watches football on TV and shouts a lot.

B: My brother plays on the computer all the time.

C: My mother keeps telling me to tidy my room.

Unit 2 PLACES AND BUILDINGS

LISTENING

3 〓 15

Conversation 1

Man: Good morning, how can I help you?

Woman: Hello, I'd like some information about your facilities.

Man: OK, well we have a swimming pool, squash courts, a gym and we have a couple of outdoor tennis courts too. You may have seen them on the left as you came in. Now, our website tells you how you can become a member and how much the yearly fee is. Do you want to make a note of the address?

Conversation 2

Bank clerk: Good afternoon, can I help you?

Customer: I'd like to open a new account please.

Bank clerk: Certainly – now, is it a basic account you're looking to open or a savings account?

Customer: A savings account.

Bank clerk: Right – we can complete your application online. I'll just get the form up on screen now. It won't take long.

4 〓 16

Conversation 1

Man: Good morning, how can I help you?

Woman: Hello, I'd like some information about your facilities.

Man: OK, well we have a swimming pool, squash courts, a gym and we have a couple of outdoor tennis courts too. You may have seen them on the left as you came in. Now, our website tells you how you can become a member and how much the yearly fee is. Do you want to make a note of the address?

Woman: Oh, yes please. I'll just put it on my phone now.

Man: OK, it's W W W dot getactive dot com. That's G-E-T-A-C-T-I-V-E dot com.

Woman: 'Get active' – is that all one word?

Man: Yes, that's right.

Woman: OK, I've got that. Thanks very much for your help.

Conversation 2

Bank clerk: Good afternoon, can I help you?

Customer: I'd like to open a new account, please.

Bank clerk: Certainly – now, is it a basic account you're looking to open or a savings account?

Customer: A savings account.

Bank clerk: Right, we can complete your application online. I'll just get the form up on screen now. It won't take long. So, I just need a few personal details. Can you give me your full name, please?

Customer: James Clarke.

Bank clerk: Is that Clark with an 'e' or without?

Customer: It's got an 'e' at the end. C-L-A-R-K-E.

Bank clerk: And where do you live? What's your address?

Customer: 2 Waddington Road.

Bank clerk: Can you spell that for me?

Customer: That's W-A-double D-I-N-G-T-O-N Road.

Bank clerk: Is that Waddington with a double D, did you say?

Customer: That's right.

Bank clerk: OK, so I just need a little more information about …

5 🔊 17

Man: Do you want to make a note of the address?

Woman: Oh, yes please. I'll just put it in my phone now.

Man: OK, it's W W W dot getactive dot com. That's G-E-T-A-C-T-I-V-E dot com.

Woman: 'Get active' – is that all one word?

Man: Yes, that's right.

…

Bank clerk: So, I just need a few personal details. Can you give me your full name, please?

Customer: James Clarke.

Bank clerk: Is that Clark with an 'e' or without?

Customer: It's got an 'e' at the end. C-L-A-R-K-E.

Bank clerk: And where do you live? What's your address?

Customer: 2 Waddington Road.

Bank clerk: Can you spell that for me?

Customer: That's W-A-double D-I-N-G-T-O-N Road.

Bank clerk: Is that Waddington with a double D, did you say?

Customer: That's right.

9 🔊 18

A: I really enjoyed that little place we went to last weekend – there was a really good choice of meat and fish, wasn't there?

B: Did you really think so? I wish I could say the same, but actually, I thought it was pretty limited. There were far too many fish dishes on the menu and I can't stand seafood. There just wasn't enough meat.

A: Oh, come on Jo! We really enjoyed the steak we had, and you said that the beef the people on the other table were eating looked delicious too.

B: Well, I won't be going back. It was much too expensive.

A: Well, I thought it was pretty reasonable. In fact I couldn't believe it when the bill arrived. £40, including a tip. That's only £20 per person. You can't get steak for less than £15 anywhere in town.

11 🔊 19

David: Hi, Leila! Where are you? We need to leave for the party soon.

Leila: I'm on my way home – I'm still waiting for the bus. I was going to get a taxi back but I've just checked my phone and there's a bus due in about 15 minutes – 7.50 pm to be exact. And it seems to be running on time. It left the railway station a couple of minutes ago, so it's not too far away.

David: Do you want me to pick you up? I've got the car, so it's no problem. Where's the bus stop exactly?

Leila: It's the one on Blythe Road.

David: Blythe Road? I'm just checking it on my phone. Is that B-L-Y-T-H?

Leila: There's an e at the end of Blythe.

David: Got it. OK, I won't be long.

Leila: Actually, David – no need to pick me up. The traffic lights have just changed and I can see the bus coming now. I'd better go – I'll see you at home in a few minutes.

12 🔊 20

Darren: Hi there, Alicia! How was your weekend? You were on a sailing course down at the harbour, weren't you?

Alicia: That's right – I really enjoyed breathing in all that fresh sea air. It was only two days but the time flew by! The instructor began by teaching us safety rules, which was necessary, but not very exciting. But then on the first morning we learnt how to open the sails and I even learnt how to turn the boat. The water wasn't as calm as it looked, I can tell you – I lost my balance a few times!

Darren: Sounds like you had a lot of fun. I'd love to learn to sail.

Alicia: Well, there are plenty of courses and I think they run them once a month – so just let me check the website here. OK, so this was my course here – see – 4th and 5th of August. Now you could sign up for the next one, at the beginning of September. And it looks like there are still some spaces available.

Darren: So, the next one starts on 1st of September? I think I could do that.

Alicia: Well, let me give you the name of the course leader so that you can give him a call. He's a really experienced sailor … OK, it's Jon Galloway.

Darren: Is that the usual spelling of John?

Alicia: No, there's no H – he's just J-O-N.

Darren: OK, got you. And did you say his surname's Galloway? Can you spell that for me?

Alicia: Yes – Galloway – that's G-A-double L-O-W-A-Y. And I've got his number too. Why don't you give him a ring?

15 🔊 21

Jon: So, how's your very first week at university going, Rita? It's Orientation Week for all you new students, isn't it?

Rita: Yes, that's right – Orientation Week. Yes, it's great fun – there are so many different events going on to help us make friends and find our way around the university. And to get around the city, come to that! But you'll remember all that, Jon. You were a new student once!

Jon: That's true. I remember I went on a walking tour of the city on my first day. And I think some students did a bus tour.

Rita: Well, I did a bike tour – I was sent an email about it and I decided to sign up. There were only eight places and there were seven other names on the list already, so I got the very last place.

Jon: I didn't know you had a bike.

Rita: I *don't* have a bike but that didn't matter. We all hired them – from a little cycle hire shop on Barkway Street. You probably know the place.

Jon: Barclay Street? Do you mean the 'Barclay Street' on campus?

Rita: No, it's Barkway Street – B-A-R-K-W-A-Y. Number 22 Barkway Street, to be exact. It was great – we could choose a traditional bike or an electric one.

Jon: So I take it you went electric!

Rita: Yes, of course I did! Well, think about it – why ride a traditional bike when you can get around the city much faster on an electric one! And because there was a group of us, it wasn't too expensive. In fact the cycle hire was only a $120 for the whole group. So the cost was only $15 per person and that was for three whole hours!

Jon: Did you say $50?

Rita: No, $15. So I thought it was really quite cheap. And I didn't have to bring along a helmet to wear either. That was included – and we also got a lock, so it was easy to park our bikes safely when we wanted to stop and take a break!

Jon: Sounds good. Have you got the website address of the place you got your bike from? I quite like the idea of doing a bike tour.

Rita: Yes – it's a really easy one to remember. It's tradelectric.com

Jon: Can you say that again?

Rita: tradelectric – T-R-A-D-E-L-E-C-T-R-I-C all one word dot com.

Jon: Thanks, Rita.

Rita: No problem. Hey, maybe we can do a bike tour together. I'd love to cycle as far as the harbour next time.

Jon: Great! That's a date then!

SPEAKING

3 22

Boy: Well, I live in a small town in the north of my country. It has quite a few interesting places to visit. For example, in the centre of town, on the north side of the square we have the historic town hall, which was built in 1895. In front of it, there's a beautiful fountain. Opposite the town hall there's the library. Then if you go over the bridge, we have the art gallery, a big modern building, which often has interesting exhibitions. The art gallery is actually between the cinema (to the north) and a big shopping mall, where I often meet up with my friends.

To the south of the town, there's a harbour, where you can take a boat to the islands. And then next to the harbour is the stadium, where people go to watch our local football team. And just behind it is the public swimming pool. It's an outdoor pool – lovely in summer, but very chilly the rest of the year.

10 23

1 **Examiner:** Where were you born?
   Candidate 1: I was born in Dubai, in the Middle East. It's situated on the north-east coast of the United Arab Emirates.

2 **Examiner:** Where did you grow up?
   Candidate 2: I was born in a small village in China, but I grew up in Chengdu, which is a very big city in south-west China.

3 **Examiner:** Has your home town changed much since you were a child?
   Candidate 3: In the last ten years Baku has changed a lot. Ten years ago we didn't have so many tall buildings and there wasn't as much to do then. The biggest problem is that everything is more expensive now.

4 **Examiner:** Is there anything that you used to do in your home town that you don't do now?
   Candidate 4: Well, I used to go to the beach every summer when I was younger, but now I don't have time. One summer, I even went fishing. I'd like to do that again. Perhaps I'll have time next summer, after my exams.

12 24

1 Our family bought an apartment in the middle of town.
2 The statue was built in 1985.
3 Our town is situated on the Yangtze river.
4 The shopping mall is called 'the Galleria'.
5 The library is located across from the swimming pool.
6 Many things have changed over the years in my home town.
7 A number of new apartments were developed by the harbour.
8 The bridge was designed by a famous architect from London.
9 Recently, scientists discovered a large cave near our village.
10 Recently, many young people have started to leave my home town to look for work.
11 A long time ago many people used to work in factories in my town.
12 A tourist who visited recently said our town is a great place to visit.

14 25

Speaker 1: In my city there are a lot of things that people can do to enjoy themselves. I personally enjoy visiting the many parks we have, but only in summer when the weather is fine. In winter, people like to visit the cinema or sometimes it's possible to go ice skating on the lake.

Speaker 2: Well, I'm really keen on sport, especially swimming. I live in quite a small town, so we only have one swimming pool and I spend as much time as I can there, when I'm not studying of course!

Speaker 3: Most of the city is pretty modern, but there's an ancient castle where the Emperor used to live. It's just a place for tourists to visit now, but in the past it was the most important place in the country and it's over 1000 years old.

Speaker 4: It depends. There are a lot of traffic jams in the morning and evening when everybody is going to work or school, but the public transport is very modern and the underground's fast and cheap.

Unit 3 EDUCATION AND EMPLOYMENT

LISTENING

5 26

Conversation 1

Manager: Come on in. It's Anna, isn't it?

Anna: Yes, that's right. Anna Scott.

Manager: Ah yes. Take a seat, Anna. First of all, we're delighted that you'll be joining us as a store assistant at the beginning of next week.

Anna: Thanks very much. I'm really looking forward to the challenge.

Manager: That's good to know.

Conversation 2

Receptionist: Good morning, you're through to Milton College. How can I help?

Student: Oh, hello there. I'd like to book a place on the Food Photography course.

Receptionist: OK. Now, is that the one that starts on the 18th?

Student: No, that's the date of the Food *Technology* course – I want the Food *Photography* course. It's the day after.

Receptionist: OK … got it right up on screen now. Food Photography – Saturday the 19th of September. And it looks like you're in luck – there are only a couple of spaces left. We've taken ten bookings already, so you've just made it – the course is limited to 12 participants. It's very popular.

Student: That's good to know! Now can I just check the details of the course?

8 27

Manager: Come on in. It's Anna, isn't it?

Anna: Yes, that's right. Anna Scott.

Manager: Ah yes. Take a seat, Anna. First of all, we're delighted that you'll be joining us as a store assistant at the beginning of next week.

Anna: Thanks very much. I'm really looking forward to the challenge.

Manager: That's good to know. Now, we know you've just finished a course in Information Technology, so we've decided to put you in the computing and phones section of our department store.

Anna: That's great. Now, that's next to the radios and audio equipment, isn't it?

Manager: That's right. All our radios and audio are in a part of the store we used to call the 'Sound Station'. But as I've just said, you'll be based in the computing and phones section. Now we've recently made this area of our store much bigger so that we can sell a much wider range of computer equipment, such as smart watches.

Anna: Mm. Smart watches!

Manager: Yes, we really want to attract a younger group of customers. And we haven't just given this whole area a completely new look – we've re-named it too!

Anna: Re-named it?

Manager: Yes. From next week it's going to be known as 'Moving Images'.

Anna: 'Moving Images'? Cool! I like it.

Manager: Now, do you have any questions before we move on?

15 〰 28

Student: Now can I just check the details of the course?

Receptionist: Sure, go ahead.

Student: Now it says on the leaflet … um, let me find it … OK, got it! Right, so it's called Food Photography, and I've got here that it begins at nine thirty.

Receptionist: That's right – it's an early start. It begins at half past nine and it goes on until four thirty. Most of our weekend courses are quite short and so they're over in a couple of hours – this course is longer. According to the information I've got up here on screen, it's seven hours long.

Student: Oh, I'm glad it lasts for more than a few hours. I don't think I'd be able to learn how to take good pictures in *less* than seven hours.

Receptionist: Now, I'll just give you a bit more information about the course itself. Basically, you'll learn how to take good photos of food using a digital camera. So it'll train you in the basics of using a range of camera angles.

Student: Camera angles?

Receptionist: Yes, you'll learn how to photograph food using close-up shots, wide-angle shots and shots taken from above, that sort of thing.

Student: What about learning to edit pictures on my computer? Will that be covered too?

Receptionist: No, I'm afraid not. The purpose of the workshop is to teach you how to take good photos in the first place. It's a really hands-on session – in fact, you'll spend some of the day on location in a local hotel. It's just round the corner from the college – the Lincoln Hotel – so you'll have the opportunity to practise taking photographs using real dishes!

Student: That's great – a practical course is exactly what I'm looking for!

Receptionist: Now just a few more things. The full fee of the course is $55 and that includes a light lunch and refreshments at the hotel.

Student: Oh, that's really good. That means I don't have to worry about bringing along my own drinks and snacks on the day. That would probably cost me at least $10.

Receptionist: OK, I think that's everything, so I'll just take your details so that we can confirm your place on the course.

SPEAKING

7 〰 29

Examiner: What do you do? Do you work or are you a student?

Nina: I'm a student. I'm doing a part-time fashion and textiles course. I'm at Milton College, in the centre of the city. I'm in my third year and at the moment I'm studying 12 hours a week.

Examiner: Are you enjoying it?

Nina: Oh yes, I am. I think it's great. I particularly like working with different materials like wool and leather. And I've just made a beautiful scarf and it's made out of plastic. It looks very strange but I think it's great! It's pretty amazing in fact!

Examiner: Would you like to learn anything new in the future?

Nina: Yes, I would. I'd really like to learn how to use computer software to create new designs. This should also help me create new shades of colour. Using technology in this way would be really challenging for me, I think.

Examiner: And is there a job you'd really like to do in the future?

Nina: Yes, there is. I'd love the chance to become a fashion photographer. And if I do well on my course and get some experience of taking pictures at my college fashion shows, perhaps my dream will come true. I've just bought myself a new digital camera and I've already learnt how to take some great close-up shots!

18 〰 31

Nina: I'm going to tell you about a time when I learnt something new. What did I learn? Well, I've always been an active and sporty person and I really like cold weather – I love it when it snows in my country. That's why I decided to learn something that mixes these things together – winter, sport and snow! So, I decided to learn to ski!

I learnt with an instructor. There was a big group of us – we had a great instructor. It was really exciting when we were on the chair lift on the first day. We started on the nursery slope – I couldn't even walk on my skis at first and I fell over many times. It took me a long time to learn how to keep my balance. It really is much more difficult than it looks! It was great fun! I really liked learning in a group – much better than learning individually.

In fact, I was in a skiing competition recently and I won! I got a silver cup. So, I think that's quite a good result.

How did I feel about the learning experience? Well, it was really thrilling to ski downhill for the very first time – I loved the feeling of speed. It was very exciting! I was so proud of myself when I reached the bottom of the slope and I was still standing! It was a great feeling!

Unit 4 FOOD AND DRINK

LISTENING

3 〰 32

Mike: So, what type of meal do you think we should have at the party, Jane?

Jane: I don't know, Mike. Do you have any ideas?

Mike: What do you think about preparing a Mexican meal?

Jane: I really like Mexican food and we could have some fun Mexican party games, but I think it might be too spicy for some people.

Mike: That's true. We could have pizza. Everybody likes pizza.

Jane: Hmm, I think we should have something healthier.

Mike: I know! We could have salad and roast chicken.

Jane: That sounds like a good idea. And it's fairly simple to prepare. Let's do that.

4 〰 33

A: So do you think that we now have everything ready for the meal?

B: Almost, I was just wondering what would be the best way of preparing the potatoes.

A: Well, you could just boil them and serve them with the fish.

B: That would be easy, but I don't think it would be very exciting.

A: What about frying them? Everybody likes fried potatoes.

B: They aren't very healthy though, and I haven't got much oil left.

A: You could bake them and serve them with the salad Elly's preparing.

B: That would taste good, but it takes ages to bake potatoes in the oven. I know, I'll boil them and then put them with Elly's salad.

5 📻 **34**

A: Before we go back to the flat, I think we need to check we have everything that we need.

B: OK, well you went to Arcadia, so I imagine that you got the strawberries and apples from there?

A: Yes, I did.

B: Did you notice if they had any cucumbers while you were over there?

A: I'm not sure. I thought *you* were going to get them.

B: Well I went over to Best Buy, and I got some nice carrots and peas, but I didn't like the look of the cucumbers.

A: Oh, I suppose we can go there on the way back to the station.

B: Don't forget we need to get some cakes and pastries too. We can get those after we've been to Hampton's to get the lamb and chicken.

A: OK, good plan.

6 📻 **35**

A: In this new series of 'Talk of the Town' we'll be looking at the different restaurants in and around Ogdenville and getting some tips and recommendations from our resident food critic, Chris Griffin. So Chris, where have you been this week?

B: Well, one restaurant that I really enjoyed is Adam's. It's on the Town Square. I ordered a steak au poivre and it was perfect.

A: What's that?

B: It's a steak in peppercorns – it's quite a typical French dish.

A: So, is it a French restaurant or a steakhouse?

B: Well, the chef is French, but it serves food from all over the world. It has a wide variety of dishes. One word of warning though, it gets really busy at weekends, so you should check they have places before you go.

A: Have you got any other recommendations for us this week, Chris?

B: Oh, yes. I can really recommend the Duke on Smith Street. I had lobster and it was really tasty. It also has a few vegetarian dishes, but it's the fish dishes that make it famous in the town. The food isn't that low-cost though, so you might want to save going here for a special treat.

A: What about people who are on a budget? Have you got any suggestions for them?

B: Yes, I have. The Tower in Market Street is a fashionable restaurant where people can get a good meal at a reasonable price. I had a pizza, but it isn't a fast food restaurant, it specialises in all different types of food from Italy. I've heard that the lasagne is especially good.

A: Thanks, Chris. You certainly have given us all food for thought.

11 📻 **36**

Chef: I suppose one thing that everybody knows about Japanese, Chinese and Korean cooking is that they all use chopsticks rather than knives and forks like people in the West. The chopsticks that people use in the different countries are quite different though. In China the chopsticks tend to be made of wood and are round at the end, whereas in Korea they're made of stainless steel and are rough at the end. This is because in the past the emperor would use silver chopsticks, as they changed colour if there was any poison in the dish. They can be quite tricky to use, but in Korea people use a spoon to eat their rice. In Japan they use a variety of things to make chopsticks. Wood and plastic are the most popular now, but you can find bone, metal and even ivory ones.

If we look at the food of the different countries, it's very difficult to talk about China in general terms because it has many different cuisines. So it might be better if we look at Korean and Japanese food a little more. It's well known that Koreans tend to like spicier food and red peppers can be found in a wide number of dishes. I suppose that everybody thinks of sushi when they think of Japanese food, but you can also find a lot of influences from all over Asia and even Europe, for example tempura, which came to Japan from Portugal. Those aren't present in Chinese and Korean food.

Traditionally, in both Japan and in Korea meat plays less of an important role than in Europe, perhaps because it's so expensive due to the lack of space for keeping animals. That said, both the Japanese and Koreans enjoy meat. Barbecues of all types are popular in Korea and beef forms the basis of many special meals in both of the countries. Now moving back to Chinese cuisine …

12 📻 **37**

Interviewer: Today in the studio I am pleased to have with me the famous chef, Graham Shepherd. Graham has just come back from Beijing in China, where he was making a TV programme on the food you can try in this historic city. So, Graham, what can you tell us about your trip? Was it how you expected it to be?

Graham: It was quite surprising really. I suppose that most people think of Beijing duck when they think of Beijing and I did try some of this tasty traditional dish, but with so many people from all over the country living in Beijing there really are a lot of different foods from all regions of the country. One dish that I really enjoyed and I didn't expect to find was kebabs. These tasty snacks are originally from north-west China, but they're very popular street food in Beijing. They're especially popular as a tasty snack at lunchtime for school pupils. They have less meat and more vegetables than we are used to, so they're a bit healthier.

Interviewer: I'm sure that most people have tried kebabs, but did you try anything that might be unusual for our listeners?

Graham: Oh, yes. One of the things that I had was jellyfish. It added a nice texture to the dish, but I thought it didn't taste of much. One dish that did have a strong taste was hotpot. The dish I had was made in the Sichuan style, so it was very spicy. What I found interesting was that the hotpot was put on a hotplate in the centre of the table, and we were given a dish of raw food and we chose what we wanted and put it into the pot ourselves, and got it out when it was ready. It was great fun and very sociable. And very tasty!

Interviewer: I'm sure that you tried some of the dishes that we all know and love too. Can you tell us something interesting about them?

Graham: Of course, everybody knows about noodles and dumplings, but I doubt many people know how many different types there are! One of the highlights for me was learning how to make fresh noodles with a chef from Northern China. The recipe of egg, salt and wheat flour is quite simple, but to make the noodles by hand you need to be quite a skilful chef.

Something which is much simpler to make are dumplings. The basic ingredients are flour and water, but the beauty of this dish is that it's very flexible. You can fill them with whatever you like. I especially enjoyed one with raw prawns, but all sorts of meat and vegetables can be put in them.

Interviewer: Thanks Graham, that's really interesting, but unfortunately we've run out of time. If you'd like to know more about Graham's adventures, the series will be starting on Thursday at 7 o'clock on Channel 9.

SPEAKING

4 📻 **38**

Examiner: What kind of food is popular in your country?

Mohammed: These days a lot of young people actually enjoy Western food like pizza and fried chicken. Our national food is often too spicy, especially for children and foreigners, and also it takes too long to cook. I think that it's delicious though!

Examiner: What do you think of Western food?

Mohammed: Well, I suppose Western food is quick to make and is tasty too, so everyone can eat it without too much trouble. I think that a lot of people like food to be convenient because they're so busy nowadays.

Examiner: Is there any kind of food you don't like?

Mohammed: Yes, I'm not keen on sushi at all. It's so strange eating something that hasn't been cooked. I know it's very fresh and healthy but I just don't like the taste and I can't stand the texture – it's too chewy for me.

6 ▅▅ 39

Angelica: I'm going to talk about an Italian dish – risotto. It's a rice dish and most people in my country enjoy it. Unlike in most countries, we fry the rice with onion in olive oil before we add any liquid. We don't cook it in water, but a kind of soup or broth, which can be made of meat, fish or chicken. I'm from Milan, and our traditional risotto is made using saffron, which gives the dish a beautiful yellow colour. It's a very creamy and delicious dish. We usually have it as a starter, not as the main meal.

Firstly, I think that it's popular in my country because – and not a lot of people know this – but Italy's one of the biggest producers of rice in Europe. It's very simple to cook, and as I said before, you can use all types of ingredients. Anything that you can find in the fridge! Also, Italians don't like to waste food, so if you have some fish or some meat and it isn't enough for a meal, you can always make risotto.

I love it first of all because it always reminds me of home. My mother's very fond of cooking risotto and if I was unhappy, she used to make it for me and it always cheered me up. I don't live at home now and so when I'm feeling homesick and missing my family, I always try to find an Italian restaurant and have some risotto! And secondly, I like it because it's a great meal to make for friends – easy to prepare, but very tasty.

You can get risotto everywhere nowadays, but it isn't always that good. If you visit my country, especially the northern part, I recommend that you try to taste risotto there. It really is special and I promise that you will find it different to any risotto that you have tasted before.

Unit 5 CONSUMERISM

LISTENING

2 ▅▅ 40

Recording 1
Whatever you do, don't miss our Summer Sale. This weekend, and this weekend only, we're reducing all our prices right across our store. So, on our first floor you'll find women's jeans at just $20 a pair. And, just in time for the holiday season, our T-shirts and swimwear are on special offer too.

And if you're looking for shoes, you'll want to visit the fourth floor. You'll find a good selection of styles and colours in our footwear department situated right next to the coffee shop. This weekend, they're all half price and that includes a wide choice of sports shoes in most sizes! So, hurry before they're all gone! Sale ends Sunday! Miss our sale? Miss out!

Recording 2
Dan: So, Jess, what do you think of my hat?

Jess: It's very nice – I like the colour, and it'll definitely keep the sun off your face. Actually, I didn't notice the clothing stalls.

Dan: I know you didn't! That's because you spent most of your time there looking at all the jewellery! And relaxing in all that fresh air, of course!

Jess: That's true – but actually, I managed to find a really nice necklace. And you'll never guess how cheap it was! Do you want to have a look?

Recording 3
A: So what did you think of it? It only opened a few weeks ago, didn't it?

B: Yes, that's right, so that's why it was very busy. In fact, it was a bit like being at a football match – there were so many people! But I really liked it – it's very convenient because there were at least 50 different shops all under one roof and there's a car park too. I'd really like to go back.

A: Then how about going along there together next weekend? I'd really like to see it for myself. I also need to buy a birthday present for my mum. You could help me choose something for her. And we can go for a coffee afterwards! I'll pay!

3 ▅▅ 41

Recording 1
And now for the local news … A new branch of Sports World, the Danish sporting goods company, is opening on Saturday. Most of you will be familiar with the branch in the south of Grinstead that opened two years ago and which has enjoyed a lot of success. There was talk of them opening a new store in the Meadows Shopping Centre in the north of the town, but they have finally decided to open in the east, near the football stadium. As a special treat for fans, Grinstead Town's Danish striker Jesper Nielsen will be opening the store ahead of their home match at the weekend.

Recording 2
That's the end of our tour of the city, so you now have a couple of hours to spend exploring the city centre. If you want to buy souvenirs, you might find them cheaper near the hotel. However, if you're feeling a bit tired, there are plenty of teashops nearby and they also sell boxes of tea that make really good presents. A word of warning, you'll find a lot of cheap electronic stores offering cameras at really low prices. They might seem good quality, but we've had a lot of complaints from tourists who have bought them, only to find they break after about a week.

Recording 3
Thank you for calling the Eastgate Shopping Centre. The centre is currently closed. Our opening days and times are as follows … Monday to Saturday we are open from nine o'clock until six o'clock and on Sunday, our doors open at eleven o'clock and we close at five o'clock.

Recording 4
When I first opened the shop three years ago, we mainly sold shirts and jackets that I had designed, and these proved very popular. However, we added more products as the business started to grow. We also started selling online. The jackets and shirts are still really popular, especially online, but in the shop itself, we sell trousers more than any other item.

6 ▅▅ 42

We also sell a lot of T-shirts. When I first opened the shop, I had a lot of designs that I'd worked on at university and in general these had writing on the front. I thought that it might be fun if people could put a photograph on the T-shirts as well. I invested quite a bit of money in this and they were popular at first. We sometimes have young children who come in with their parents and they buy T-shirts with photographs on. I've stopped designing T-shirts with writing on them, because I don't have the time, so now we sell more T-shirts with nothing on them at all. If fashions change, I might go back to designing them and if you want a photograph on your T-shirt, you know where to come.

7 📊 **43**

Calling all fans of Sam West! This famous adventure writer will be in Westfield shopping centre tomorrow in Bookworms Bookshop on the first floor. He will be signing copies of his latest book, *Timed Out*. He's expected to get there at quarter past two and will stay until half past three. Get there as soon as you can because queues will start to form as early as noon. Don't miss this great opportunity to meet everyone's favourite writer!

8 📊 **44**

I had a great day in that new shopping centre but I would complain about one thing – and not the usual kind of thing – the service in all the shops was good, and I had a delicious lunch in the café on the third floor. No, the annoying thing was the amount of rubbish I saw around me. I think it was because there weren't enough rubbish bins for people to put their empty cans and sweet wrappers in. But, apart from that, I would say that it's well worth a visit.

9 📊 **45**

Hello everyone. So can you all hear me and see me? OK, my name's David Edwards and I'm your tour leader for your shopping tour today. Now, as you can see, we're parked just in front of the main theatre. If any of you would like tickets for tonight's performance, we can arrange that for you. We're just round the corner from the railway station. If you want to come on our Historic Buildings tour tomorrow, the coach will leave from just outside the station. And if you want to go for a drink at the end of our tour today, there are plenty of cafés just behind the station.

We're still waiting for a few people, but while we wait I can tell you a little about the theatre. Although the building is very modern, in fact a theatre has existed on this site for over 200 years. The original theatre used to be very popular because of the musicals it put on. However, it had to be rebuilt after a fire. Some people love the striking modern design, others hate it. These days, its popularity is mainly due to the fact that it attracts a lot of well-known performers.

Now, in a few minutes' time – at 9.30 – we'll be starting our tour. First we're going to make our way down to Market Place, which is one of the most famous squares in the city – that should take us about ten minutes. There's not too much traffic on the roads, so we should get there at quarter to ten at the latest.

Market Place was the city's old food market. People used to come in from the countryside to sell their fresh fruit and vegetables. Remember that these were the days before supermarkets! You won't find any food here now though. It's now a craft market and I think you'll find lots to interest you – especially if you want to take presents home. You'll see all kinds of things like hand-painted local pottery and leather goods. Personally, I suggest that you visit the jewellery stalls. You really won't find anything like it anywhere else! But if you're looking for clothes, I'm afraid you'll be disappointed. Wait for this afternoon's visit.

We'll stop at Market Place for an hour and a half and then continue the tour with a visit to the Regional Food Centre. Here you can find over 50 types of local cheeses! There is also fresh fruit juice on sale – orange juice, peach juice, pomegranate juice, produced in the villages of the region, and local jam too. You're welcome to buy things to take home with you, but the real reason for our visit is lunch. The idea is that you buy food and drink from the stalls and take it to eat in the lovely open-air dining area.

And finally, in the afternoon we will be visiting the Fashion Fair in the exhibition centre on the outskirts of the city. This is a huge venue, so try not to get lost. There is a whole hall devoted just to footwear – every kind of shoes and boots you can imagine. You can easily find it because it has a green roof. Just don't go through the blue doors at the entrance of the centre – you have to pay for that part of the exhibition. And if all that shopping has exhausted you, there's a café where you can rest your weary feet! That's in the building with a red sign. But don't worry, I'll remind you all about that later.

Right, everyone's here now, so, if you've all got your shopping bags, let's go!

2 📊 **46**

The place where I really enjoy shopping is Covent Garden Market. It's very convenient because it isn't far from where I live. It isn't a traditional food market, though at one time it used to sell fruit and vegetables. Now, it's a collection of all sorts of independent shops and stalls. There's an amazing selection of things to buy – clothes, jewellery, books, art and crafts. I love it because it has a great atmosphere. There are cafés outside in the square, and often you can see street performers. It's very lively and friendly. I avoid the big malls because they're often out-of-the-way – you need a car to get to them.

And what do I enjoy buying? Well, I'm keen on fashion and like to go clothes shopping whenever I can. I love trying on clothes even if I can't afford to buy them! And I absolutely love going to the sales! Sometimes I manage to find great designer shoes at very reasonable prices. And I like shopping for really fun and original gifts for my friends – things that nobody else has. Covent Garden's a great place to do that.

7 📊 **47**

You asked me to describe a place where I like going shopping, so I'm going to talk about a department store in my town. It's called Judies and it's a very old store. In fact, it's about a 100 years old, so it's very famous. I would say that it's a landmark because everyone knows it. It's very large and spacious too, with four floors and more than 30 different departments to visit. You can find anything you want here, such as unusual presents for your friends, and you can buy really good food too. For example, you can buy traditional cakes and sweets that are famous in my area and they are delicious. It's an amazing shop but it's not cheap. In fact, it's one of the most expensive shops in the area.

I think it's in a good location because it's right in the centre of the town, which is very convenient. It's also very close to the railway station and a multi-storey car park too, so that's good for you if you have lots of shopping bags to carry.

What do I like to do there? Well, I really like spending time in the jewellery department and this is on the ground floor of the building. I love looking at the different rings and necklaces. I enjoy trying them on too! I like gold jewellery the best but I can't afford it.

Why do I like it so much? Well, I like the atmosphere in the store because it's very traditional. All the sales assistants are very friendly and helpful too. Yes, it's a really good store, so that's why I spend a lot of time in it!

Unit 6 LEISURE TIME

LISTENING

4 📊 **49**

Melissa: Thanks for offering to drive us all to the concert. It's really kind of you and makes getting there much easier. I don't live far from you at all. First, you need to turn right onto Maple Avenue and drive to the bottom of the road, passing the supermarket on your left. Then, you need to turn left at the traffic lights and then take a sharp right onto Main Street. You can also go straight on here, past the surgery, but I usually drive down Main Street. Follow this road until you reach a roundabout – you'll pass a park and some shops on your right. When you get to the roundabout, take the first turning on the left, onto Silver Street. As you approach the crossroads here, my house is the first on the corner.

5 🎵 50

Melissa: Sorry, I've just remembered, I told Sarah you would collect her on the way. Forget the route I just gave you, I'll give you another set of directions. This route might even be easier. Again, you need to turn right onto Maple Avenue, and go up to the lights. Instead of turning left here, turn right, with the park on your left. Then after the zebra crossing, take the first turning on your left onto New Road. Drive along New Road until you reach the bridge. Sarah's house is the second house after the bridge. That's on the right; there are shops on the left. Once you've picked up Sarah, take the first turning on the left, onto Silver Street, and go straight ahead until you reach the roundabout. Go straight ahead at the roundabout and then take the first turning on the right, Oak Avenue. My house is number 1. It's on the corner.

7 🎵 51

Tanya: Hi Jane, this is Tanya. I'm calling to make arrangements for the concert on Saturday. I can't believe you've never been to the Arena before. I often go at the weekend. There isn't just the Arena concert venue, there are also lots of other things to do: shopping, restaurants, exhibitions. I'm giving Melissa and Sarah a lift, so shall we all meet up for a coffee before the concert? I'll give you directions. OK, listen carefully.

As you walk through the main entrance, you come to a square with a big fountain in the middle. This is where people usually arrange to meet up and sometimes they have live music here. Beyond the square, on Main Avenue, on your right, there are several restaurants, and opposite these on your left is an exhibition centre. There used to be a cinema here, but they moved it when they finished building the Arena.

So there are several coffee shops to choose from, one near the fountain and one in the north end of the building, but I suggest that we go to the one at the end of Main Avenue, because it'll probably be less busy than the others. It's right at the end, after you pass the art gallery on the right. So shall we all meet there at seven o'clock?

Then, after we've had a coffee, to get into the Arena we just need to go through the shopping centre, which will be on our right once we go back down Main Avenue. It can be a bit tempting, but there's no other way to get there, as the Arena is the other side of it. Oh, and there are toilets beside the entrance if you need them. And then after the concert, they open the door opposite and you can go straight out into the car park, which is very convenient.

Let me know if you can make it for seven. I'm looking forward to seeing you – it's been a while.

9 🎵 52

First of all, welcome to our activity summer camp. I hope you enjoy all the activities we have on offer. We start our tour at the outdoor theatre here, where we hold many of our evening activities. From here you can see our various watersport activities. Directly in front of the campsite, on the edge of the lake, we have the kayaking centre. And then in front of the beach, we have an area reserved for diving. Swimming isn't permitted here.

If you like racket sports, just behind the beach you can practise badminton in the large building. That's quite popular in the evenings. We also have some outdoor tennis courts. We used to have basketball in the building too, but now you can play it on the court behind the building. And if these activities make you hungry, the path from there takes you straight to the café and dining hall.

However, we'll continue our walk along the lake shore and I'd like to draw your attention to two other areas. One is this part of the lake, which is perfect for swimming, but, for safety reasons, only when an instructor is present. Unfortunately we can't offer sailing as an option here this year. And I also want to point out, just across the lake, a track for cycling. Some people in the past have also gone running on the track, but there were a few accidents because there isn't enough space for runners and cyclists, so now running isn't allowed.

So now let's take this path here, towards the tennis courts. On our left, you can see there's a football field. Gary's our coach and he'll be organising tournaments during the week. He'll arrive tomorrow, because he's taking part in a rugby game today.

And now if we walk up to the right of the tennis courts, we can see the archery field, surrounded by trees. And in the building just to the right of this, you can hire equipment for the archery and buy snacks and drinks. It also has some table tennis tables, so you can go there and have a game if the weather turns bad.

10 🎵 53

Good morning. I'd like to thank the council for agreeing to this meeting and for welcoming us here today to explain to you our plans for Pine Woods Centre. Our aim is to make Pine Woods a place where people of all ages can come and enjoy their free time. The centre will feature our Tree Tops Challenge – only for the brave and fearless! For the less brave, and for families with children, there will be adventure playgrounds, indoor and outdoor, and a feeding area for farm animals and we will also offer cycle trails through the woods.

I'll give you an overview of Pine Woods first and then tell you more about each area in more detail. This first slide shows the overall layout of the centre and where all the activities will be situated. As you can see from the map, the entrance to this attraction will be on the south side. As visitors enter from the car park, they will walk along this path leading them to the café and gift shop. The gift shop will be where tickets are on sale and therefore needs to be near the entrance. So this building here on the right will be the café and the building on the left will be the gift shop. There will also be a picnic field behind the café for the warmer months. It's the area just to the right of the café as you look at the map. And in the bottom right-hand corner of the picnic field we're planning to have a barbecue area, where people can hire a barbecue and bring their own food to cook. It'll be great for parties. In summer we plan to have bands performing here in the evenings.

To the west of the gift shop is where the Tree Tops Challenge will take place. There's a path here winding through the forest, and up in the trees there will be all sorts of high-level adventure apparatus – rope swings, awesome rope bridges and tunnels, and zip wires where you can fly way above the forest floor. This adventure experience will only be open to those aged 15 and over.

Beyond the Tree Tops Challenge there will be an adventure playground. To get to it, you go along this path from the entrance until you reach the crossroads, then you turn left. The young children's playground will have a fence around it, making it safer and keeping them away from the lake. The indoor play area, only for the very young, will be on the east side of the farm, near the café and just inside the picnic area.

And finally, let's turn our attention back to this area here, where the paths meet and form a crossroads. This path leading to the east end of the farm will take our visitors to the area which houses the farm animals. Children will be able to watch the animals being fed and cared for, and in some instances they will be able to feed the animals themselves. The sheep will be in this first area on the right here, directly opposite the pigs, and the goats will go at the very end there. We haven't quite decided on the other areas yet.

So those are our plans. We hope they will be approved, and we look forward to welcoming you back in the not too distant future to see the final result.

4 54

I'm going to talk about a hobby I'd like to take up in the future. I really want to learn ballroom dancing. This is because I love Latin music and I love the way the dancers move and shake. I also want to give myself a challenge and learn something new. Watching ballroom dancing always makes me feel excited. I don't think it'll be too difficult for me, because I already do ballet and tap dancing. I like learning new steps. For example, I really want to learn the tango or the samba because these are exciting and look good to people watching. I've tried Flamenco dancing but I'm not very good. I'm also worried about finding the right dance partner, because I'll be a little slow to learn in the beginning. So I might fall over sometimes. In fact I'll probably fall over quite a lot!

7 55

I'm going to tell you about a leisure activity I'd like to do in the future. I'd really like to learn how to play the acoustic guitar. This is because I love music and I love the beautiful sound this kind of guitar makes. I also want to give myself a challenge and learn something new. I don't think it'll be too difficult for me because I already know how to read music. I play the piano but I'm not very good. I think playing the guitar will be easier. I also like the fact that you can carry a guitar round easily and play it anywhere. For example I can play it in the park or on the beach.

I can't think about learning it at the moment because I'm too busy. I need to focus on my studies and prepare for my exams. I think that I'd like to take up the guitar next year. All my exams will be over by then, so I'll have more time, and more money too. In fact, I'll need money to pay for lessons! I think that learning the guitar would change my life in a positive way. If I learn to play it really well, I'll start my own band. I'd love to perform live on stage at a concert. I think that would be fantastic!

8 56

Examiner: Do you generally enjoy trying new things?

Candidate 1: Yes, I would say I like to try new things, meet new people. It's something that is very important to me.

Examiner: Is there any other activity you would like to try one day?

Candidate 2: Yes, I've always thought about windsurfing, I mean, I'm a big fan of the ocean and love water sports, so it's next on my list of things to do.

9 57

to: I want to go now.

and: You have to wear a shirt and tie.

a: Wait a minute.

of: Get me a glass of water.

some: Will you lend me some money?

for: This is for you.

from: I come from London.

Unit 7 FAME AND THE MEDIA

LISTENING

2 59

Justin Bieber's rise to fame is an interesting story. He was interested in music from a very early age and he taught himself how to play a whole selection of musical instruments, which I think is rare in youngsters these days. Like a lot of teenagers who want to be pop stars, he learnt the guitar. But, whereas very few of those teenagers put in the effort needed to be successful, Bieber, on the other hand, not only learnt how to play the piano as well, but also mastered the drums and even the trumpet! One day he hopes to learn the violin.

He was clearly gifted, and his mother used to arrange for him to take part in local competitions. He came second in one, and his mother posted his performance on YouTube. She kept posting other clips of him singing, and soon these attracted a number of fans who started following him, though at this point he still hadn't found fame.

His big break came when a music executive came across these videos by accident when he was looking for a performance by a different artist. He immediately recognised Bieber's talent and gave the teenager a contract with his recording company. His first record was a worldwide hit. He shot to fame in just two years and is now a global superstar, one of the most well-known performers the world has ever seen.

5 60

A: I wouldn't like to be famous. I would hate people to recognise me all the time. You would always be followed by journalists and never able to have a private life. Being followed on a good day, when you've been to the hairdresser and are wearing your best jeans, is perhaps acceptable, but can you imagine how it would make you feel on a bad day?

B: I would love to be famous. I would adore all the attention and the special treatment. Everywhere I went, people would know my name and I wouldn't need to queue any more. The best part, though, would be meeting other famous people. I can imagine that would be so interesting. They would come to my private yacht and I would visit their mansions.

7 61

Interviewer: So, you've been a famous singer for over three decades now. What advice would you give to someone wanting to become famous?

Celebrity: Well, my first piece of advice is – don't try and become famous. Instead focus on being good at something. Choose something you enjoy and then work hard at doing well in that area.

Interviewer: What did you do to become such a successful singer?

Celebrity: Well, a good way to be the best is to learn from the experts. Find people you admire in your area of interest. Try to get as close to them as possible. Observe them carefully. If possible, talk to them. Ask lots of questions. Don't copy them, but try to learn from them. And don't be afraid to experiment, try something new.

Interviewer: Being the best is one thing, but how did you get yourself known?

Celebrity: Getting yourself known is indeed another skill you must work on. One thing is for sure, nobody is going to come to you. You have to make opportunities for yourself. You have a product to sell and the product is you. It's much easier to do that these days, especially with the internet around. Many people use social media for this.

Interviewer: Any other piece of advice?

Celebrity: Yes, the last thing I would say is, if you want to be really successful in something, you will most likely experience a certain amount of failure. People who fail at some point often say that the experience has been a great lesson and helped them on the road to success. Try to learn from these moments instead of being frightened of them. In fact, some of the most successful people have often failed countless times before reaching their end goal. What makes them successful, is that they kept on trying regardless.

10 62

If you're going to take film-making seriously, you need to learn how to get the best from your camcorder. Many people use camcorders these days, to make short videos of their friends and family, and often people just use the automatic functions. These work well enough for those types of occasion, but if you want to take a more professional approach for the production of your short film, you should have some knowledge of the camcorder's manual functions too.

In this tutorial I will start by discussing three of the most basic functions: the focus, the iris and the zoom. The focus control is usually the manual focus ring at the front of the lens, well certainly with professional cameras. It's a particularly useful function if used correctly. The ring turns anti-clockwise for a more distant focus and clockwise for a closer focus.

Next, I will talk about the iris ring. This is also located on the lens. It manages how much light appears through the lens, through the adjustable opening called the aperture. As you let more light into the shot, it naturally becomes brighter.

Finally, I will talk about the zoom function. Many people use this function and it's often over-used! Used in moderation, however, this very popular feature can be a really useful tool. It moves your perspective closer or further away from your chosen subject. I would advise, however, that whilst shooting a long zoom, you use a tripod.

11 〰️ 63

So welcome to Film-makers' Club. I hope you're excited at the thought of making a film and that you're bursting with great ideas. I've put you all into groups, so here's what you're going to do. Now you might think the first thing that you need to do is to come up with an idea for a story, but even before that you need to think about what *type* of film you want to make.

Remember that a film is really a story in pictures. There are lots of ways of telling a story. So choose a style of film that suits the talents of the group. If you have talented artists, but no good writers, or actors, you might want to make your film in the style of a cartoon or some other kind of animation. Last year a group made an excellent film using Lego bricks.

So having decided that, you can start to think of your idea for the story. Think about the movies you like to watch. What is it that makes them interesting? Is it the characters, the plot? As regards plot, my advice is – don't be too ambitious, don't make it complicated. Keep it simple – the simplest ideas are often the ones that work the best. Initially you just need to find the basic concept. You can fill in the details later. It's a good idea to keep a notebook in your pocket and carry it everywhere. You never know when a great idea will suddenly come to you! And the more ideas, the better, in my opinion.

The next stage is to write the screenplay – for this you need to divide the story up into a series of scenes. For each scene, the screenplay should begin with a short description of where it takes place and the time of day, that is day or night. Then the rest consists of the script – the lines the actors will speak, and it should also describe the camera movements, and give directions to the actors about how they should move.

Before you can start filming, you need to prepare a storyboard of your film to help everyone involved to imagine the scenes clearly and to understand what you are trying to achieve. This is similar to a comic-book version of your film, but without speech balloons.

And at this point you need to appoint a director. This is a major role and it's vital that he or she is a good communicator, as they are the key link between the actors and the rest of the team. This person will have responsibility for the creative side of the project. He or she will have the final say in the choice of the main actors and in directing the action of the film.

That brings me to the next stage – casting your film – finding the actors. Don't just rely on your friends. Be creative! Perhaps you could advertise on social media. Or if your film needs a doctor, perhaps you could ask one from the local hospital if they could spare a couple of hours for you?

And then before filming finally starts, you will need to assign other jobs, such as director of photography – in your case this will be the person who operates the camera; someone in charge of sound and music, and someone in charge of costumes and props (including furniture and any other objects needed) and also someone to look after hair and make-up. But we'll look at these roles in more detail in our next session.

2 〰️ 64

Well, for this task I'd like to talk about Bill Gates. He's the brilliant computer programmer who created Microsoft and the Windows operating system. I first saw Bill Gates on television in 2001. He was talking about Windows XP, which came out that year. I remember thinking that he is the richest man in the world, but if you look at him, you'd never know that. He just looks like a typical computer programmer.

I like Bill Gates because he's responsible for bringing computers to millions of family homes around the world with his Windows operating system. This made computers easier to use for everyone and also at a price that many families could afford.

I also like him because he was the world's youngest self-made billionaire at the time. If he could do it, I like to I think I could do it too.

Finally, I admire him because he's very generous and uses his money to help people. He has given away a huge amount of his money to charity, and I believe he plans to give most of it away in the end. I think this is an excellent idea and I hope this can show other rich and powerful people that they should also help others.

3 〰️ 65

Well, the famous person I'm going to describe is David Beckham. He was a footballer who played for Manchester United, and he also played for England. I first saw him play for United when I was only seven, so that was probably in about 2002. I remember it as one of the most exciting days in my life!

David Beckham became famous because he was a very talented footballer. His speciality was scoring amazing goals from free kicks. But he wasn't well-known only for his football skills. He became even more famous when he married a pop star – Victoria, one of the Spice Girls. And another reason for his fame was his good looks and his style. I think almost every boy in the world wanted to have a David Beckham haircut! I know I did.

I adored him as a boy because I was mad about football and he was my hero. The reason why I still like him is that in spite of his fame he behaves like a normal guy. I heard a story from someone whose car was broken down in the middle of the countryside. And then a car stopped and a man got out and asked him if he needed a push. It was David Beckham!

Unit 8 NATURAL WORLD

LISTENING

2 〰️ 66

Speaker 1
This creature is found in the mountains of Central Africa. It has black hair all over its body, which is much thicker than that of other members of the species. This means that it can live in colder temperatures. There are only about 900 of these apes in the wild. A lot of the green plants they eat have been destroyed, and they have also been killed in the past for their fur.

Speaker 2
This creature lives in the ocean from Australia up to Japan. Many of them are quite small, with a body that grows up to five centimetres long, and they have long tentacles, or arms. Its name comes from the bright blue rings that show up when it's frightened. You need to be careful in the sea around them as they are very poisonous.

Speaker 3
These creatures live mainly in desert areas and can survive in both mountains and valleys. Their tails help them to balance when they are climbing or sleeping in trees. Their black and yellow coats help them to hide in the places where they live. Unfortunately, there are only about 250 of these beautiful big cats left in the wild today.

Speaker 4

This strange-looking animal lives in wet areas and comes from the area south of the tropics in China. There are very few in the wild now. As you can see, it has antlers like most deer, but it has a neck like a camel and hooves or feet like a cow. They eat mainly grass and live partly on land and partly in water.

8 ▊▊▋ 67

Hello everyone. Today I'm going to talk about a project I've done about the mountain gorilla. I think it's a truly fascinating animal. They originate in Africa – Central Africa, in fact.

So now I'm going to talk a little about where they live. As you can probably guess, and as you can see in this first photo, their name reflects the environment they live in – tropical mountain forests.

Now just like all other apes, they build nests out of leaves. But they don't make their nests high up as other species do – mountain gorillas make them on the ground instead. And they sleep wherever they end their day and they rarely sleep in the same bed twice!

So, I'll move on to talk about the physical features of the mountain gorilla. In other words, what it looks like. So here are some more photographs on screen for you all to have a look at. This gorilla here on the left is a male gorilla. We know that he's an older male gorilla because of the colour of his coat. As you can see, his coat is grey. He's called a silverback. Younger male gorillas are called blackbacks. And there's an obvious reason for that! Yes, a young adult male has a black coat. As he gets older, his coat turns from black to grey.

Next, I'm going to tell you a little about the diet of the mountain gorilla. Interestingly, mountain gorillas are herbivores. In other words, they survive on a diet of plants. As you can see from this next picture, this gorilla is eating leaves. They also eat fruit and flowers. They occasionally eat insects too, but only when they're very hungry! And it might interest you to know that mountain gorillas very rarely drink water, even though they live in a very warm climate. It appears they get all the water they need from plants.

I'd like to conclude by talking about some of the threats that mountain gorillas face. They are in serious danger of disappearing from our world altogether. Let's have a look at two reasons why they're in such danger. And both of these reasons are connected to human activity. Firstly, people are damaging the mountain forests where these gorillas live. They're cutting down the trees to build farms and towns. Mountain gorillas live in close family groups and this means that it's difficult for them to get enough to eat in the small areas they now have to live in. Secondly, gorillas are also suffering as a result of hunting. Sadly, some people find and kill them to sell. So it's a very sad situation indeed for these beautiful animals.

11 ▊▊▋ 68

Good morning, everyone. In today's lecture I want to talk to you about a very unpopular animal here in Britain. In fact, you could say that it's one of our least loved animals! It's called the American bullfrog and yes, it does in fact come from America – the east of America, to be exact – and it was brought to Britain in the early 19th century, so you could say that it's been here for quite a long time. It wasn't brought here on purpose – it actually arrived in a big container of aquatic plants. In other words, it was accidentally introduced into Britain.

Now, I'll tell you a little about its appearance. The American bullfrog is a very large – and ugly – species of frog. And when I say it's large, I mean *large*. Interestingly, female American bullfrogs are usually much larger than the males. In fact, they can weigh up to 750 grams, whereas the males only go up to about 600 grams. Take a look at its head – it's really broad and flat, isn't it? And you can see its mouth – just here – that's quite large too.

Now, both the male and the female American bullfrogs have green or brown bodies and have dark spots on the top. But there's one important difference between them – the male's throat is yellow but the female has a white one instead. And the other difference is their eardrums, here just behind their eyes. Those of the male are much larger than the female's.

So, let's move on to why we so dislike the American bullfrog. Well, this is because it has threatened our own native species of frogs. Firstly, it breeds very quickly indeed. For example, female bullfrogs can lay up to 25,000 eggs every single season. And secondly, the American bullfrog is very greedy. In fact, they eat just about anything they can put into their mouths! As well as other frogs, they eat insects, fish and have even been known to eat birds and snakes! So, in other words, they eat the food sources of our own native species. Thirdly, they carry a disease that is dangerous to other frogs. And finally, they don't just damage our natural world, they cause financial damage too. Around £100,000 has been spent monitoring the American bullfrog in the wild.

So, as scientists, we can learn a lesson from this about the dangers of introducing any living species into a new environment.

13 ▊▊▋ 69

OK everyone, I think we're ready to make a start. Now, when you think of a dangerous animal, what do you think of? A tiger perhaps? Or maybe a leopard? Most people think that all dangerous animals live on land, but in fact, some of the *most* dangerous animals on the planet live in our seas and oceans. I'm going to talk today about one of these – the box jellyfish.

There are different types of box jellyfish, and they are found in warm coastal seas anywhere from the Indian Ocean to as far north as Japan, but the most dangerous ones are found in the oceans around Australia.

OK, so now let's examine what these box jellyfish look like. There are no prizes for guessing why it's called a box jellyfish! You can see that it's shaped like a box or a cube, with four sides and rounded corners. And you can also see that its body is light blue.

So, let's take a look at the tentacles of the box jellyfish more closely. It's got 15 of these growing from each of the four corners of the box. Now, you may be surprised to learn that these tentacles *can* grow to a length of *three metres*! And another surprising thing is its large number of eyes, that's six eyes on each of its four sides, so 24 altogether.

So now let's move on to talk about the sting of a box jellyfish. What is it? Well, a jellyfish has a lot of tentacles, and each tentacle has thousands of cells which can produce a poison. If the tentacles come into contact with a fish, or a person, they stick to their skin. If the tentacles are very long, they are in contact with a lot of the body, giving a bad sting which hurts terribly. This can be dangerous to the victim.

There are two ways that people can die as the result of a jellyfish sting. Firstly, a very severe sting can cause a person to have a heart attack. This can happen within minutes. Secondly, sometimes a swimmer goes into shock and can't make it back to the beach because they are in such extreme pain. If they're in the water alone, they'll die.

And now I'd like to conclude with advice on how to help someone who has been stung by a box jellyfish. If they have had a heart attack, of course the most important thing is to try to revive them first of all. And then, the best thing to help is vinegar. Yes, the same vinegar you use when you're cooking! Many Australian beaches keep bottles of it near the jellyfish warning signs. You should pour a bottle over the tentacles for 30 seconds, and then the tentacles can be removed. However, if you get stung and don't have any vinegar, you should pour seawater on the skin. This will help to ease the pain before you can get further medical help.

SPEAKING

5 🎚 70

1

Examiner: What can governments do to prevent illegal hunting?

Student 1: There are two things the government can do to prevent illegal hunting. The first is to be more serious about punishing hunters, for example …

2

Examiner: Should the government provide more money for zoos?

Student 2: They definitely should. It seems to me that zoos need money now more than ever. Many of them have very old facilities for the animals …

3

Examiner: How might we be able to protect wildlife in the future?

Student 3: Well, in the future, it might be a good idea to use technology to track where wild animals are …

4

Examiner: Is there any difference in how children learn about wildlife now than in the past?

Student 4: There's a big difference, I think. In the past, we used to go on more field trips to places to see wild animals, but now we mostly just see them on the internet.

7 🎚 71

1

Examiner: What should be done to people caught hunting illegally?

Student: Well, if you ask me, I think people caught hunting should pay all the money they made to charities that help to protect animals. And the same for people caught buying these animal products. For example, I read that the government in Kenya took money from people who were caught buying animals' furs. The reason why is that it will help charities better protect wild animals, and hopefully make hunting more difficult.

2

Examiner: Is there anything we as individuals can do to prevent hunting?

Student: Yes, there are many things we can do, and perhaps the most important one is to stop buying things made from animals. A good reason for this is that it might cause the demand for things made from animals to drop. For instance, many of the world's most famous fashion designers have stopped using real animal fur in their clothes.

3

Examiner: Will there be more or less hunting in the future?

Student: In my opinion, there will be less hunting in the future. The reason for this is that many of our animals are already close to becoming extinct, so when they are gone, there will be nothing left to hunt. By way of example, the white rhino in Africa was hunted for many years, but now there are almost no white rhinos left to hunt.

Cambridge University Press
www.cambridge.org/elt

Cambridge Assessment English
www.cambridgeenglish.org

This publication is in copyright. Subject to statutory exception
and to the provisions of relevant collective licensing agreements,
no reproduction of any part may take place without the written
permission of Cambridge University Press.

Cambridge University Press is part of the University of Cambridge.

It furthers the University's mission by disseminating knowledge in the pursuit of
education, learning and research at the highest international levels of excellence.

www.cambridge.org
Information on this title: www.cambridge.org/9781316640050

© Cambridge University Press and UCLES 2017

First published 2017

20 19 18 17 16 15 14 13 12 11

Printed in Poland by Opolgraf

A catalogue record for this publication is available from the British Library

Additional resources for this publication at **www.cambridge.org/mindset**

Cambridge University Press has no responsibility for the persistence or accuracy
of URLs for external or third-party internet websites referred to in this publication,
and does not guarantee that any content on such websites is, or will remain,
accurate or appropriate. Information regarding prices, travel timetables, and other
factual information given in this work is correct at the time of first printing but
Cambridge University Press does not guarantee the accuracy of such information
thereafter.

**The authors and publishers would like to thank the following people for
their work on this level of the Student's Book.**

Alyson Maskell, Helen Forrest and Jock Graham for their editing, project
management and proof reading.

Design and typeset by emc design.

Audio produced by Leon Chambers at The Soundhouse Studios, London.

**The publishers would like to thank the following people for their input
and work on the digital materials that accompany this level.**

Dr Peter Crosthwaite; Jeremy Day; Natasha de Souza; Ian Felce; Amanda
French; Marc Loewenthal; Rebecca Marsden; Kate O'Toole; Emina Tuzovic;
Andrew Reid; N.M.White.

Cover and text design concept: Juice Creative Ltd.

Typesetting: emc design Ltd.

Cover illustration: MaryliaDesign/iStock/Getty Images Plus.

The authors and publishers acknowledge the following sources of copyright material and are grateful for the permissions granted. While every effort has been made, it has not always been possible to identify the sources of all the material used, or to trace all copyright holders. If any omissions are brought to our notice, we will be happy to include the appropriate acknowledgements on reprinting and in the next update to the digital edition, as applicable.

Key: B = Below, BL = Below Left, BR = Below Right, BC = Below Centre, C = Centre, CL = Centre Left, CR = Centre Right, L = Left, R = Right, T = Top, TR = Top Right, TL = Top Left.

Illustrations
by Ana Djordjevic (Astound us) pp12 (except map), 13, 15, 61; Sam Parij (Eye Candy Illustration) pp12 (map), 20, 34, 40, 118, 119, 120.

Photos
p. 8 (header): Hill Street Studios/Blend Images/GettyImages; p. 9: Bloom Productions/Taxi/GettyImages; p. 10–11, p. 54 (photo A): Trevor Adeline/Caiaimage/GettyImages; p. 12 (header): Tanya Constantine/Blend Images/GettyImages; p. 13: ANUPAM NATH/AFP/GettyImages; p. 16: Willie B. Thomas/Taxi/GettyImages; p. 17: SolStock/E+/GettyImages; p. 18: Blend Images - Hill Street Studios/Brand X Pictures/GettyImages; p. 19 (header), p. 54 (photo G), p. 70, p. 156 (photo A): Image Source/GettyImages; p. 19 (BL): Juanmonino/E+/GettyImages; p. 19 (BR): Tom Merton/OJO Images/GettyImages; p. 19 (CL), p. 64 (photo 3): Todd Wright/Blend Images/GettyImages; p. 19 (BC): Miroku/Taxi/GettyImages; p. 20 (family), p. 86 (CR): Image Source/DigitalVision/GettyImages; p. 20 (BL): Purestock/GettyImages; p. 20 (BR): monkeybusinessimages/iStock/GettyImages; p. 21: Ty Allison/The Image Bank/GettyImages; p. 22 (BL): Eileen Hart/E+/GettyImages; p. 22–23 (B): Lyn Balzer and Tony Perkins/Iconica/GettyImages; p. 24 (header): chinaface/GettyImages; p. 24 (CL): Fotosearch/GettyImages; p. 24 (CR): Spaces Images/Blend Images/GettyImages; p. 24 (BR): Mark Bury/robertharding/GettyImages; p. 25 (photo A), p. 96 (TL): VisitBritain/Pawel Libera/Britain On View/GettyImages; p. 25 (photo B): FooTToo/iStock/GettyImages; p. 25 (photo C): Marka/Universal Images Group/GettyImages; p. 25 (photo D): Peter Ptschelinzew/Lonely Planet Images/GettyImages; p. 26–27: Heinz Wohner/LOOK/GettyImages; p. 29: Daniel Schoenen/imageBROKER/GettyImages; p. 30: Robert Daly/Caiaimage/GettyImages; p. 32–33: Universal Images Group/GettyImages; p. 35: Hans Blossey/imageBROKER/GettyImages; p. 37: Silvia Otte/The Image Bank/GettyImages; p. 38: travelgame/Lonely Planet Images/GettyImages; p. 39 (header): Insung Jeon/Moment Open/GettyImages; p. 39 (CL), p. 54 (photo B), p. 54 (photo F), p. 59 (photo F), p. 65 (photo A), p. 112 (header), p. 123 (BR): Hero Images/GettyImages; p. 39 (CR): Archive Holdings Inc./Archive Photos/GettyImages; p. 39 (BL): Barry Winiker/Photolibrary/GettyImages; p. 39 (BR): Tom Cockrem/Photolibrary/GettyImages; p. 41 (photo 1): Spencer Platt/Getty Images News/GettyImages; p. 41 (photo 2), p. 115: John Elk/Lonely Planet Images/GettyImages; p. 41 (photo 3): Xavier Arnau/iStock/GettyImages; p. 43: Eric Raptosh Photography/Blend Images/GettyImages; p. 44 (header): chinaface/E+/GettyImages; p. 44 (CR): Venturelli/WireImage/GettyImages; p. 44 (BR): Roy Mehta/Iconica/GettyImages; p. 46: momentimages/GettyImages; p. 48: Huntstock/GettyImages; p. 49: JGI/Jamie Grill/Blend Images/GettyImages; p. 53: John Lund/Marc Romanelli/Blend Images/GettyImages; p. 54 (header): Gary Burchell/Taxi/GettyImages; p. 54 (photo C): Juice Images/Cultura/GettyImages; p. 54 (photo D): Hero Images/Stone/GettyImages; p. 54 (photo E): kupicoo/E+/GettyImages; p. 55: Peter Dazeley/Photographer's Choice/GettyImages; p. 56: Glow Images, Inc/Glow/GettyImages; p. 57: Danil Rudenko/EyeEm/GettyImages; p. 58 (header), p. 63 (L), p. 114: Steve Debenport/E+/GettyImages; p. 58 (photo D): Monashee Frantz/OJO Images/GettyImages; p. 58 (photo A): JOSHUA ROBERTS/AFP/GettyImages; p. 58 (photo B): Erik Dreyer/The Image Bank/GettyImages; p. 58 (photo E): Seb Oliver/Cultura Exclusive/GettyImages; p. 59 (photo G): Tooga/Stone/GettyImages; p. 59 (photo C): Gary Conner/Stockbyte/GettyImages; p. 60 (photo A): Monty Rakusen/Cultura/GettyImages; p. 60 (photo B): YinYang/iStock/GettyImages; p. 60 (photo C): Goodluz/iStock/GettyImages; p. 60 (photo D), p. 69, p. 75 (header): Zero Creatives/Cultura/GettyImages; p. 62: Lucidio Studio Inc/Photographer's Choice RF/GettyImages; p. 63 (TR), p. 107 (kabaddi): ROSLAN RAHMAN/AFP/GettyImages; p. 63 (BR): Zero Creatives/Image Source/GettyImages; p. 64 (header), p. 96 (BL): Betsie Van

Der Meer/Taxi/GettyImages; p. 64 (photo 1): JoeGough/iStock/GettyImages; p. 64 (photo 2): Davies and Starr/The Image Bank/GettyImages; p. 64 (photo 4): Tony Robins/Photolibrary/GettyImages; p. 64 (photo 5): Paul Blundell/StockFood Creative/GettyImages; p. 64 (photo 6): Magone/iStock/GettyImages; p. 64 (photo 7): Daniel Cole/Hemera/GettyImages; p. 64 (photo 8): Judd Pilossof/Photolibrary/GettyImages; p. 65 (photo B): PBNJ Productions/Blend Images/GettyImages; p. 65 (photo C): Kiratsinh Jadeja/Stone/GettyImages; p. 65 (eating daal): Dinodia Photo Library/StockFood Creative/GettyImages; p. 65 (photo D): Robin Skjoldborg/DigitalVision/GettyImages; p. 65 (photo E): Jamie Grill/GettyImages; p. 66–67: Ray Kachatorian/Blend Images/GettyImages; p. 68 (TR): New York Times Co./Archive Photos/GettyImages; p. 68 (BL): FOX/FOX Image Collection/GettyImages; p. 71: Alina Solovyova-Vincent/E+/GettyImages; p. 75 (photo A): Ryerson Clark/E+/GettyImages; p. 75 (photo B): Cornelia Schauermann/Image Source/GettyImages; p. 75 (photo C): Radius Images/GettyImages; p. 75 (photo D): Brian Curtiss/EyeEm/GettyImages; p. 76: ML Harris/Iconica/GettyImages; p. 77: Wavebreakmedia Ltd/GettyImages; p. 78 (T): Klaus Vedfelt/DigitalVision/GettyImages; p. 78 (B): PeopleImages.com/DigitalVision/GettyImages; p. 79: sunstock/iStock/GettyImages; p. 80 (header): Mariemlulu/iStock/GettyImages; p. 80 (L): yuliang11/iStock/GettyImages; p. 80 (CR): Steve Brown Photography/Photolibrary/GettyImages; p. 80 (BR): Jennifer Valencia/EyeEm/GettyImages; p. 82: martinturzak/iStock/GettyImages; p. 83: Merten Snijders/Lonely Planet Images/GettyImages; p. 84–85: Thomas Barwick/Stone/GettyImages; p. 86 (header): fiftymm99/Moment/GettyImages; p. 86 (CL): Alex Wong/Getty Images News/GettyImages; p. 86 (BL), p. 158: Panoramic Images/GettyImages; p. 86 (BR): Lester Lefkowitz/The Image Bank/GettyImages; p. 86 (C): MAISANT Ludovic/hemis.fr/GettyImages; p. 87: Klaus Lang/All Canada Photos/GettyImages; p. 89: Luis Davilla/Photolibrary/GettyImages; p. 90 (clothes market): Tim Graham/Getty Images News/GettyImages; p. 90–91 (food market): Bob Pool/Photographer's Choice/GettyImages; p. 90–91 (handicrafts market): AGF/Universal Images Group/GettyImages; p. 90–91 (flea market): Stuart Dee/robertharding/GettyImages; p. 92 (header), p. 112 (CR): Lonely Planet/Lonely Planet Images/GettyImages; p. 92 (BL): Eva Katalin Kondoros/E+/GettyImages; p. 92 (BC): Jeff Titcomb/Photographer's Choice/GettyImages; p. 92 (BR): Izabela Habur/E+/GettyImages; p. 93: Andrew Olney/DigitalVision/GettyImages; p. 95, p. 140: Bloomberg/GettyImages; p. 96 (TR): Jupiterimages/Stockbyte/GettyImages; p. 98 (header): erhui1979/DigitalVision Vectors/GettyImages; p. 98 (photo A): Ken Welsh/Photolibrary/GettyImages; p. 98 (photo B): Olaf Protze/LightRocket/GettyImages; p. 98 (photo C): Insights/Universal Images Group/GettyImages; p. 98 (photo D): Oktay Ortakcioglu/E+/GettyImages; p. 98 (photo E): Floresco Productions/Cultura/GettyImages; p. 100 (TR): Robert Alexander/Archive Photos/GettyImages; p. 100 (CR): VisitBritain/Grant Pritchard/Britain On View/GettyImages; p. 101: Siqui Sanchez/Moment/GettyImages; p. 102 (CR): Dwi Janto Johan, Lie/Moment/GettyImages; p. 102 (header): Christer Fredriksson/Lonely Planet Images/GettyImages; p. 102 (BR): goir/iStock/GettyImages; p. 104: Linda Lewis/Photodisc/GettyImages; p. 105 (CL): Neil Setchfield/Lonely Planet Images/GettyImages; p. 105 (CR): Peter Zoeller/Design Pics/Perspectives/GettyImages; p. 105 (BL): sturti/E+/GettyImages; p. 106 (header): Shaun Botterill/Getty Images Sport/GettyImages; p. 106 (photo A): Adam Kazmierski/E+/GettyImages; p. 106 (photo B): Andy Crawford/Dorling Kindersley/GettyImages; p. 106 (photo C): Lou Jones/The Image Bank/GettyImages; p. 106 (photo D): Christof Koepsel/Bongarts/GettyImages; p. 106 (photo E): VisitBritain/Britain on View/GettyImages; p. 107 (bossaball), p. 121 (photo A): NurPhoto/GettyImages; p. 107–108 (BL): Anadolu Agency/GettyImages; p. 107 (chess): DIBYANGSHU SARKAR/AFP/GettyImages; p. 107 (BR): Chip Simons/Stockbyte/GettyImages; p. 110 (T), p. 110–111 (B): Darryl Leniuk/The Image Bank/GettyImages; p. 111: AFP/GettyImages; p. 112 (BL): Mike Harrington/DigitalVision/GettyImages; p. 112 (BR): Monkey Business Images Ltd/GettyImages; p. 116: ViewStock/GettyImages; p. 117: narvikk/E+/GettyImages; p. 121 (header): Thomas Barwick/Taxi/GettyImages; p. 121 (photo B): Jan-Otto/iStock/GettyImages; p. 121 (photo C): Jake Curtis/Iconica/GettyImages; p. 121 (photo D): LIU JIN/AFP/GettyImages; p. 121 (photo E): Robert Daly/OJO Images/GettyImages; p. 122 (BR): Westend61/GettyImages; p. 122 (CL): Peter Muller/Cultura/GettyImages; p. 122 (CR): Photo and Co/The Image Bank/GettyImages; p. 122 (BL): Ascent Xmedia/The Image Bank/GettyImages;